An American Cutting Garden

An American

Cutting Garden

A Primer for Growing Cut Flowers
where summers are hot and winters are cold

Suzanne McIntire

UNIVERSITY PRESS OF VIRGINIA

Charlottesville and London

The University Press of Virginia
© 2002 by the Rector and Visitors of the University of Virginia
All rights reserved
Printed in the United States of America on acid-free paper

First published 2002

1   3   5   7   9   8   6   4   2

Library of Congress Cataloging-in-Publication Data

McIntire, Suzanne, 1951–
   An American cutting garden : a primer for growing cut flowers where
summers are hot and winters are cold / Suzanne McIntire.
      p. cm.
   ISBN 0-8139-2062-0 (cloth : alk. paper)
   1. Flower gardening—Middle Atlantic States.   2. Cut flowers—
Middle Atlantic States.   3. Flowers—Middle Atlantic States.   I. Title.
   SB405.5 .M53 M35 2002
   635.9′66′0974—dc21

                                                                2001002487

for my mother,
and the memory of my father,
whose corn won first prize at the county fair

Contents

Preface

This book is for all those who love a garden and like the company of flowers in the house. It covers fresh flowers from herbaceous plants, or those plants that die back in winter and do not develop persistent woody tissue above ground. It includes annuals, biennials, perennials, and bulbs, but not roses, shrubs, or trees. The first five chapters help you get a cutting garden off the ground, or into the ground, I should say, and also suggest interesting material for cutting. Chapter 6 provides detailed information on those plants and many more; I hope readers will forgive me for any that have been overlooked. I grow only a small portion of these plants in any one year.

I've referred to most plants throughout this book by both their common and Latinized botanical names. An example is *Salvia leucantha*, also known as Mexican bush sage. Some of these common names are not commonly heard, but as they offer an alternative for those with a disinclination for Latin, I've included them anyway. A few other plants, such as delphinium or boltonia, have no well-known common names in the United States and are generally referred to in garden talk by their botanical names, used colloquially. The reader will probably want to become familiar with both names of the plants we grow, even though most of us are still learning to pronounce the botanical names. With botanical names, you'll know what everyone is talking about at a garden lecture; you can order precisely the plant you want, even without a picture; and you can ask for the same plant in another part of the country where gardeners use a different common name, or another part of the world where a different language is spoken. However, common names allow us to move easily in the local gardening scene and to speak with neighbors and gardeners who may never have read a garden book, yet have accumulated a wealth of cultural information, not to mention collections of interesting plants. I hope both beginning gardeners and those who are more advanced will find something here to enjoy trying out in their bit of earth.

Every garden book that has its origin in a garden has the imprint of place, and knowing where that place is makes the book more valuable to the reader. When I sit down with a new garden book, I like to turn to the preface or dust jacket to discover where the author gardens. If a gardener from Connecticut says a certain plant blooms in June, then I suspect it may bloom in May in my garden. If a plant thrives in North Carolina, it will probably survive the heat here. So I'm sure it will help readers to know that this book was written in Arlington, Virginia, just across the Potomac River from Washington, D.C., in cold-hardiness zone 7a, and heat zone 7. Almost all of my note taking took place in the garden, in fact in my two gardens: one in the unavoidable shade at my home, and the other in full sun at a community garden about a five-minute drive away.

A number of people helped me along the way, in the garden, with the manuscript, and with photography. Thanks go to Augie Scheele, Jim Stark, Sandy Austin, Carol Fonteyn, Dan Newman, and Roger Foley. More thanks to gardeners Joanne Hutton, Mary Ellen Kemp, Clarence Mahan, Becky Heath, John Roe, Vicki Bowen, Alice Nicolson, Marjorie Olsen, Elaine Faucher, and my many colleagues at Ten-Barton Gardens. And especially to my agents Kirsten Manges and Clyde Taylor, and my editor Boyd Zenner, project editor David Sewell, and copyeditor Gary Kessler.

An American Cutting Garden

1

Ground Work

I have always liked to visit the immense cutting garden, almost equal in size to the herbaceous border, at Washington, D.C.'s Dumbarton Oaks. It was designed for Mildred Bliss by Beatrix Farrand in 1922. The extensive beds lie within pretty stone walls on three sides, with a charmingly roofed toolshed, flanked on each side by lead cisterns and built into the west wall. To the east, the cutting garden is framed by the Plum Walk, and through there fall the steps to the even larger kitchen garden. Still a working garden, it supplies flowers for the educational institution now in residence.

However marvelous such a garden may be, many a gardener in times past was a guest in his or her own cutting garden, estranged from work by propriety and a huge staff. I am mindful of this when I'm dirtying my hands in my own plot, making my own plans for the season. It was probably such a gardener who penned the sentiments of "The Seeds of Love," my favorite song for singing in the garden. British music historian Cecil Sharp sparked the revival of the folk song when he took it down in 1903 after hearing a gardener singing in a Somerset garden.

> My garden was planted well
> with flowers everywhere.
> But I had not the liberty to choose for myself
> the flowers that I would wear,
> the flowers that I would wear.
>
> The gardener was standing by
> and I asked him to choose for me.

> He chose for me the violet, the lily, and the pink,
> but those I refused all three,
> but those I refused all three.*

She finally chooses a red rosebud, yet "gains but the willow tree."
Thomas Hardy has a sheepshearer sing this song in the garden at the
shearing supper in *Far from the Madding Crowd.* The supper table is
set with one end through the parlor window, so that Miss Everdene
can sit inside like a lady, with the shearers sitting in chairs on the
grass.

Not many of us will have a cutting garden designed by Beatrix
Farrand, a full 60 by 75 feet, beautifully sited, and staffed by gardeners; but neither will we be shut out of participating. Our gardens will
likely be smaller, but the reward will be enormous. The work begins
with choosing a site, preparing the soil, and selecting the flowers
that will grow best there.

The Site

An ideal cutting garden boasts full sun and a small area of partial
shade that isn't overly dry, but areas of half shade or wet soils offer
the welcome chance for other interesting plants. A garden under deciduous trees will likely produce its best arrangements for spring, as
the preponderance of shade-tolerant plants bloom in spring. In fact,
a shady cutting garden will be in full swing in midspring, while
a garden in full sun may appear to have barely begun to grow. (See
chapter 5 for "The Shady Garden.") The further south the garden,
the more useful the shady spot will be.

Sometimes there is too much shade, and removing lower branches
from your trees will bring in more light. You should have all tree
work done before installing the garden, as a falling limb can take
a year off a plant's life in an instant, and if the limb doesn't do it, the
tree men will.

It's a challenge to find space for a cutting garden on a small property. (See chapter 5's "The Small Garden.") Some gardeners also
have trouble cutting flowers they can see from the house, which fur-

---

*A version of this song by John Langstaff may be heard on *The Seeds of Love,*
Minstrel Records, JD-208, 1987.

ther reduces the likely sites for the garden. Behind the garage and the sides of the house often are neglected places where you could locate a few cutting plants out of sight. Or you might want to position your cutting garden so that passersby can enjoy the view; many people never notice a garden, but others are enormously cheered by the sight without expecting it to resemble an English garden.

While it's tempting to locate a cutting garden in the most useless or leftover part of your property, make sure the spot can be reached by a hose and is safe for growing things. I've seen a fellow hanging storm windows for my neighbor and trampling her ferns, found a deliveryman driving over the daylilies along our driveway, and caught the painter throwing the washwater on the hostas. In earlier years, I hoped there would be leaves left, now I just pray the roots live. Such incidents are less easy to take when they involve special strains of seed-raised delphinium, an astrantia you finally got established, or ammi that made it to three feet tall.

Don't locate any part of your cutting garden under the eaves of the roof where it will get no rainfall, or under a maple or other demanding tree where competition from tree roots may prevent the garden from ever becoming established. Another common error is to plan a cutting garden as a three-foot strip against a fence or wall, providing no room to walk behind the plants, and leaving the plants unable to grow upright as they lean away from the structure. Many gardeners find it convenient to grow cut flowers in the vegetable patch instead of a separate cutting garden, and some flowering plants, like marigolds, will have a beneficial effect on neighboring vegetables.

Any plants that still look good after considerable cutting—usually because they have a lot of basal foliage—can also be kept in the ornamental border rather than the cutting garden, if the border is large enough that taking flowers doesn't spoil the display; baptisia and columbines are two of those plants whose pretty foliage almost requires that they be located in the border. A large border in medium shade can also flower so heavily in spring that a separate cutting garden might not be necessary for spring flowers. Areas of deciduous woods can sometimes host plantings of daffodils, ferns, Solomon's seal, and other wildflowers for cutting, although make sure you don't plant anything invasive.

For those without space at home, growing cut flowers in a municipal community garden is very rewarding. It's a pleasure to be relieved of keeping the cutting garden presentable—at our community garden, the weeds only need be kept under 12 inches—and wonderful for the friends to be found, and the exposure to plants and gardening methods you might otherwise miss. It's amusing to attend the annual meeting and hear it asked who has lost their dentures in the mulch pile, or the scuttlebutt about seeds taken from somebody's zinnias. Outside the fence one day, a man approached me with the extension service map in hand for choosing a community garden. Obviously an old hand, his first question was "Is there a lot of fighting in this garden?"

Soil

One of the marks of a good gardener is careful soil preparation, vital when first establishing a cutting garden, when whole beds should be dug and prepared at one time, even if only one small bed can be prepared per season. The payoff is bigger plants and extra flowers. A soil test will provide you interesting information about pH, organic content, and mineral composition, and often the tester will make specific suggestions about treatment. Here in Virginia we get small cardboard collection boxes from the Extension Service and mail them to the specified university testing lab.

If you can, prepare the beds some weeks before the optimal planting times of fall or spring. Midsummer is a good time to work the soil to be ready for fall planting. Fall is an ideal time to prepare the garden for planting in spring. Waiting until spring to prepare the soil for the first time can sometimes delay planting for weeks, if the soil fails to dry out sufficiently, and digging in very wet soil can be counterproductive, as it's easily compacted.

The heavy clay soil we have here doesn't have to be removed, as new gardeners sometimes think, but it does need to be amended, as does sandy soil elsewhere. Garden centers offer a range of products such as humus, composted manure, sand, greensand, organic fertilizers, and gypsum, and together with your own compost and a layer of mulch, they will make a vast improvement in the average soil. If you have access to aged cow or horse manure, this can also be used to amend the soil. You don't need to make a life's labor out of improving your soil except for keeping it loose and replenishing organic material. I've learned to seek plants that like clay loam in order to limit the number of failures caused by poor soil.

When rototilling, spend enough time to allow the tiller to dig in deeply and take the amendments as far down as possible, which may make the job take twice as long, but tilling may not be required again for years. When you replace a plant, dig up the larger area where the plant will go, rather than only gouging a rootball-sized hole. Planting is a pleasure when the soil is loose—never walk on it after it has been turned. You'll relish pulling a weed from soft soil and love the look of it as it crumbles under your shovel; there are few odors better than the smell of freshly dug earth in spring.

You'll often have dispensed with mild-tempered annual weeds just by turning the soil, but persistent weeds need to be dug out individually. If you have a serious weed problem, you might consider planting that area only with vigorous annuals until the nuisance is resolved. Weeds can invade desirable perennial plantings and lurk permanently among the roots, while an annual bed provides many more opportunities to continue weed eradication. Since sunflowers sometimes suppress the growth of weeds around them, perhaps a planting of the wonderful new cut-flower varieties of *Helianthus annuus* would be a help. For more on weeds, see chapter 3 on "Weeding and Mulching."

Garden Layout

You may find it helpful to separate the cutting garden roughly into areas for bulbs, annuals and biennials, perennials, and invasive plants in order to simplify garden maintenance.

The care of bulbs is simpler if those of similar culture are planted together; this can be a corner of the cutting garden or elsewhere on the property. Most hardy bulbs, like daffodils and alliums, like to be in well-drained soil that is dry in the summer, and you can plant drought-tolerant annuals such as tithonia above them. Because of poor winter drainage in my only sunny area, however, I've always had tulips planted in a terraced shady border, where they receive a fair amount of summer watering. This is not ideal for tulips. Nonetheless, the drainage there is so excellent they often repeat for several years. The site has also proved better than a poorly drained sunny location, as the deciduous trees allow in a considerable amount of light in spring.

Hardy bulbs that like summer watering and that you hope will return, like lilies and camassias, can be planted in a well-drained perennial bed. The spring-planted tender bulbs or tubers like *Gladiolus callianthus* and tuberoses, which also appreciate summer watering and will be either lifted or abandoned at the end of the season, may be conveniently planted with the annuals.

Annuals and biennials present a changing scene, sometimes twice yearly where the growing season is long. You may choose to grow only one crop of annuals a year in a particular bed. Or in Zone 7 and further south, you can plan a September planting of a hardy annual like pansies or cornflowers for bloom in April and May, followed by a sowing of zinnias or sunflowers for August. Don't sprinkle perennials here and there among the annuals, particularly if they're the type that don't like to be moved, like peonies, gas plant, or baptisia. A perennial that needs dividing every year or two for best performance (like asters and mums) and so can be moved easily, could be thought of as an annual for locating purposes.

You can also plant tender perennials in the annual section. These are perennials that are killed by frost in much of the United States. They're usually grown from seed or found in garden centers, herb nurseries, and the more intriguing mail-order nurseries, and include salvias, flowering tobacco, and bloodflower. Also, you might plant here those few hardy perennials like gloriosa daisies that are grown as annuals, because, though they will survive winter, they flower best their first year.

The perennial section of the cutting garden changes less often, with plants divided or replaced at intervals. If your new cutting garden will be devoted largely to perennials, you might plant it half with annuals the first year, as some perennials are stingy with flowers the first season. Sometimes in an expansive cutting garden, it makes sense to create a rich-soil area for plants like delphinium or astilbes, rather than overimprove the entire garden, and conversely, you might set aside a poor-soil area for plants such as cosmos and gaillardia. Lastly, a corner devoted to invasive perennials will keep them away from smaller and more fragile plants.

My cutting garden rarely looks very nice, because often I've cut all the flowers. If yours will be visible from the house or street, you might want to locate prolific long-blooming plants along the front to hide the eyesore that your garden may occasionally become. Choices could be hollyhocks, cleome, castor bean, snow-on-the-mountain, wheat celosia, bushy sunflowers like 'Italian White', Shirley poppies,

or anything that will produce more flowers or foliage than you'll
want to cut.

Paths

For my first sizeable cutting garden, I couldn't bear the thought of
giving over any space to paths, and I just walked about between the
plants. Of course, the soil became so compacted the weeds could
scarcely be dug out. The next year the winter drainage had been so
poor that raised beds had to be created. But because I resisted devot-
ing much space to the trenches, I dug only a perimeter trench and
two interior ones, and of course, I walked in the raised beds, too.
A certain weed with a brittle root plagued me, and new little plagues
sprang from the tiniest bit left behind in hard soil. It therefore was
clear I'd have to stop tramping through the beds. Little by little,
I moved the perennials to create paths and resisted the temptation to
sow rows of annuals down those inviting spaces. It seems you can't
have a garden without a path through it.

The paths don't have to be any wider than you or your wheelbarrow, and they work best if they occur every three or four rows. It's
a pleasure to cut flowers without bending over from five rows away,
or being stung by bees while wedged between plants. Sometimes
a plant dies and leaves a good space to place one's bucket, park the
wheelbarrow, or store a bag of compost, so the paths don't become
blocked.

Raised Beds

A raised bed is a useful feature for growing a wide range of annuals,
perennials, and bulbs, providing better drainage for such plants as
acanthus, sea hollies, dahlias, gypsophila, or tulips, while offering
roots a deeper purchase. A raised bed in areas of high rainfall may
make the difference between death and a fine harvest. It doesn't
need to be edged beautifully with railroad ties or constructed like
a box. Sometimes building up the soil in the bed six inches higher
and digging a small gutter around it will suffice. This raising may
happen naturally as you improve your soil with organic matter, as
well as with sand, if need be, in clayey soil. A bed at the top of a terrace wall, or on a slope, may function like a raised bed, though in

some places raised beds in full sun can't be too high or they will dry out quickly in hot summers.

Fences

Occasionally there's a need for perimeter defenses. Gardens in many areas are destroyed by deer, a problem so severe that stockades can scarcely provide a remedy, but in our community garden it has always been children and thieves. A happy fact is that our garden is fenced, or things might be worse. There are charming characters who appear at the fence to ask for flowers for their girlfriends, and I'm grateful to have the chance to give, rather than have it stolen from me. But the most enjoyable giving of flowers is to the old women from the crowded apartments of this varied community who stop at the fence and gaze at the gardens. I imagine they're thinking of their homelands and gardens past, and when they bring a daughter-in-law to translate the request for flowers, no one enjoys the gift of flowers more than I do.

I once went to visit the home of a friend who had two massive dogs but who was still interested in establishing a cutting garden. The weather had been wet and then freezing, and it was evident from the sea of frozen paw prints that without a fence there would be no garden. I could only recommend a plant named live-forever.

Ready for Planting

If you've prepared your garden beds in early spring, they are ready for almost any kind of planting, and in the North the planting may continue longer into summer. But if you've not prepared the beds until late spring in a hot summer area, and it's now six weeks past the *average* last frost date (April 15 in my garden, but you can find out your approximate date by calling your county extension service or by inquiring at local garden centers), all is not lost for the season. You can plant durable perennials, including tender perennials like the salvias, if you water carefully and offer some shade for a few days. You can sow seed for quick-growing and heat-tolerant annuals such as tithonia, cosmos, castor bean, zinnias, sunflowers, celosia, snow-on-the-mountain, China asters, and marigolds if you pay attention to keeping the seedbed moist. In the cooler North, you should also be able to sow those quick-growing annuals recommended for repeat sowings, including dill and gypsophila. Dahlia tubers should be planted in late spring anyway, as early rains make them susceptible to rot. In hot summer areas, annuals that need cool weather to grow well, like sweet peas, Shirley poppies, or bupleurum, should be saved for the following year's bloom.

When your beds have been prepared in summer, most planting in hot summer areas should be delayed until fall, though you might sow zinnias, cosmos, tithonia, and sunflowers immediately, as they'll bloom in 60 days. If you've prepared your cutting garden in autumn, you can either plant the beds then or rest them over the winter. Hardy perennials and bulbs are suitable plantings in autumn, as are sowings of seed for biennials and the hardiest annuals, if it's still early fall. (See chapter 5 for "The Garden in Fall.") Leave plenty of room for sowing more seed in spring and adding tender bulbs and perennials. You'll find certain perennials such as bearded iris, oriental poppies, and peonies are sold for planting in fall, and others such as hardy mums and asters are best planted in spring. Leave space to install these plants at the proper time.

Keep a garden journal with yearly diagrams of what was planted where and the dates you sowed seed. Make notes on why a plant failed and lists of plants to try in the future. Use full names so that you'll know what you have and so that when friends ask for a division, you can tell them what it is. Make note of peak bloom dates in the garden, so you will know when to take pictures or schedule a party. Write a paragraph late every fall describing the essence of the garden year: the dry spring or wet summer, spectacular successes or failures, and events like the 17-year locusts or the new tiller. Staple in your soil tests. Your journal will be your best reference and will give you enormous pleasure, while also making you a better gardener.

Enjoy your cutting garden. You might want at first to avoid plants that demand special attention because they're unsuited to your climate or soil. If you rarely grow plants that are sensitive to the cold in your area, you can get away with never tying them up in particular ways, or laying evergreen boughs and heavy winter mulches. If you avoid plants that require a lighter soil, you won't need to truck in loads of soil amendments. But for the gardener with lots of energy, all these challenges may be part of the fun.

2

Choosing Plants

If there are essential flowers for the cutting garden, they're probably those most commonly known and loved. Daffodils have been gathered and sold as cut flowers since the time of Shakespeare, and tulips so affected the Dutch in 1635 that the government intervened to end the speculation in bulbs. So it's not surprising that daffodils and tulips almost always begin the year in the cutting garden, followed by favorites like iris, peonies, poppies, delphinium, and colorful summer phlox. If there are children in your home, you'll need at least one of the flowers that children fancy, like bleeding hearts or sunflowers. Most people want white daisies, whether Shasta daisies or ox-eye daisies, among others. And lilies, zinnias, dahlias, and fall chrysanthemums.

Connoisseurs will want hellebores and euphorbias, aconitums and astrantias, but it's not long before you realize there are many more plants out there than you can grow in a lifetime. I still haven't grown that *Smyrnium perfoliatum* I've been wanting for years. How do you begin to choose among them?

Climate and Garden Conditions

The more you garden, the more painful it may be to talk about gardening. I ask a gardener what he'll be growing this summer. It's late April and 86 degrees during the usual spring heat wave. He leans on his shovel and reveals his intention to plant ranunculus—he found it in a catalog. It's a bulb. He has ordered it and it should come soon. Dumbfounded, I don't even have the presence of mind to say "That certainly is a beautiful flower," which is the only kind and polite thing to say, because it's not right to take hope away from a gardener. It's unfortunate that many catalogs don't make clear what climatic conditions are necessary for good results (in this case, a long period of frost-free cool weather), but this gardener should do some simple research before sending in his check. Chapter 5's "Easy Garden for Beginners" has suggestions for new gardeners, and chapter 6 provides detailed information on hundreds of plants.

Regional garden writers (such as Elizabeth Lawrence, Henry Mitchell, and Allen Armitage for those of us in the upper Southeast) are the most useful to read for gardening advice; it was from them I learned that it was probably not my fault *Allium caeruleum*, globe-flowers, goat's beard, monkshood, and most of the gayfeathers were failing in my garden. You may also discover that plants from certain parts of the world do well in your area. Here in Virginia, it's worth trying plants native to Japan and Korea, but much less so those from South Africa.

You can thus pare your list first by selecting plants with a likelihood of success in your garden. Consult the USDA cold-hardiness zone map included in many seed and nursery catalogs for your zone. The American Horticultural Society has developed a new heat zone map, which you can find in their recent publications, on their website, and in some garden catalogs. Most catalogs note the hardiness zones of plants they offer, and we can hope soon they'll include the heat zone, too. Remember also that every locale and garden has its microclimates created, for example, by rivers or hills and, on a smaller scale, by such garden features as a south-facing wall that absorbs heat.

Shade reduces the plant list too, especially if it's dry shade. In a cutting garden, however, partial shade may be a boon, because some plants, such as monarda, often have better flowers in light shade, particularly in hotter areas of the South. Plenty of water in full sun may help, but very light shade tends to produce fuller blooms with better color on longer stems from plants that tolerate light shade. For specific recommendations for shade, see "The Shady Garden" in chapter 5.

While most books and catalogs are careful to provide information on cold hardiness, it's less simple to discover relative heat tolerance when selecting a plant, which is an important consideration for gardeners in Zone 7 and further south. Many perennials for cutting are difficult to grow in hot summer areas, and gardeners in those parts of the country will need to avoid them or decide which are valuable enough to replace every year. Northern catalogs commonly list plants for full sun that may burn to death in full sun in the South. Russell lupines, delphinium, monkshood, and geum are among those that need a long period of cool weather to flower well and that may become dormant or die in hot, humid weather. Other perennials, described as blooming throughout summer in Great Britain or cooler areas of the United States, will flower heavily in June and then stop blooming abruptly until the next year.

Many hardy annuals won't grow well in hot summer areas if you sow them in spring, because the spring there isn't long enough before the heat sets in. Cornflowers and larkspur are examples of extremely hardy annuals that may perform much better when they are planted in fall. You'd choose them for late spring cutting rather than all-summer cutting. Other annuals, like stocks, aren't cold hardy enough here in Virginia to be sown in fall and yet need cool weather to grow well, and so we have to search for heat-tolerant varieties and start them early under lights. For the same reason, when choosing sweet peas (or even peonies) for a hot-summer garden, you'll want to choose early-flowering varieties to escape the heat. And half-hardy annuals that prefer direct sowing, such as the beautiful *Trachymene coerulea,* are the most difficult of all: while they need a cool growing season, they can't be sown in fall where winters are cold, and yet they can't easily be started indoors, because they resent transplanting.

The hot summer does seem pretty burdensome until you appreciate its advantages, not the least of which is a long growing season. Those gardeners who envy the British their climate may be surprised to realize many sun lovers we take for granted can't be grown well there. A visit to England to see them desperately trying to grow tomatoes in tiny greenhouses *in summer* is instructive. I commented to one gardener that I'd never before seen those remarkable "grow bags" of special soil everyone had their tomatoes staked in. She said in disbelief, "You *don't* have *grow bags*?" I answered, as modestly as possible, that we don't *need* grow bags. I didn't tell her that, in fact, I don't always start my own tomatoes anymore, since decent plants just volunteer up from the ground or the compost heap. Certainly many cut flowers, not just tomatoes, thrive on sun and moderate heat. Among these are helianthus, eustoma, tithonia, hyacinth bean,

China asters, bloodflower, and zinnias. I'm still amused by the story I read somewhere of the English gardener who was delighted when he could get more than one plant of cleome from a packet.

Season

Unless you're away from your home for a portion of the year, you'll want flowers from spring through fall, making season of bloom a major factor in choosing plants for the cutting garden. "A Sequence of Bloom" (see appendix 4) lists cutting plants in order of their median date of first flowering through the year in Zone 7, from which you can determine roughly when flowers might bloom in your garden.

The bouquets of early spring are small, but charming; their short stems seem more welcome at that time for cutting than later in summer when the truly long-stemmed flowers are plentiful. It's trickier to plan flower combinations for spring than for other times of year, as variable weather can cause plants that usually bloom together to bloom weeks apart. It's best simply to have a nice variety among the many spring bulbs and perennials and be awake to possibilities.

Daffodils are the preeminent flower of March and April in my garden, followed by tulips. Other spring flowers not to miss include bleeding hearts, hellebores, primroses, and euphorbias. Unfortunately, spring plantings are sometimes ruined by poor weather; crocuses melt in the rain, daffodils bow to the ground splashed with mud, a late snow breaks the stems of *Helleborus foetidus*. You rinse and dry your flowers indoors and wait for the sun to reappear.

In earliest May, when the plants associated with early spring end, flower production slows briefly and the cutting garden will rely heavily on bearded and Siberian iris and peonies. These are important plants to have at that time, but others that keep the garden going include cornflowers, hesperis, painted daisies, coral bells, poppies, lady's mantle, and alliums such as *A. aflatunense*. The second or third week of May is the first time I carry in brimming buckets of flowers, and through June it's the season of most abundant flower production, tapering off to the few true friends of fall.

June supplies so many possibilities that the cutting garden fills quickly if you haven't given thought to the rest of the year. Handsome plants for June are Japanese iris, astilbe, summer phlox, delphinium, lilies, hollyhocks, and foxgloves. July brings flowers with strong personalities, like gloriosa daisies, celosia, crocosmia, and sea hollies, but also cleome, stokesia, and snow-on-the-mountain. If you like to be amusing, you can have red, white, and blue flowers on hand for a July Fourth picnic. August is the ideal time for zinnias and sunflowers, as so many other plants have finished; plan their sowing for late May or early June to avoid a slow month. Joe Pye weed, goldenrod, golden aster, China asters, and oriental lilies also make their appearance in August.

September should not be a time of just waiting for chrysanthemums. You should have dahlias and perennial asters in bloom as the mainstay of the month, but other annuals and perennials will still be around from summer. In October dahlias continue and mums begin. The last few substantial flowers here, before the cutting garden shuts down for the year, are the remaining chrysanthemums of November. For more on your garden in autumn, see "The Garden in Fall" in chapter 5.

Fashions for certain flowers come and go and may affect your choices strongly. A certain lily now is in every florist arrangement; seeing it so often, I'd never want to grow it, and in fact the scent repels me. But the rage for baby's breath has been gone long enough that my big crop of *Gypsophila elegans* 'Giant White' this year was a pleasure.

Annuals

In some places, the craze for perennials has created a bizarre bias against annuals. An annual is simply a plant whose life span is shorter than a perennial; this doesn't make it a less desirable plant, or more time consuming to grow. In fact, just the opposite could be said, as an area devoted to annuals can be planted or tilled at one time in thorough swoops. I'm always astonished by the notion that perennials are less work than annuals; just the contemplation of dividing a four-year-old boltonia is enough to make me call for help. I can't easily discipline Joe Pye weed or gooseneck loosestrife the way I can pull up rows of expiring zinnias or globe amaranth, and that giant clump of overgrown iris will still be sitting there long after winter has done the work of clearing my annual bed.

You can easily grow an enormous number of annual plants from seed for a fraction of the cost of perennial plants from a nursery, and without those annuals, you won't have as many flowers certain weeks of the year. I noticed one August that out of a vaseful of flowers I particularly enjoyed, only one of seven was a perennial, despite half my garden space being devoted to perennials. That year, out of 70 different kinds of flowering plants in my garden, 20 percent of those coming into bloom in May were annuals or biennials; in June, 22 percent; in July, 25 percent; and in August, 40 percent. Annuals also provide variety: a certain monotony sets into a perennial collection in a few years, when space is filled and there's little room for new plants. I don't care for growing the same thing too many seasons in a row, or I find myself using buckets of flowers as doorstops because I never got around to arranging them.

Biennials

Biennials are of particular interest because they're usually more cold hardy than most hardy annuals—they're especial friends of gardeners in the North. They have neither the permanence of perennials nor the immediacy of annuals. They're unknown plants to many gardeners, because they're excluded from books about annuals as well as from books about perennials, and possibly because they require patience. It's not unusual to meet someone who has been gardening for years but has never grown sweet rocket or honesty (money plant) or Chinese forget-me-nots. I once saw the help at a well-respected garden center cut back a large potted Canterbury bells *(Campanula medium)* that had finished flowering, and quite innocently put it back out for sale; the poor soul buying such a plant undoubtedly will think he killed it when it disappears. Of course, confusion is understandable, as short-lived perennials may appear to behave like biennials, and hardy annuals that are sown in the fall for spring bloom may leave a similar impression. A biennial like wild parsnip *(Pastinaca sativa)* may self-sow so reliably that the gardener has never even noticed what its life cycle is. A few, such as sweet William and some hollyhocks, flower after a shorter period of growth than another like honesty *(Lunaria annua)*, which requires a full year. Biennials are best undertaken by the gardener who doesn't mind waiting and who has space to devote to plants that don't bloom for a year and are dead the next. Anyone who wants to grow interesting cut flowers, however, will want to try these beautiful plants.

Because biennials have an aura of rarity to them and have to be held by nurserymen for as much as a year, they're sometimes quite expensive compared to annuals. It may only be worthwhile to buy hollyhocks, foxgloves, verbascums, and other biennial plants at the same price as perennials (as they usually are) from a nursery catalog or garden center if you can't start them from seed yourself. I've seen year-old potted foxgloves, ready to bloom, for the same price as two perennials. To have the desirable conditions to permit them to self-sow is the best hope.

Perennials

Perennials, for most cut-flower gardeners, are dependable friends whose reappearance every year is taken for granted, yet they form the backbone of the garden. The old iris and peonies that were there when you bought the house, the Shastas and asters you divide when you remember to, the Joe Pye weed at the back of the garden—all these supply flowers regularly without much thought. A number of perennials, and even a few annuals, grow to such a grand size that they're not suitable for small gardens; see chapter 5's "The Small Garden" for suggestions on this common problem.

Some genera, such as *Primula* and *Euphorbia*, contain so many interesting plants that you may enjoy collecting special varieties for the cutting garden. Perennial vining plants are also good choices and include perennial sweet peas and hops. Many herbs make pretty bouquets, with or without flowers, including sage, agastache, feverfew, artemisia, chives and garlic chives, nepeta, echinacea, fennel, tansy, lavender, and angelica.

Some perennials are better grown as annuals in difficult climates. Where it's cold, of course, such perennials may be called "tender." Tender perennials (better said as perennials tender to your area) such as Mexican bush may require replanting each year, but it's worth the effort to locate them from time to time. Where heat is the problem, instead of trying to keep alive a purchased anthemis or delphinium for another year, you can grow the plants from seed and pull them up after they have flowered or allow them to self-sow.

Other perennials such as columbines are also grown from seed by nurseries, and you can attempt this too. Good seed catalogs offer marvelous perennial seed such as lychnis, tellima, verbascums, and penstemons, selections you may not even be able to find from nurs-

eries. But be sure to note the information on germination, invaluable
when selecting unfamiliar seed. If I read "germination in 90 days to
one year," for example, I don't order that seed, as it's too difficult
to provide suitable conditions. I'd rather order the plant.

Invasive plants may present unwanted additional digging and
hoeing for weekend gardeners, because some plants grow so quickly
they require division almost immediately. *Achillea millefolium* 'White
Beauty' is one that outran my efforts to remove weeds around it and
had soon entombed them. If you're not put off by invasive plants,
however, locate them in a separate spot. It can be distressing to discover in spring that the little slip of tansy you set out in fall is now
inches away from a demure coral bells. Since you're going to be cutting the flowers, plants that are invasive by means of self-seeding are
less of a worry, unless you leave town at the crucial time. If you can't
rely on yourself to cut back the seedheads of a plant like *Chasmanthium latifolium*, don't get it.

Bulbs

A gardener's eyes are often too big for the garden when it comes to
bulbs. Practiced gardeners who've struggled in the past to get their
bulbs planted, learn to limit the fall's bulb purchase to 6, 30, or 100,
depending on the circumstances. Busy people might well begin with
no more than 30 bulbs and gauge their satisfaction in spring.

The indispensable daffodils and tulips have a long season of bloom
and great variety of color, form, and size; every cut-flower garden
should include these two bulbs somewhere. Because daffodil bulbs
are longer lasting in the ground than tulips, I think of daffodils as
my best bulb investment, and tulips as my best bulb indulgence. The
smaller flowering bulbs of spring, such as crocus, Spanish bluebells,
and muscari, are excellent for little bouquets with the other small
garden flowers of the season. Some of the less familiar fall-planted
bulbs the cutting garden should include at some time are various alliums, camassias, *Anemone coronaria*, *Nectaroscordum siculum*, *Leucojum*
'Gravetye Giant', and *Gladiolus byzantinus*. Expensive bulbs you may
like to treat yourself to on occasion include foxtail lilies and the giant
alliums.

Spring-planted bulbs for summer cutting such as nerines, tuberoses, and a gladiolus relative like *G. callianthus* aren't familiar to
most people, so they're quite interesting. However, the long warm

growing season that many require to flower makes some of them more difficult to grow in cold winter areas. Dahlias, which grow from tubers, are often listed with bulbs for spring and should be included in every sunny cutting garden. The bigger seed companies often offer spring-planted bulbs and tubers for purchase along with your spring seed order.

Self-sowers

Self-sowing plants that aren't invasive can lighten the work of propagation. They're especially valuable in the South, where the long growing season allows them to come and go at their leisure. While plants vary by climate as to whether they self-sow, here in Virginia some good volunteers are myosotis, anthemis, Shirley poppies, snow-on-the-mountain, and columbines (a more complete list of self-sowers in my area appears in appendix 2). You'll notice which are self-sowers in your garden and can take the opportunity to encourage them by using only light mulches and by going easy on the hoe. Get to recognize seedlings and think twice while you're weeding.

If you allow annuals to seed year after year, observe them to notice if flower quality is deteriorating. Cornflowers may become smaller, larkspur may revert to only one or two shades of color, columbine colors become muddy. The solution is to bring on fresh seed and rogue out the reverted types.

Fillers

Fillers are flowers or foliage that fill out a vase without overpowering the featured flowers and that sometimes make the best sort of arrangement just by themselves, without any showcase flowers at all. They are necessary in any cutting garden and include small green and acid-yellow flowers such as patrinia, bupleurum, fennel, dill, wild parsnip, and various euphorbias. They also include the familiar small white flowers of gypsophila, feverfew, and Queen Anne's lace. Add to that the less well-known angelica, valerian, ammi, Jerusalem oak, kalimeris, centranthus, *Calamintha nepeta, Euphorbia corollata,* and *Aster pringlei* 'Monte Cassino'. Other tiny flowers of various colors include *Limonium latifolium, Briza media,* myosotis, tellima, some thalictrums, and heuchera. (All of these flowers and many more are described in depth in chapter 6, "Two Hundred Choice

Plants for Your Cutting Garden.") Modest larger green flowers like the zinnia 'Envy', bells of Ireland, "white" marigolds cut while still green, and the green and white viridiflora tulip 'Spring Green' will be a similar aid in arranging. You can use green flower heads of sedum and goldenrod before they show color, as well as many other flowers in bud. Grasses and the more ornamental among the weeds, such as mustard and wild onions, are also worth gathering for arranging in their season.

The foliage from a number of perennials and some annuals is useful for greenery in the vase. Examples of foliage you can pick from the garden border or vegetable garden, as well as the cutting garden, are artemisia, Egyptian onion, galax, tellima, epimedium, Solomon's seal, orach, hosta, bergenia, ballota, liriope, ivy, hops, and the strappy leaves of iris.

Variegated leaves are especially desirable. You can take green seed-heads and pods from such plants as iris, agapanthus, agrostemma, poppies, tulips, lilies, honesty, euphorbia, butterfly weed, perennial sweet peas, hellebores, and nigella. You can also use mature stems of ferns in arrangements, but fiddleheads and immature fronds will usually wilt irrecoverably.

Form and Interest

It's surprising to find that some plants may be better looking in the vase than you anticipated in the garden. Gaudy tulips and loud dahlias are examples of flowers usually better appreciated once they come indoors.

When selecting plants for the cutting garden, try to provide a range of flower forms for harmony and interest: spiky, like veronica or obedient plant; rounded like peonies; daisy-form like China asters; large like summer phlox and small like forget-me-nots; in sprays like solidaster, and single on long stems such as globeflowers; modest like tellima, and bold like sunflowers; tight-headed like achillea and in loose clusters like boltonia. *Penstemon barbatus* and bells of Ireland are two of those whose stems arch and twist endearingly at the tips. Some flowers' natural carriage is drooping, like checkered lilies and hellebores, and you'll want to include them. Naturally curving stems such as those of crocosmia, old-fashioned bleeding heart, or *Gladiolus byzantinus* make arranging seem effortless, and like the vines of nasurtiums and hops that trail so satisfyingly from pedestal vases, they'll dip toward the table as though still heavy with dew.

Some flowers particularly invite inspection indoors. I could look at Canterbury bells *(Campanula medium)* for hours, which is more easily done in the house than by bringing a chair up to the plant. You'll want to see up close the exquisitely furled buds of eustoma, the crinkled petals of poppies and beautifully packed petals of ranunculus, the insides of tulips, the prickly balls of globe thistle or castor bean, veins of malva and iris, spurs of columbines and tendrils of sweet peas, the spots of foxgloves and lilies, the geometric pattern at the center of sunflowers, and the dangling oats and tears of grasses. Children are enchanted by snowdrops, tiger lilies, and snapdragons, and it's more than names that inspire their interest.

We often want bold or "masculine" flowers or foliage for a certain place or event. Good choices for such occasions are brushlike, thorny, or spiky flowers like acanthus, sea holly, torch lilies, teasel, globe thistle, various grasses, safflower or *Centaurea macrocephala*. Interesting fruited or seed-pod carrying plants are castor bean and Chinese lanterns. Bicolored and strongly zoned flowers command attention: two-toned dahlias or gloriosa daisies like 'Sputnik'. Dark and "black" flowers make unusual displays, for which black tulips, black dahlias, black hollyhocks, dark brown sunflowers, or brown iris are especially good. Red stems and leaves such as those of amaranthus, hardy begonia, hyacinth bean, *Atriplex hortensis* 'Rubra', or *Celosia* 'Wine Sparkler' are striking in glass vases, to show off stems as well as flowers.

Flowers as well as foliage can be intriguingly variegated: tulips, bearded iris, and dahlias such as strongly colored 'Vernon Rose', are usually striped with red, but sometimes with white. Curiosities like Thompson & Morgan's *Rudbeckia* 'Green Wizard', a coneflower with green sepals but no petals, appear in catalogs from time to time and provide a nice opportunity to display something unusual. Of course, you can always include in arrangements the branches (even twiggy branches without leaves) and berries of shrubs and trees found outside the cutting garden, and fruits and vegetables, such as artichokes and colorful peppers, from the vegetable garden.

Color

Color is often cited first when deciding whether to grow a plant. Blue is a popular color for flowers, although what passes for blue with nurserymen is often violet or purple. I've heard many people say they don't like yellow or red flowers, and even fewer like orange or salmon. This means there are people who don't like sunflowers in the house. It does seem true that few elegant flowers are yellow, and frequently the shades of yellow are crude, like the construction-paper yellow of zinnias. Lemon-yellow flowers on occasion do not look good with golden yellow.

But the gardener who has no yellow is missing something important. Some more refined yellows are found among daffodils, primroses, Iceland poppies, Carolina lupine, globeflowers, columbines, lilies, cephalaria, dahlias, and collard greens gone to flower. If you prefer lemon-yellow sunflowers like 'Lemon Queen', rather than gold, read catalog descriptions carefully to find them.

Red is sometimes difficult to work into an arrangement, but red is also the surprise that a bouquet often needs: a red *Anemone coronaria* in a spring basket of pink, blue, and green, or stems of *Crocosmia* 'Lucifer' in a country arrangement of yellow and white. Orange and salmon you may have to use alone unless you're clever, but a vase of salmon poppies or orange zinnias makes a great show. Very pretty oranges for orange-haters to try come from the *Geum* and *Trollius* clans.

If you want exquisite color, some plants have especially nice color ranges: stocks, tulips, poppies, peonies, larkspur, delphinium, penstemon, godetia, sweet peas, ranunculus, iris, the hollyhock 'Indian Spring', and dahlias. When you're tired of pink, it might be time to try the buff-colored verbascums of 'Southern Charm Hybrid'. Green flowers are particularly intriguing.

Very dark flowers show up poorly indoors, unless the natural light in your house is exceptionally bright, but so many of the sophisticated "black" flowers are impossible to resist. Loud colors are wonderful, but choose too many for the garden and you'll later find you can't put them together in a bowl. When in doubt, get white. In fact, white sets off other colors, for which reason it's often used for filler, though masses of white flowers may need a green companion.

Length of Bloom

Plants known for a long bloom season are appealing, but they may not have that long a harvest time in the cutting garden. Even with sincere efforts at deadheading, many plants become more and more difficult to harvest from because of mildewed foliage (heliopsis), innumerable seed heads among the flowers (malva and nigella), increasingly smaller flowers and shorter stems (veronica), fading colors (sidalcea), or stems dirtied by sticky juices and insects (nicotiana and cleome). Some plants may be almost impossible to deadhead, such as calliopsis and golden aster. All these plants are best cut when first blooming, and so are not necessarily better in the cutting garden than plants that bloom for only a short time.

A related consideration is the vase life of flowers, some lasting much longer than others and mattering much more to the owner of a small cutting garden. Two supremely long-lasting flowers are prairie gentians *(Eustoma grandiflorum)* and Canterbury bells *(Campanula medium)*. Length of life in the vase is something that becomes less important the more flowers you grow; there is always something new coming into bloom.

Fragrance and Night Closing

Most people prefer the sort of fragrance you notice at the flower rather than a smell that fills the house. You'll probably only want a plant known for its strong scent, such as *Phlox divaricata,* in small amounts for bouquets, and in the case of lilies, probably never for the dining table. Sometimes you can trace an unpleasant smell in the house to flowers like cleome or ox-eye daisies that you had otherwise trusted. Patrinia, valerian, and *Eryngium planum* are others that may smell slightly off-putting in the house, and some bugbanes (though you can use their beautiful buds) quite simply reek and would never come indoors. For arrangements in spacious rooms in situations where people won't be in prolonged proximity to the flowers, strong flower scent is less a problem.

Tradition says that a flower that closes at night can't be a good cut flower, but that would eliminate stokesia or the glowing *Aster novae-angliae* 'Alma Potschke', two of my favorites. Just don't put them on the dining table or any other place you'll especially notice in the evening. Yet other interesting flowers open fully only at night and are fragrant, like *Hosta plantaginea,* the August Lily.

Stem Length

Most of us like long stems in a cut flower. Some spring-flowering plants such as primulas, doronicum, and English daisies *(Bellis perennis)* begin the season flowering on short stems that gradually lengthen toward the finish, and if the weather has been cool and favorable, with plenty of moisture, almost any plant will have longer stems. A little shade for some plants lengthens their stems, sometimes dramatically. To the new gardener's disappointment, though, it's next to impossible to reproduce the very long stems of many florist flowers in the home garden—stocks and snapdragons are two examples—as many growers manipulate light and temperature in greenhouses to achieve their length. The shorter stems of home-grown plants are much simpler to arrange, however.

Deciding on the size of bouquets you'll be arranging will also make it easier to select plants for the garden. Stem length is an important consideration for large arrangements, or if you detest short stems past spring. During spring, I'll use flowers with stem lengths of only 6 inches, but later I like stem length to be at least 12 inches. Gardeners with high ceilings and open spaces will use flowers with very long stems or large arrangements to much better effect than those with small rooms—tall, long-stemmed arrangements in low-ceilinged rooms only call attention to the low headroom.

Don't forget that there's more to cut than just the contents of your cutting garden. While you wouldn't pick rare wildflowers, there are interesting plants to be found at the road's edge, and even in your own yard. I rarely remember to cut the ivy and vinca we have everywhere, and I forget how nice the leaves of iris can be in an arrangement, but I do see the wild pink sweet pea in overgrown lots and like to put it with the 'White Pearl' I grow. You can find Queen Anne's lace or thistles by the roadsides, along with Joe Pye weed and other wild plants, like mustard. And the slim stems of dogwood or serviceberry trees are especially nice, as, of course, are many shrubs and roses.

While it's difficult to imagine a cutting garden without certain classic cutting flowers, like phlox or lilies, every garden will be different according to the taste of the owner and the nature of the garden. You may find you want only a few choice plants for your cutting garden. When I first began to garden, I was so desperate for flowers, any would do, and the more the better. Now after years of gardening, the flowers must be special, as I'm more willing for the house to be without flowers between harvests. It's a great pleasure to grow something new, perhaps something difficult, or masses and masses of a favorite, flowers to feast the eye rather than just decorate the house.

3

Garden Proceedings

Gardens change from year to year, and so does the work they require. Some springs I wear the skin off my fingers pulling up sprouted acorns from the oaks overhead; other years there is scarce a one. Another season, the 17-year cicadas emerge, leaving deep holes into which we watch the "gardener" snakes, as my young son called them, disappear. After picking our way through cicadas to the garage, there'd be more sitting on the handles of the garden tools, and one on each picket of the fence, like birds in a frightening movie. There are years you never get out the hose, and others when the entire gardening activity seems to be moving around sprinklers. There have even been years when my roses did not have blackspot. I find, like an old farmer, I can recall the dates of heat waves and spring droughts. This kind of connectedness to the earth is only one of the great blessings of a garden.

Another reward is work for the body and peace for the mind. Anyone who has weeded for long stretches, or dug up a patch, knows the tranquilizing effect of the effort, the pleasure of looking up to see a squirrel or goldfinch hard at work on a sunflower head, and hearing the voices of children in the distance. And of course, there's the pleasure of working in dreadful old clothes in which you're thoroughly comfortable as you are nowhere else. In these times, you can buy special gardening attire from mail-order catalogues, but I don't know if I could treat new garb with the disregard that is the special joy of wearing old clothes in the garden.

Once the cutting garden is established, there will be less work, especially if the garden is shady. Weeds grow slowly in shade; a shady garden may need a good weeding only three or four times a year. It's another matter in sun, however, and weeding may constitute the majority of work in an established garden in full sun. Planting, propagating, maintaining the soil, removing finished flowers to prevent seed setting ("deadheading"), disposing of detritus, battling insects, and watering are the other essential jobs in the garden.

Planting

Setting new plants in the garden is a pleasant task when the soil is in good condition. A major reason for failure with annuals and perennials is poor cultivation of the soil before sowing seed or planting. Perhaps the smallness of the tiny plant or seed lulls the gardener into thinking the digging requirements are minor as well. If you find yourself using a hand trowel when putting in plants, and they later don't flower like they should, you might want to get in the habit of planting even small plants with a shovel instead. You'll also avoid the embarrassment of discovering that the plant you've concernedly been coddling for several years has been growing in only four or five inches of soil over a buried flagstone or drainpipe. This kind of idiocy happens less often when the gardener uses a shovel and not a trowel. Keep soil amendments on hand so they're more likely to be used.

The right tool makes all the difference in turning soil and digging planting holes. A garden fork turns large amounts easily for protracted digging. For those not so strong, and for young assistants, a shovel called a "perennial shovel" by some catalogs and a "lady's shovel" in hardware stores makes work much less tiring. The blade is smaller, eight to nine inches long, and digs less soil at one time. Get the long handle when possible, and see that the blade is turned over at the edge for your foot. Wear a thick-soled shoe while you dig, so that you don't damage your feet. If you garden so that large areas can be cleared and turned at one time, you'll be able to use a tiller.

Plant on cloudy days, if possible, as strong sun is a strain on a new plant; you can rig up temporary shade for a few days to prevent transplant shock. Cut back the foliage to match the root loss if it seems appropriate, especially if it wilts. If the plant is heavy with flowers and buds, it may establish better if the blooming stems are cut at planting, a practice that's difficult to bear in the border, but right up the cutting garden alley. Water regularly, and once the plants are established, water deeply but infrequently to encourage deep roots. You can locate plants that benefit from afternoon shade to the east of a north-south row of tall bushy plants like hollyhocks and tithonia, or a line of tomato cages, if you're growing vegetables too. Interweaving tall, airy plants like calliopsis can also create light shade on neighboring sufferers.

The plants in a cutting garden can usually be spaced more closely together than in a display garden. This may cause them to be slightly smaller, but it should increase the number of flowers per given area, and when you cut the flowers, space will open up between plants. You may choose to crowd some of the bigger sunflowers deliberately to reduce the size of their flowers, but species that have special requirements for good ventilation, such as summer phlox and zinnias, shouldn't be crowded, nor should sun lovers that are particularly intolerant of shade, like cornflowers or globe amaranth. Squeezing in single specimens isn't a good idea either, as you may forget some are there, and they'll pass their flowering time before you remember to cut. I have a goat's beard behind tall lilies and bushy bugbanes, and I often discover in June, too late, that it has almost finished flowering.

Avoid growing annuals every year in the same place; a few do less well in only the second year in the same location. Crop rotation should be practiced in the cutting garden, too. When you grow two different crops a year in the same spot (succession planting), such as cornflowers followed by celosia, or larkspur followed by zinnias, or where plants are grown closely, you must pay particular care to maintaining fertility. Fertilizing of perennials should begin in earliest spring, not when all new growth is above the ground, but if you amended the soil well when you first dug the bed (see chapter 1, "Ground Work"), you may not need much fertilizer for a while. A compost pile is a useful garden project for sidedressing plants during the growing season.

Be ready with stakes in the cutting garden, as high winds will topple even the calliopsis and sunflowers, and they must be righted within a day or two or they'll suffer bending of their stems from turning up to the light. Some plants, like dahlias, must be staked from the beginning, easier to do then than to correct the problem later. Sometimes a tomato cage can be set down over a smaller plant when it flops, with the plant threaded up through the wires. You can salvage good pointed stakes from old picket fences, but as they're hardly unobtrusive, what I think of as a find may be someone else's eyesore.

We all know planting bulbs is arduous work in unprepared soil. Often you can use a shovel with a back-and-forth rocking motion to open a slit in the ground into which to place smaller bulbs. Bulb planters are a help, but a heavy electric drill and auger—some specially sold for planting bulbs—makes quicker work of hard ground.

To do a better job of planting a bulb bed, dig the entire space to a depth of 12 inches and amend the soil well. The results will make the work worthwhile, and the planting painless. Where squirrels dig up bulbs, you can place large rectangles of wire "hardware cloth" over the area to keep them out while still allowing rain in. Lift the screens in spring when growth shows. When bulbs disappear, mark the location of empty spaces before the foliage is gone in June, so that in fall you'll know just where to put new selections; a metal marker pushed deep into the soil lasts the longest.

Dividing Perennials

You'll save space in the cutting garden and not find yourself caring for unwanted flowers if you keep your perennials only as big as you need, dividing plants as soon as they're too large. Some years I find I have more achillea, chrysopsis, or boltonia than I can even give away. A number of plants like Siberian iris or gas plant don't require division, but others like chrysanthemums and asters become sparse flowering or weedy without it. A somewhat simplistic rule of thumb is to divide plants in the spring that bloom in the fall, and for those that bloom in the spring, divide after flowering or in the fall. Always take the opportunity to amend the soil before you replant.

Digging up and dividing large perennials is hard work, and sometimes you need to find help to get the job done. Good luck. Few people really want to dig, especially not in somebody else's garden. One year a heartwarming sign went up along the road, the kind of sign that makes my car screech to a stop. It read:

GARDENING
Nick

Even more promising were the little flowers painted around the edges. I called the number and explained I had an old torch lily, a boltonia, and a huge bearded iris clump that needed digging up and dividing, and after that I wanted to deeply dig and weed the whole area and amend the soil. Nick promised to let me know when.

More calls to Nick were unreturned. Somehow I suspect Nick had really hoped to cut the grass and put in a few annuals from the garden center.

Sowing Seed in the Garden

Spring brings the seed-sowing season most people know. Some gardeners only sow annuals in April and May, then leave off gardening when the plants quit on them in September. You can, however, be sowing seed of a wide variety almost all year around, in the garden or indoors under lights (see appendix 1, "Growing Seed under Lights"), and many climates will require you to adjust conventional wisdom on when to sow.

Over the years, I've worked up several pages of indoor and outdoor seed-starting instructions to myself, which have everything I need to know in one place. Each plant I frequently sow has its own line with planting depth; need for light or dark; optimal temperature; whether hardy, half-hardy, or tender; annual, biennial, or perennial; and notes like "peat pot," "chill 24 hrs.," or "chip and soak." I've put these notes in plastic sleeves, so they're easy to take into the garden. Get this information from seed catalogs, books (see the suggested reading list at the back of this book), and the Internet, and then adjust it on the basis of your own experience in your specific growing area.

You can save the printed plastic labels that come with purchased plants, and long after the original plant is gone, you can use them as markers in the garden for rows of sown seed or the location of bulbs. Since they do break and get pulled up by mistake, I use them only as markers and record on a plan in my notebook what's planted where for each season.

Some types of seed are best sown in rows: those that come up slowly or erratically, are small for a long time, or look like grass, such as bupleurum. Sowing in a row, though unimaginative, makes identifying seedlings easier among weeds and permits hoeing and mulching between plantings. Quick-growing reliable plants with big easily recognized seedlings like zinnias and sunflowers are fine for putting into odd spots here or there, or spaced over an irregular area. Broadcasting over a large patch works well for small plentiful seed that shouldn't be covered, like Shirley poppies, and even for dill and *Verbena bonariensis*, which can come up between other plants.

When the seed has germinated abundantly, you need to thin the seedlings, a difficult chore for many people to do. It can even be difficult for people to watch. Some seed is expensive and there is little in the envelope: sow it thinly, as you wouldn't want to waste many seedlings by unnecessary thinning. Gaps left in the row from poor germination can be filled in later by purchased plants or last-minute sowings of foolproof seed like zinnias. Occasionally, I receive seed I cannot germinate indoors or out, but it's worth trying another pack from a different source before concluding that it's too difficult to grow.

Perhaps one out of five of my seed-growing efforts failed when I first began gardening, and many still do. I may get only a few or no plants at all, or stunted plants, or plants that die prematurely, but it's always enjoyable, every season, to try growing something difficult, or something that came to little the year before, bells of Ireland, bupleurum, or *Campanula pyramidalis,* for instance.

In Fall

Autumn finds me sowing certain hardy annuals and biennials, and some perennials, in the cutting garden. Many popular annuals can't successfully be sown in spring in hot summer areas, but autumn sowing usually produces a fine crop for the cutting garden the following spring. Even in cool-summer areas where fall sowing is not essential for success, hardy fall-sown plants should bloom weeks earlier than spring-sown plants.

Starting hardy annual seed outdoors in the fall isn't always a foolproof method. Plants that were there in November may not be there in March, and warm spells in January may induce plants to grow rapidly and promptly freeze back. But I've had terrible results as well with seed sown in spring, weather again being the culprit. (What can't the gardener blame on weather?) Lavatera has been washed away by spring rains, and godetia burned by early heat. When it works, though, as it usually does, planting certain hardy annual seeds in the fall produces spectacular results.

Agrostemma, cornflowers, nigella, gypsophila, some poppies, and larkspur are a few of the annuals that especially profit from fall sowing, as they require a long period of cold before flowering. Be sure to sow them at least six weeks before your cold weather gets under way. However, many perennials and some biennials, such as foxgloves or honesty (money plant), grow so slowly from seed that you must start them in the previous spring rather than fall, so they have a chance to develop to a good size before winter appears. For the best show, always give biennials as long a growing season as you can.

The surface of recently dug or tilled soil in fall may dry out more quickly than expected. Check more frequently than in spring for soil dryness, even after germination. You can water the bed well *before* sowing seed, too. I only mulch the fall seed bed lightly, as mulch may smoother seedlings and delay my garden from drying out and warming up in spring, and some plants like agrostemma and gypsophila are particularly vulnerable to winter sogginess. It's also difficult to prepare a seed bed and sow seed where squirrels are active, as they're attracted to disturbed earth; you may have the best results broadcasting seed over lightly scratched or undisturbed soil.

It's best to complete fall sowing in my garden by the end of September to get the plants established before winter, though some plants like poppies won't germinate until cooler weather of about 55 degrees appears, sometimes not until October. Another reason for not sowing most seed late is that it's difficult to hoe or mulch while waiting for seed to emerge, and not getting a good last hoeing in November can mean a terrible weed problem in March and April. Further north, fall sowings of hardy annuals may purposely be done just before the freeze to delay germination until spring, as young seedlings are vulnerable to deep winter. Such a "cold treatment" may actually improve germination of some types of seed—often it's the self-sowers like larkspur or cleome that like a good chilling.

I always buy more seed and plan more plantings than I actually have room for. Invariably something fails to germinate or doesn't survive the winter, and that's where you can later sow celosia or China asters, or plant purchased *Salvia farinacea* or *Eustoma grandiflorum*.

In Winter

January and February, I'm in the basement first starting perennials like delphinium, verbascum, and gloriosa daisies under lights, and later the hardy and half-hardy annuals like blue lace flower and calendula. In March, during the daffodil time, I may be out in the garden sowing hardy and half-hardy annuals such as Shirley poppies, cleome, sweet peas, and *Verbena bonariensis*, which appreciate a spell of chilling and do well sown in place in late winter or earliest spring.

You begin to feel your efforts have failed when the seedbed is blank week after week, but in perhaps the week or two before the average last frost date, the seedlings reward patience and generally all begin to appear at once. If nothing has shown in a few weeks after that, you'll want to sow another selection, although this time, particularly in the South, it may need to be a heat-tolerant annual. And a couple of weeks before your frost date the seedlings begun indoors under lights can be brought out for gradual hardening off.

In Spring

Midspring after the *average* last frost—about April 15 here, an easy date to remember, but it varies from place to place—and for the following month, is the best time to sow most annuals directly in the garden (half-hardy annuals like lavatera and bells of Ireland in the first weeks and tender annuals like gomphrena or celosia in the later). It's also the time to plant out seedlings begun indoors. In colder areas where spring comes late and the ground is unworkable for a long period, creating a shorter growing season, gardeners have greater difficulty sowing in situ and must rely more on purchased plants and plants started under lights, though several plants with brief flowering periods such as *Gypsophila elegans*, nigella, and dill are often suggested for successive sowings two or three weeks apart to keep flowers coming through summer.

I have a fondness for the easy direct-sown seeds that leap into plants almost immediately, such as zinnias, sunflowers, castor bean, and calendula. They're especially good for new gardeners (see "The Easy Garden for Beginners," in chapter 5). Poppies and others like godetia don't appear for weeks, while weeds are sprouting everywhere and rooting firmly. Sowing directly in the garden is the easiest way to start plants, though in preparing the seedbed and providing regular moisture, you're also creating ideal conditions for the germination of weeds.

Put aside some seed for zinnias or other quick-growing annuals for sowing in very late spring, even if it can be sown earlier, to be assured of having new plants coming into flower in August, a month that otherwise is rather tired. For that same reason, you may not want to start too many tender annuals early under lights, unless you need greater variety of bloom earlier in summer or you garden in an area with a short growing season and find that, for example, ageratum takes too long when sown direct (garden talk for "directly in the garden"). In the South, however, one is well advised to sow many of the hardy or half-hardy annuals early under lights to get a jump on the heat.

In Summer

Where it's hot, only a few kinds of seed can be sown successfully in early summer for late summer and fall bloom (amaranthus, sunflowers, China asters, and tithonia are some), and it may be difficult to keep the seedbed moist. Indoor lights are especially valuable for starting plants during summer for planting out in fall, as the conditions indoors in your basement or another room may be cooler and permit germination of the biennials and perennials, like stocks, violas, Chinese forget-me-nots, and Canterbury bells, that dislike hot weather.

Collecting your own seed is a great way to keep down garden expenses, and such fresh seed often gives better results. Take a paper lunch bag (for big seed) or white china mug (for fine seed) into the garden and cut the ripened seedheads into it whole. Clean and remove the pods and any chaff left behind, and keep the seed in an unsealed bag or glassine envelope in the refrigerator. You may not get what you expect, however, as I found when I collected seed from off-white zinnias one year, and got every other color possible the next.

I sometimes read advice that's simply impossible and obviously intended for gardeners in Britain or Canada, or at least at higher altitudes, such as to sow biennial poppy seed in summer at 55 to 60 degrees. I can't imagine how that temperature could be arranged in summer in Virginia unless Luray Caverns agreed to take the seed trays for a week. Sometimes you'll read a recommendation to sow in summer in a cold greenhouse! Who has heard of such a thing in most of the United States?

Weeding and Mulching

Total weed removal before winter arrives is the best assurance against unwanted flora in spring. In a sunny garden, weeds take over quickly, even when the garden is otherwise asleep. The gardener I know with the most weed-free soil achieves it in part by covering his vegetable and annual patch with heavy black plastic in winter, tilling once in April. However, there's no substitute for persistent attention to weeding, by hand or hoe, through the growing season. Pull them after rain or watering, and you'll get more of the root. Apply a good mulch for the summer to conserve moisture as well as prevent weeds.

Loose soil aids weed removal, though it's true that rampant plants are sometimes held in check by difficult soil. A passion flower vine became a terrible menace in my deeply dug soil, while my neighbor, Mary Ellen K., grows hers sedately in unimproved clay, which, she says, is about the same as growing it in a clay pot.

It's a little more important to keep a perennial bed weed free than an annual bed. Many weeds are perennials too, and letting them invade a perennial planting can be rather like growing a yarrow inside a phlox. With the annual bed, of course, once a year you can dispose of everything. But if you keep the worst weeds out of the perennials, you can give divisions to friends or the garden society plant sale.

Frequent, timely mulching works well against weeds. Thick layers of black-and-white newspaper covered with salt hay have been an effective mulch here on paths, but they are difficult to apply around individual plants. When salt hay can't be found, straw has to do, though it brings a few weeds with it. Shredded leaves make a simple mulch to use around small plants, though it degrades quickly. Heavier mulches include shredded or chipped wood and pine bark, but a disadvantage of such mulching is that it may discourage desirable volunteers. I wouldn't heavily mulch any plant I hoped would self-sow, or only mulch with a short-lived material such as the shredded leaves. Some plants like gaillardia and penstemon should rarely be mulched, because they're prone to crown rot. Mulching may eventually cause nitrogen loss, which you can remedy with fertilizers or cottonseed meal and dried blood.

Pests and Disease

There are days in August when, mercifully, there is little that needs doing in the garden but killing bugs. I was taught to kill aphids between my fingers by Mary Ellen K., but it was a full summer before I was able to bear it. They squash easily by running your fingers down the stem, and you need a hose nearby to rinse your fingers afterward. I rather like aphids compared to those creatures that do their dirty work underground. The plastic grocery bags I despised so much at first are excellent for collecting slugs, then tying the handles tightly and tossing in the trash. A birdbath brings birds into the garden to banquet on insects.

I'm often late to diagnose insect damage. Usually I have enough plants that I may just pull out such a plant. But if a prized specimen needs treatment, you will have to consider using insecticidal soap and hope it will work. I once asked a group of codgers in a garden center about the efficacy of insecticidal soaps, and their raucous laughter was apparently their answer.

Sometimes an ailing plant is diseased, and again, quick removal is the easiest solution. Shasta daisies seem to die of an affliction here, to the point that it's simplest not to plant them, though the plants I grew from seed myself have been long lived. Keep the garden clean. Rotting iris tubers or fallen iris foliage should always be removed promptly. China asters and hollyhocks sometimes get a soil-borne disease, but rotating their position in the garden should prevent it. If possible, avoid watering the leaves of plants like phlox that are prone to foliar diseases; soaker hoses and drip irrigation take water directly to the root zone. But I confess to being an old overhead waterer who likes doing it that way best.

The Garden Grows

Sometimes the cutting garden feels like it has grown too big. You know your garden has become big when you come across plants while weeding in the spring and wonder what they are, or find yourself wrenching them out by mistake. It helps to take a yearly inventory in fall and to keep a sketch of your garden in your notebook. Save your nursery receipts and shipping lists in a file. Also save your empty seed packets for a couple years back, rubber-banded together by year. You've always grown more things, and more often, than you remember.

You might want to keep a bulb book in which all your bulb plantings are entered by year. You could just keep the receipts, which I also do, but those are never as readily at hand as your bulb book. I make my entries in a little blank book with a lovely painting by Redoute on the cover, given me by a gardening friend. It struck me one spring that I could not identify half my daffodils and tulips, so I went in to research my receipts and fill out the book as long as five years back. Now it's on hand to annoy me with the information that I really did plant twelve *Anemone coronaria*, though only three came up, that two orders of *Allium caeruleum* have now failed utterly, and that I've been planting fancy lilies with only one success for five years now. There's also the welcome reminder that *Tulipa clusiana, Muscari botryoides album,* and the camassias are still there eight years later. If you're an aficionado of a particular bulb, such as daffodils, you can keep a plan that locates each variety by name. That way you won't know your friends' faces but have forgotten their names.

The End of the Garden Year

Autumn is a lovely time in the garden. The days are cooler, the bees slower, and the spiders are still terribly busy and grown very big. More birds than ever visit the garden, and the zinnias lean south to catch the last of the sun. Gardeners are there too, removing weeds and plant debris, turning soil for fall plantings, and hoeing and mulching to keep down weeds during winter. I leave the skeletons of perennials as a handy reminder of just how big a particular plant is for decisions in spring about dividing or moving it, or putting something precious next to it. Remove the old stalks when new growth first appears, cutting low to the ground, or they'll stab your fingers when you reach in to take flowers.

When the work of the fall garden is done, there comes the time to put away the tools and sharpen the pruners. On my list of favorite handymen, there with our retired plumber Dusty and Tim the dishwasher repairman is the fellow who sharpens tools. I drop off my clippers and pruners at the hardware store, and later they return like new. I once lost my pruners in the garden for two months and they were stiff with rust when I came upon them again. They reappeared looking like they did when I first bought them, and the joy in my heart was something I can only compare to seeing your house newly roofed and painted.

Winter is welcome in my garden year, like a good sleep at the end of a long day. I appreciate the chance to tidy up and close things down, to anticipate the arrival of new seed catalogs, to feel impatient for new growth and assuage that by starting seedlings in the basement. I enjoy the annual meeting of community garden members in February, talking about dates for tilling, making payments for water and mulch, seeing gardening friends, and feeling friendships blooming again along with the garden after the long winter.

4

The Flower Harvest

As winter wears thin and I wonder again just when it is that spring begins, the first white snowdrops make their show, followed within weeks by crocus. Later in the cutting season, you might scoff at cutting anything so small and apparently insignificant, but in February and March, these little heralds in their tiny vases on the kitchen windowsill and dining table announce that spring is coming. It's easy to forget there's work to be done in the garden even in late winter, and cutting tiny flowers in earliest spring takes you into the garden when otherwise you might be inside waiting for a bigger show.

Careful scrutiny of the garden as the days pass reveals more small plants ready for cutting, especially the little bulbs. English daisies *(Bellis perennis)* may have been flowering sporadically all winter, but they put on a burst now, and hellebores may escape your attention unless you pay them a special visit.

Daffodils will be your first experience of the year with flowers that give off a sap, or latex, when cut; after standing them in water for a few hours, change their water before arranging with other flowers. Several other plants give off latex (a skin irritant to some people), notably euphorbias, and you may need to burn or sear the stem ends to stop the flow. You'll also notice a thin rainbow of oil on the water when you cut sunflowers. I like to see these little clues to the chemistry of plants.

Midspring sees the first great explosion of flowers for cutting, particularly from a shady cutting garden. At this time of year, flowers may well be wet and dirty when you cut them. Bring them indoors and hold the muddy ones upside down under a thin stream of water in the sink, rubbing spots lightly with fingers. Shake the water off gently, and stand them up in the vase to dry.

Hellebores and honesty (*Lunaria annua*) are two of the first plants of the year to produce attractive seed pods good for fresh arrangements. The pods of some others are not thought so pretty, but a green seedhead of columbine here and there won't spoil an arrangement, and you might choose to leave on many of the whiskered seed pods of cleome when cutting.

The advent of ox-eye daisy reminds me that some flowers don't always smell good indoors. Cut smaller amounts of these or test them indoors first. Outdoors on the picnic table, or in rooms with open windows, they may be fine. Conversely, some flowers, like lilies or the scented daffodils, may smell very sweet, but too many overwhelm the room.

Flowers that fill up with bugs, like goat's beard and Queen Anne's lace, are best cut early in the morning before the insects are very active. Plants with sticky stems like nicotiana may attract dirt and small insects, but they can be rinsed or rubbed off indoors. I'm afraid bringing flowers into the house means bringing in bugs, too.

Don't forget many vines carry short-stemmed flowers you can cut away from the vine: sweet peas, clematis, nasturtiums, hyacinth bean. Sometimes you can use sections of vine to trail attractively from the container.

Keep picking the flowers if it's a plant that needs it to keep blooming, as most do. If you can't get it done yourself, or you're going away on vacation, ask friends to help—it's wonderful how nicely friends can keep a garden picked. Phlox, helenium, goldenrod, Joe Pye weed, and *Veronicastrum virginicum* are examples of plants that produce a set of smaller new flowers at the point of the first cut, usually flowering a month later as a second flush of bloom. Some plants, like globe-flowers and painted daisies, may have a true second flush of flowers, on new stems, weeks to months later. Throughout their season, zinnias and gloriosa daisies produce new flowering laterals (branches) along the stems if they're kept picked.

June finds large numbers of plants in bloom for mixed bouquets of many kinds, but from late July, there will be less and less to cut, with arrangements depending increasingly on masses of an individual plant such as zinnias, dahlias, or Mexican bush sage than on mixed flowers. Foliage becomes more likely to be unsightly with mildew, but the coming cooler weather will improve the appearance and color of many plants. Late in autumn the garden may look finished long before everything is truly gone. If you can be happy with small vases once again, *Chrysanthemum pacificum* and calendulas, among the last flowers of the year, will produce flowers into a quite cold November here in northern Virginia.

Cutting

I have a good-quality pair of small pruners for cutting, which can be disassembled for cleaning and sharpening or for replacing the blade. Before these, I had pruners that couldn't be sharpened, and cheap ones that fell apart. In the kitchen, I keep a pair of sharp needle-nose garden scissors for reaching into a vase to cut out finished flowers.

When cutting, always leave enough foliage on a perennial plant to support life. Some plants have few basal leaves, or even none at all, like lilies and liatris, and are easily robbed of their life-sustaining foliage. If you must have long stems or want to take all the stems from such a plant, get more plants. As with pinching and deadheading (the removal of spent flowers to tidy up and prevent the setting of seed), cut above a growth point, just above a leaf or pair of leaves, to assure production of more stems and flowers. You may not want to pick or deadhead everything, as some seedheads and pods are good to have later.

The first flowers of any plant are frequently the best for cutting. Among the exceptions are cleome, wallflowers, and *Leucojum* 'Gravetye Giant', which flower early but should develop a reasonable length of stem first before cutting, and those like coreopsis and heuchera, which continue to have fine flowers when deadheaded regularly. The stems of many spring bloomers, primroses for example, become longer as the days pass and the weather warms. When the weather is dry, a deep watering will sometimes induce a hesitant plant to open its buds a day or two sooner.

It's vastly easier to deadhead an entire plant first and then cut from it than to cut the stems and deadhead while arranging. The first way, the plant holds the stem for you while you work on it. Prolific plants like emilia can be cut back entirely to just above the basal foliage, rather than deadheading individual stems, and a new crop will appear.

In the garden, put the flowers immediately into several inches of warm water in a clean bucket as you cut. Don't crowd them. You can wedge plastic cups or deli containers in the bottom of the bucket to separate the stems and prevent shorter stems from falling sideways into the water. I once had a floor-mopping bucket with two compartments that also was handy for this purpose. Old plastic juice pitchers with handles will carry smaller numbers of flowers conveniently. These are homemade alternatives to fancier methods of carrying cut flowers.

While it's best to cut flowers in the early morning or late evening when they're refreshed from their long day in the sun, we all must cut when it's convenient. I often pick flowers in the heat of the day because that's when there is time to do it, and worse, drive them home in a hot car. Usually, they do quite well and only sometimes need to be taken down to the cool dark basement because they've wilted. Stand them in a tall jug or bucket of deep water for a few hours or overnight.

For the longest vase life, learn to tell newly opened flowers from older ones by looking at centers rather than petals. The petals of certain plants, such as heliopsis and rudbeckia, don't show their age as quickly as, for example, Shasta daisies, but newer flowers have centers that are smaller, flatter, and tighter.

I first cut stems in the way of paths or other plants, unless they're dirty or broken, in which case they go to the compost pile, then I move on to other areas of the plant. Anthemis, painted daisies, and others with slender stems that bloom profusely can be cut efficiently by grasping bunches of stems in the hand to cut at one time. When cutting from a large floppy-stemmed plant such as *Achillea* 'Moonshine' or *Salvia azurea,* I like to take some stems from the center, where they're likely to be straighter, and others from the sides, where they may have developed a graceful curve. Curved stems are most effective arching over the edge of the container, even displaying the pretty undersides of the flower. *Gladiolus callianthus,* tulips, tellima, lady's mantle, and sweet peas can be counted on for an occasional good swoon.

Certain flowers, such as Shasta daisies and zinnias, need to be cut when fully open, because the buds won't open in water, but the deliberate cutting of buds, say a half-opened zinnia or the pretty green "raspberry" buds of scabiosa, adds a just-picked freshness to an arrangement. The buds of eustoma or sweet peas are especially beautiful, and those of gloriosa daisies, dahlias, and sunflowers are large and robust. If you've grown a lot of a particular flower, you can afford the luxury of cutting more buds.

Removing the excess foliage from a cut flower, or in some cases almost all the foliage, prevents wilting by increasing the amount of water in the stem that is available to the flower. A long stem cut with too much foliage or too many flowering side branches is more likely to wilt than a shorter stem: salvia, ageratum, baptisia, cornflowers, and some rudbeckias are vulnerable. You may often want to cut the laterals off separately to have shorter, but more numerous, stems. Painful though it is, buds and little side shoots often have to be trimmed off to get a reasonably long stem. Sometimes the trimmings can make up a smaller nosegay for a bathroom or bedroom, or to give away.

Stripping the foliage completely off below the water line lends a much cleaner look in glass vases and prevents decay and fouled water. Trim the leaves and laterals onto the compost heap to save bringing them into the house; the detritus from plants like hollyhocks or yarrow can be substantial. You can easily strip the foliage of flowers like larkspur, yarrow, and chrysopsis by moving your thumb and forefinger quickly down the stem, taking the leaves with them; others, like cleome and globe thistle, require use of the shears.

Conditioning

Poppies and hollyhocks, and some plants from *Campanula, Asclepias,* and *Euphorbia,* require burning the stem ends soon after cutting to prevent wilting; this is discussed fully in their respective sections in chapter 6. You sometimes see elaborate advice on various flowers, such as plugging the stem ends of foxgloves with cotton wool, and it's worth experimenting to see if you can do without these drudgeries. I never plug stem ends, or prick stems with pins, or insert wire into stems.

In the house, give the flowers additional water; warm water is better than very cold. Recutting under water is almost never necessary, as most flowers do nicely with a minimum of fuss. If they are wilting badly in water and showing no signs of recovery, trim off additional foliage and lower branches. I put the more vulnerable flowers in our cool dark basement to condition, standing them in a container of deep water just under the high basement window, to induce them to stand up as straight as possible toward the light. If you wish, you can support big flower heads by wrapping the stems in stiff brown paper and standing them in deep water. Flowers like *Euphorbia polychroma,* which you can almost count on wilting, should be cut before you need them and left a few hours or overnight in a cool dark place to revive; it's amazing how much better they look the next morning. Occasionally, you can restore a just-wilted flower by recutting: if you discover the water level is too low in a bowl of freshly cut zinnias, for example, quickly recut the stem and place it in warm water.

Sometimes I leave flowers in the bucket for several hours and return to find the stems have grown curved or bent. This may be attractive on long stems, but it may make short ones, particularly short-stemmed spring flowers, unusable. Stand them up straight while they're conditioning, unless you're purposely inducing curves.

Arranging

Keep your vases, containers, and garden shears clean, and change the vase water when it becomes cloudy. Products for increasing the vase life of flowers are available at florist shops and garden centers, and may double the life of some fresh-cut flowers. An often-recommended home recipe is warm water with a tablespoon of sugar, a shot of bleach to prevent the growth of bacteria, and a squirt of lemon juice, or more simply a tablespoon of corn syrup and a half-teaspoon of bleach to a quart of water. As it happens, I never use these products, but if I had a very small garden and wanted to make my flowers last as long as possible, I might. Recutting stem ends after a few days may also prolong flower life.

Successful flower arranging will come to you the more you do it. I prefer to spend only a few minutes to help flowers look their best, and often it comes down to selecting the right vase, choosing good vase companions for a given flower, and adjusting stem lengths by shortening where necessary. Experience is a good teacher, but almost everyone can benefit from, and enjoy, a flower-arranging class.

Filler flowers, green flowers, and foliage take arrangements to another level of artistry. You'll notice something missing in your bouquets if you never use them. I often realize later how much better a bouquet would have looked if I had used some sedum, ballota, or honesty seed pods. An extensive list of fillers is included in chapter 2.

Some flowers, especially the smaller and finer ones, should be bunched in an arrangement rather than distributed evenly throughout; cut the stems to slightly different lengths to make the flowers easier to see. Large flowers, like peonies or oriental poppies, are usually located low in the composition. You don't need to use every flower you have just because they're there, often the best designs use only a few varieties. Locate a few flowers within the bouquet to give it depth, so there is something to see if your eye travels into the center.

A few flowers turn strongly to the light, so occasional rotating of the vase after arranging may prevent lopsidedness. The ability of flowers to do this also means you can add interesting turns to flower stems before arranging, by leaving the flower lying on an angle in the bucket for several hours after cutting. Torch lilies, hosta, and snapdragons are three that will assume a curve.

Your arrangements will look better longer if you remove individual flowers once they are finished. Snip the flower off the stem and leave the stem in place if that's less disruptive. When pollen falls on the tablecloth, or on your clothing, vacuum it up with a small hand unit, or shake it off outdoors. Don't try to wipe or wash it first, or it will become more permanent than otherwise. Avoid this situation by moving the vase once the pollen becomes prominent, as happens with sunflowers, and by cutting off the anthers on lilies.

The ethylene gas produced by ripening fruit and vegetables can shorten the life of cut flowers; some are much more susceptible than others. I always had a vase standing by the fruit bowl in the kitchen until I understood this. You'll also want to keep arrangements away from heat, direct sun, and drafts.

Learn which plants and seeds (such as hellebores, larkspur, aconitum, lily-of-the-valley, and foxgloves) are poisonous. If you have children and animals in the house, it's important to clean up after these plants. Once I came back to the table and found that a hellebore hovering over my placemat had burst a pod and dropped seeds into my teacup.

You'll hear of many "rules" for flower arranging, and you are free to disagree with them. If you're a gardener who likes a natural garden look, the old notion that stems shouldn't cross in the vase is absurd. This is the first rule of arranging that should be broken. As that wonderfully testy old gardener Katharine White *(Onward and Upward in the Garden)* points out, stems cross naturally in the garden. Likewise, it seems unnecessarily limiting to coordinate flower colors with house decor, matching shades in the sofa or pictures on the wall. My idea would be more that a colorful room might be a wonderful opportunity to show off big snow-white irises, or a room without yellow may need the cheer of daffodils on the table.

Vases

It is less important what your vases are made of or how they're decorated than whether they offer a variety of sizes and shapes. The easiest vases to use have relatively narrow necks and wider waists, and require fewer flowers. Another good form billows out at the top—the shape that is typically thought of as vase—but it's one that needs more flowers. Large gardens can use more large or wide vases, small gardens need more small or narrow vases. My most useful vase is medium sized, seven inches tall, fat around the middle, but with a narrow mouth opening two-and-a-half inches wide. Almost everything looks good in this very plain glass vase. Its rival for Best Vase is a rectangular modern glass vase of the same height, with a three by four inch opening.

Rules of thumb say the vase should be one-third to one-half the height of the final arrangement—if you're using 30-inch stems, consider vases 10 to 15 inches tall. Depending on the flowers you arrange, you may need tall and straight-sided for armfuls of long-stemmed calliopsis, or tall and narrow necked for a few lilies, short and wide for a mass of *Salvia nemerosa* or *Asclepias tuberosa,* and small for the early spring flowers. Vases that arch over at the sides and are more wide than deep, like a lady's fan, are useful for displaying flowers on a mantel or against a wall. A short fat vase with a little opening will be endlessly useful for that single big dahlia, lily, or peony on a short stem.

For small flowers, you can look for such devices as the pansy ring. It's a low vase shaped like a doughnut and useful for the dinner table; the sides of the ring support the short-stemmed flower heads. Gardeners who have planted a lot of little spring bulbs and ephemerals will be glad to have a collection of tiny bottles and vases for the single checkered lily or few primroses the garden sometimes is so stingy with, and you might want to have a couple of tall bud vases for those longer-stemmed flowers that are hard to grow where you live, like Iceland poppies or lupines are here. In a narrow vase, it looks deliberate that there are only a few stems.

It's lovely to have colorful vases to show off white flowers; a rich blue is excellent, or a mosaic of tiny colorful tiles, also pretty for green flowers. Mustard yellow vases set off flowers and foliage particularly well, while white and green vases graciously take back seats to the flowers. Many flowers, even the most delicate, are unexpectedly handsome to look at in black. I'm partial also to colored glass as well as to glass blown with bubbles.

While glass vases are appealing, you wouldn't want all your vases to be of glass, as flowers that require burning of stem ends (poppies and hollyhocks) and those that foul the water (zinnias and stocks) don't look as pretty in glass. To prevent water rings in glass vases, fill them to varying levels rather than always to the same spot, and never neglect them to the point of allowing water to evaporate down the sides of the vase. If a vase is difficult to reach inside to clean, always fill so the water level is at the area easiest to clean, usually near the top, and acquire a few bottle brushes of varying diameters, some angled for better reaching. You can remove a persistent film by filling the vase with full-strength vinegar overnight (place a heavy glass jar in the vase to displace the vinegar upward so you can use less of it), and using fine-grade steel wool along with the vinegar, gently scrub away the residue; it shouldn't scratch. You can also gently use a razor blade.

Some people like to display flowers almost exclusively in low baskets or dishes, but this usually requires floral foam (the larger and more formal the arrangement, the more likely it will require foam). I personally never use foam or florist's tape, preferring the drop-in-the-vase arranging method, though I do have some pin holders and glass "frogs" to help stems in the center stand up, or to weight down top-heavy flowers like hyacinths. Arranging flowers in marbles in a glass vase is attractive when the water is crystal clear, but changing the water, storing and cleaning the marbles, and carrying a vase heavy with marbles or tumbled glass is added work the casual arranger might choose to avoid, or to enjoy on a small scale. The marbles function like glass frogs, with the flower stems inserted to hold their position. Since they draw attention to the stems, a few showy flowers with strong straight stems look the best.

You need a large heavy container for supporting tall top-heavy subjects like sunflowers and castor bean. An ideal choice is the glass block style of vase, which has square proportions to flatter almost any long-stemmed flower and which you can also use for branches of holly or forsythia. Mine is 12 inches high and wide, but not even 4 inches deep, so that not a great many stems are required. These vases also come in smaller sizes. Another good, but casual, container for big masses of flowers is a galvanized florist bucket.

The best values in vases are found at yard sales and the lower end of antique shops, the "Granny's Attic" type that sell old china and glassware and have lovely finds like pitchers and sugar bowls that have lost their lids and are marked "as is." Between 5 and 25 dollars is all one should have to pay. It's possible to find wonderful old white or green wicker baskets, intended for flower arranging, which have high sides with a metal liner for water. (Put a plastic bag inside these old liners as they're likely to leak.) Even the Smithsonian has such baskets in its collection. If a favorite vase is cracked or leaks, put a plastic bag inside and fill with water; the bag will conform to the sides of the vase. Vases that "sweat" can also ruin tables; collect small coasters the size of vase bottoms to protect surfaces.

You'll want to share your flowers with friends, but it's not a great idea to take flowers, even very nice ones, to a party as a surprise. Better to call several days ahead and ask whether you can supply flowers and arrive with them before the party begins. Unexpected flowers may end up left in the kitchen as the hosts have no time to work with them. And it may be that the house is already full of artificial flowers, ghastly with fresh, or that there are no available surfaces on which to place a vase.

After the Harvest

When you've harvested all the flowers you need from your annuals and biennials, and from certain short-lived perennials, you're free to dispose of the plants, particularly at the end of summer to make way for the fall seedbed. I remove some plants right away, like teasel and Queen Anne's lace, which are nuisances by self-sowing. I take down those I want to self-sow, like Shirley poppies or larkspur, when the seed has scattered.

Many people are bothered by the idea of disposing of a plant with a breath of life left. It's at this point that gardeners at my community plot appear at my side, looking at me doubtfully, accusingly, as I explain that the plant is almost finished and won't come back. "Won't come back?" they repeat. They drag off the carcasses to attempt planting in their own gardens, or pore over them searching for a seedhead. I suppose it's the only way to learn for certain that you cannot transplant a finished hesperis here and that globe amaranth really doesn't come back the next year. When my son was young, he told me "Don't step on plants, even poison ivy has a right to live." Luckily he didn't always see me in the garden, or I'd have been in trouble.

Four Cutting Gardens

Most cutting gardens do not need a formal design. If your garden won't be in plain view, the general ideas about layout from chapter 1 will probably be satisfactory for positioning plants. But if your cutting garden is clearly visible from the house or street, you may feel obliged to give some of the care to its appearance that you might give to a border. My own sunny cutting plot in my community garden looks more like a vegetable garden than a border, and it rarely appears the same from one year to the next. At home I cut from a shady ornamental border, which has never had a formal design, either.

The following descriptions for four different cutting gardens address some common garden situations: the novice gardener's first garden, the garden with little space, the garden with too much shade, and the garden in that neglected season, fall.

The Easy Garden for Beginners

A beginner's first cutting garden, like any garden, starts with a well-drained site with as much sun as possible and thorough preparation of the planting beds. Low-maintenance gardening methods, such as choosing long-lived plants suited for your particular soil and climate, are good for beginners who are still deciding how much time and energy they have for the garden. If your plants are happy where they're growing, they'll require less care and expertise to coddle along. You may find that old varieties often prove to be longer lived and less trouble than new hybrids.

There was a time when most gardeners began gardening by sowing annual seed directly in the garden and were familiar with the
masses of bloom annuals produce for cutting. Now that perennials
have become the fashion, it frequently happens that a gardener
hasn't sown annuals outdoors until several years into the gardening
life and perhaps has to be coaxed into it by friends.

Easy annuals you can sow directly in the garden are more reliable
for beginners than those that require starting indoors under lights or
on the windowsill. What is an easy annual differs from region to region, but in eastern Zone 7, we can depend on cornflowers, Shirley
poppies, calendula, calliopsis, cosmos, snow-on-the-mountain, teasel, celosia, Queen Anne's lace, amaranthus, cleome, ageratum, marigolds, sunflowers, China asters, scabiosa, tithonia, zinnia, nasturtium, emilia, hyacinth bean, and castor bean. Read about each of
these and the following plants in their individual sections of chapter
6, and consult local gardeners or a good garden center to discover
your area's cold-hardiness and heat zones.

Cut-flower annuals that are more challenging (a relative term, as
some will be easy in certain parts of the country) but still suitable for
beginners to sow outdoors are larkspur, nigella, agrostemma, gypsophila, nicotiana, and globe amaranth. Some of these are heat tolerant, and for that reason are reliable in hot-summer areas; others despise heat but are hardy and can be successfully sown in September
to grow through winter and flower in spring. Additional rewarding
direct-sown annuals for cutting in cooler areas of the United States
include lavatera, bells of Ireland, ammi, sweet peas, dill, bupleurum,
and godetia, but for the most part these are not hardy enough to be
overwintered where it's really cold. You should be able to encourage
some of them to self-sow in an area of moderate temperatures. A list
of volunteers in my garden (where temperature extremes, particularly
heat, are more the norm) appears in appendix 2.

In the spring, garden centers often have young plants of eustoma,
snapdragons, stocks, pansies, gloriosa daisies, flowering tobacco, and
tender perennials (which behave like annuals where there is frost)
such as *Salvia farinacea,* all excellent for the cutting garden. Herb
nurseries should have fennel and more of the cut-flower salvias. Buy
taller selections, not low bedding varieties.

The biennials are the next adventure for beginners to sow or
plant, requiring a little more patience, because you must wait until
the following year for flowers. Biennials include most hollyhocks,

honesty, hesperis, cynoglossum, myosotis, sweet William, brown-eyed Susan, and wallflowers. (See chapter 2 on biennials.) You may want to try germinating one or two under lights. At the same time, you could also start several of the easy and quick-growing perennials from seed, outdoors or under lights. The obliging ones are often the type that self-sows, such as columbine, feverfew, and anthemis.

First-time gardeners will appreciate longer-lived, well-behaved perennials like peonies, tall sedums, and Siberian iris over too many temperamental or invasive bad boys. Consider how much attention you want to give individual plants, because, depending on where you garden, some may require extensive watering, staking, fertilizing, or yearly division. Others will ask little, though they may live only three or four years—it's enlightening to look back over years of nursery receipts and realize how short lived many perennials are in the garden. All perennial gardens require constant renewal, as only a few plants are truly long lived. It's also important to your sanity to accept failure, rather than replacing plants that have died repeatedly without flowering. Good perennial choices for the beginner's cutting garden include primroses, bleeding hearts, coral bells, yarrow, coreopsis, gaillardia, astilbe, phlox, echinacea, obedient plant, stokesia, chrysopsis, goldenrod, hardy begonia, boltonia, the Lenten rose, and numerous members of the aster and chrysanthemum tribes (which includes Shasta daisies). A few plants such as Solomon's seal, lady's mantle, euphorbia, or sea lavender for filler will make arranging a delight. Get all these from a local nursery or garden center or by mail order.

Reliable bulbs and tubers for planting in fall in a well-drained area include daffodils, hyacinths, Spanish bluebells, tulips, *Leucojum* 'Gravetye Giant', Dutch iris, camassia, alliums like chives and garlic chives, and Asiatic lilies; and for planting in late spring, dahlias and gladiolus. Some bulbous or tuberous plants such as iris and crocosmia are often sold as perennials, potted with growth already showing.

Seed purveyors who provide plenty of information in their catalog and on their packets, like Stokes and Shepherd's, and general nurseries that take pains to educate their customers are some of the best sources for new gardeners, even when they're slightly more expensive. Some of the mail-order sources supply bigger plants and do a better job of packing, which means the plants arrive in better condition, something that may be of extra importance to beginning gardeners. The better catalogs rarely arrive unsolicited; ask gardening friends for them (and turn to appendix 3 in this book for sources). Check their information as to which plants are hardy in your area, and learn to use botanical names, because that's the only way to be sure of what you're getting. You'll also find that good garden centers often have potted plants that transplant better than those shipped by mail, in addition to allowing you to inspect the goods before purchase. Friends and neighbors are great sources for plants, carried home in plastic grocery bags for quick installation. Consider joining a community garden or garden club where plants and information are passed around freely.

All cut-flower gardeners were beginners once, none of them born with a green or black thumb. Size your garden to keep you happily engaged and confident. A green thumb comes from the enjoyable work and attention to detail that keeps us learning in the garden.

The Small Garden

Gardening in the city or suburbs so often is small-space gardening, with all its comic, and tragic, limitations. I remember struggling with one tiny plot, the entire front yard in fact, of my little old brick row house on Capitol Hill in downtown Washington, D.C., a garden so shallow that the house's cast iron front steps descended directly to the sidewalk. Because the back received no sun, I put the cutting garden in the front, something I wouldn't usually like to do because it doesn't seem quite neighborly, but the fact is that any city garden close to the street is a cutting garden, it just may not be the owner who does the cutting. It was two-and-a-half feet deep and eight feet wide, red clay, and too near a street tree, which was, unfortunately, a maple. The entire product of that garden fit in one small vase, and foolishly proud, I brought the vase into the house one day to everyone's stifled laughter. The lesson from this is not so much that it's impossible to get many flowers from a small garden or a city garden, but at least not to site a cutting garden under maples.

If there is little space around your home to establish a separate garden for cutting, you may still be able to find out-of-the-way locations for plants: a little strip behind the garage for daffodils and magic lily, a section of fence for sweet peas, a spot of earth from where a nasturtium could wander. Use landscape plants like hosta, Solomon's seal, or bergenia around your house—the foliage can accompany flowers from the cutting garden, however few. If you have a separate border or display garden, perhaps an herb garden, and you've included plants there with handsome foliage, such as hellebores, peonies, lady's mantle, bleeding hearts, even fennel, when you pick a few flowers the plants won't look plundered.

There is usually not enough material in bloom at one time in the small cutting garden to plan on large arrangements of many kinds of flowers. You'll want to select flowers that arrange well by themselves, not narrow, stemmy flowers such as emilia, lythrum, tellima, coral bells, *Polygonum orientale,* or *Verbena bonariensis,* which need companion material and do better in mixed bouquets. Big bunches of daisies or coneflowers of any kind are excellent choices: anthemis, gloriosa daisies, China asters, sunflowers, and members of the chrysanthemum tribe like Shasta daisies, fall mums, and *C. corymbosum.* None of these require company to look great. Many other flowers you can successfully display alone include daffodils, tulips, cornflowers, sweet William, larkspur, phlox, iris, snapdragons, calliopsis, celosia, cosmos, snow-on-the-mountain, yarrow, lilies, stokesia, sea hollies, zinnias, hardy begonia, goldenrod, and dahlias. There are a few flowers that combine beautifully as filler with almost anything, such as lady's mantle, bupleurum, dill, and several of the euphorbias. Flowers with a long vase life, like Canterbury bells and eustoma, are also desirable for extending the value of a small cutting garden. Primroses, poppies, ranunculus, and the little spring flowers are ideal for smaller arrangements in little vases for viewing close up, and for which many flowers are not needed.

You may want to choose plants for all seasons of the year so that not everything is blooming in May and June, as so easily happens. When there's room for little in the garden, late summer and fall are the first abandoned. It's even possible to have an extensive cutting garden and still not have much to cut at times if the garden doesn't contain a number of prolific plants of varied bloom dates. While a long period of bloom is an attractive feature in any plant in a small garden, don't rely on them overly much, or you'll have, for example, nothing but zinnias for more weeks than you want them. For variety's sake, set aside a spot for annuals, tender perennials, or tender bulbs; year-to-year their changing faces keep the garden lively.

It's a particularly good idea to select plants that are reliable in your climate and soil conditions, as failure is proportionally more disappointing the smaller the cutting garden gets, although those of us gardeners who are hardened to death rub our hands together at the chance to scoot off to the garden center for something new. Flowers that are known for odd smells, like cleome, valerian, or ox-eye daisies, also fit into the unreliable category.

Most gardeners with quite small cutting plots should avoid too many of the truly enormous plants like teasel, acanthus, love-lies-bleeding, Joe Pye weed, perennial gypsophila, Mexican bush, *Helianthus angustifolius, Anchusa azurea, Malva sylvestris mauritiana, Rudbeckia triloba,* and *Cephalaria gigantea,* which, though good for cutting, would leave little room for anything else. Some leviathans, like *Baptisia australis,* have such extensive root systems that it is difficult to plant anything else near them. Others, like bearded irises, spread widely without offering many flowers for the space; get a Siberian iris instead. Aggressive plants will fill the garden too quickly and need frequent division (or elimination); generally, it's most productive to emphasize upright, well-behaved plants, rather than large and spreading, without limiting the garden entirely to tiny plants that would be disappointing. Vining plants like hyacinth bean and sweet peas, trained up a fence or trellis, make excellent space savers.

Where the growing season is long, Zone 7 and further south (possibly Zone 6 for some fast-growing plants), the garden will seem bigger if you succession plant to get two crops a year out of the same piece of ground, but it will also require extra fertilizing and care of the soil. In late spring, sow quick-growing annuals like zinnias, calendulas, and sunflowers, and put in started plants such as snapdragons and eustoma bought at the garden centers and seedlings you've started indoors. (See appendix 1 for "Growing Seed under Lights.") When they're finished at the end of summer and early fall, pull them up and sow hardy annuals like calliopsis, larkspur, Shirley poppies, hollyhock 'Indian Spring', or agrostemma to grow slowly over fall and winter and flower in spring. You can also plant in fall the (relatively) quick-growing biennials you've started indoors under lights in midsummer: hesperis, Canterbury bells, and sweet William are three. Biennials that require a full year's growth to perform well, such as honesty and some hollyhocks, are a true test of patience in the small garden, unless you can purchase them ready to bloom.

When you've got only the tiniest cutting plot, you have to find your pleasure in just a few stems: a bulb or two of narcissus, a tulip, a lily, a sunflower, carefully chosen and with vases that make the most of a single flower. The tulip could be a *multiflora* or parrot or peony flowered for the greatest impact, and a good increaser like the daffodils 'Ceylon' or 'Thalia' will produce more stems each year from the single bulb you planted. Find a sunflower like 'Soraya' with many handsome flowers per plant, rather than just one.

When the garden is small, the plants are all the more special, so be sure to select them to please yourself, not because they satisfy popular ideas of flower arranging. Though it's frustrating to have little space for all the plants you want to grow, one agreeable aspect of the small cutting garden is how little work it is.

The Shady Garden

Shade poses special challenges to establishing a cutting garden. You wouldn't want to locate your garden in considerable shade unless you had no choice, as a sunny or lightly shaded site will accommodate the greatest variety of plants. You will have to investigate the suitability for shade of every plant you consider, and you will have to turn many away. You'll need to be content with fewer flowers, as a shady cutting garden isn't as prolific as one in full sun. For that reason, it helps if your shady garden is large, to include more plants.

While it's disappointing to be without sun, there are many advantages to growing cut flowers in shade: the garden needs much less watering and only a tiny fraction of the weeding, and you escape exposure to the sun. In many plants, shade produces a longer stem, richer flower color, and improved foliage. It's a benefit more pronounced toward the South, as in hot summer areas many plants usually grown in full sun are better for cutting in light shade. Daffodils and lilies of strong colors fade less with a little shade. In full sun here in Virginia, *Physostegia virginica* may produce fine flowers, but its foliage often burns, making it too unsightly to cut. With too much sun, cleome rolls up its petals and doesn't unroll them after cutting, even when brought into a cool dark location. A little light shade here encourages some cool-season plants like dill, which has a wonderful spreading flower, to live long enough to bloom; and my tall sedum has a longer, thinner stem in medium shade, and a lovely looser flower head.

If you have heavy shade cast by trees, talk to a tree service about "elevating" your trees, which means to remove lower branches to create higher shade. High shade is a lighter shade than that cast by low branches. Full sun for a couple of hours a day may qualify an otherwise heavily shaded spot as medium shade. Shade that falls only in the morning, such as that cast by a house, is a brighter shade than that falling in the afternoon, because afternoon sun is felt by plants to be stronger than morning sun. Shade on the north side of a house or wall is heavy shade, as is that thrown by big evergreen trees and shrubs. It's much better if the offending trees are deciduous, as a great many plants will grow and flower before the trees leaf out, which is why a very shady cutting garden under deciduous trees is often largely a spring garden.

Soil preparation to increase moisture retention is important for dry shady areas, as few plants grow well in both dry soil and shade. A dry garden in shade should be located where you can easily reach it with a hose, and it will probably need to be mulched.

Squirrels in our trees are immediately attracted to freshly dug earth and are quite a nuisance. They dig up new seedlings and disturb rows of sown seed. It helps if the seed you're sowing can just be scattered on the surface, such as honesty, dill, foxgloves, hesperis, columbine, the taller varieties of flowering tobacco such as *Nicotiana alata* or *N. langsdorfii*, *Myosotis sylvatica*, and *Bupleurum griffithii*, which all start easily and self-sow well in a lightly shaded garden. Stokes, Territorial, and Twilley are three seed companies that allow you to order seed in bulk (in fractions of an ounce), which makes broadcasting seed in the garden more affordable. On occasion, I've laid down sections of chicken wire over areas I need to protect, or even a wire cloche of sorts standing around a new plant, but once plants are established, the squirrels generally leave them alone. There isn't as much choice among seed to be sown in a shady garden, so you don't have to battle the squirrels if you don't wish to, and in a garden of considerable shade you should probably not bother with seed at all.

For cutting plants in the heaviest shade, begin with old-fashioned bleeding heart, Virginia bluebells, hardy begonia, and various hellebores such as *H. orientalis* and *H. foetidus*. Solomon's seal, hosta, and arum are good for foliage. The first year in heavy, but deciduous, shade you may have luck with many spring bulbs, but not all will come back. Lily-of-the-valley will flower in quite a lot of shade.

In medium shade, you're able to add many more plants. Try the small spring perennials and wildflowers that bloom under the bright light of deciduous shade: doronicum, epimedium, little dicentras such as 'Luxuriant', pansies and Johnny-jump-up, *Phlox divaricata, Uvularia grandiflora,* and especially primroses. Euphorbias are as useful for greenish-yellow filler as lady's mantle, and they bloom weeks earlier.

Among the spring bulbs blooming before the trees leaf out fully are crocus, chionodoxa, fritillaries, snowdrops, *Erythronium* 'Pagoda', *Leucojum* 'Gravetye Giant', and hyacinths. The blue color of muscari is pretty for mixing with other flowers in tiny arrangements. We're quite at the upper limit for growing *Anemone coronaria* in the garden, so I plant a lot of them and am delighted with what few I get. Add some of the smaller daffodils, and the charming daintier flowers that some tulips produce in their later years, all delightful for little spring bouquets, and together with some small hostas of interesting leaf color such as 'Golden Tiara' they make a gorgeous early spring border or cutting garden.

Taller choices flowering in spring are columbines, coral bells, honesty, Spanish bluebells (the latest name is *Hyacinthoides hispanica*), and tellima. The daffodils bloom over a long season, and while they may not quickly form generous clumps in medium shade, they will flower nicely for many years. I find tulips perform reasonably well in deciduous shade the first year or two. Larger hostas provide interesting green leaves for company.

A little later in the season for the medium to light shade garden, foxgloves, goat's beard, tall perennial lobelia, and Asiatic lilies afford excellent cutting. Astilbes of a bright hue are outstanding in generous bunches, and those of a soft hue are perfect with the delphinium you may choose to grow in lighter shade. In August, Joe Pye weed has surprised me by growing vigorously immediately under an oak. Its huge flower heads are outstanding in a big glass block vase. Some hostas carry flowers useful for arranging, though they'll flower more heavily in light shade. *Chasmanthium latifolium* produces its oat-like dangling flowers abundantly in shade. Japanese anemones may cut successfully if you don't take too long a stem, as they're prone to wilting.

Light shade in the upper South helps keep alive, or in good condition, plants that are often grown in full sun in the North or cool summer areas. Globeflower, veronica, prairie mallow, thalictrum, geum, echinacea, turtlehead, delphinium, monarda, sea lavender, lythrum, oriental poppy, Russell lupines, crocosmia, Carolina lupine, obedient plant, *Lysimachia clethroides, Campanula persicifolia, Kali-meris pinnatifida, Caryopteris incana,* and *Malva alcea* 'Fastigiata' are examples of cut-flower perennials that may burn less and persist longer with a little shade in hot summer zones, though sometimes extra moisture can have the same effect as light shade in improving the appearance of a plant. None do well, however, with much more than light shade, as they require a great deal of light. In other parts of the country where heat and humidity aren't so stressful, astrantia, acanthus, aconitum, Jacob's ladder, and many campanulas bloom generously in a lightly shaded garden.

Popular cut-flower annuals for light shade are larkspur, nasturtiums, stocks, cleome, dill, snapdragons, bells of Ireland, snow-on-the-mountain, nigella, calendula, and eustoma. When it's very hot, sweet peas, poppies, and mignonette may appreciate a little relief from the sun. Among biennials, hesperis has a flower similar to honesty (also a biennial) but tidier, more weatherproof, and blooming over a longer period, but without the wonderful green seed pods. Grow both. The little blue forget-me-nots of *Myosotis sylvatica* are enchanting for small posies and self-sow nicely for flowers the next spring. *Cynoglossum amabile, Angelica archangelica,* and *Campanula medium* are three more biennials to try in light shade. Bulbous plant choices include camassia, agapanthus, *Ranunculus asiaticus,* and *Lycoris squamigera.*

Many other plants tolerate very light shade, although with adequate watering, they don't require it in Virginia. *Baptisia australis* is a desirable plant for cutting that can take a bit of shade, as are peonies, balloon flowers, summer phlox, daylilies, globe thistle, bergenia, patrinia, heliopsis, kniphofia, solidago, anthemis, iris, *Lychnis chalcedonia, Campanula glomerata, Allium senescens* and *A. tuberosum, Salvia farinacea* and *S. nemerosa, Artemisia lactiflora,* most of the *Chrysanthemum* tribe, and some from *Asclepias, Rudbeckia,* and *Helianthus* as well. Even zinnias and China asters can be grown in light shade. There will probably be fewer flowers on these plants, and they'll be more likely to flop around as their stems grow longer and thinner. Some plants, like foxgloves, take up more space in the shade than in a sunnier garden, as their leaves grow larger to increase the amount of sunlight they capture.

Since the shady cutting garden isn't as prolific as one in full sun, you'll want to use vases of a suitable size: small for spring bouquets and tall and narrow, or at least with a narrow neck, for longer stems. It might seem discouraging to arrange a few prized flowers in too big a vase, but so artful in a small one.

The Garden in Fall

With so many tempting selections for spring and summer cut flowers, autumn is often the forgotten season. Garden centers may not put out the plants that flower later in the year until midsummer (and you'll miss them if you're not there), because the enormous volume of spring inventory leaves little space for them in April and May, and because the plants sell better when in bloom. Likewise, fewer people think to visit a good public garden in September than do in May and June, and they miss the opportunity to see firsthand an interesting autumn collection; a change in habit to visit nurseries and gardens in late summer and fall may introduce you to late bloomers you've never seen before. But it's disappointing to find that many of the best public gardens shy away from dahlias and fall chrysanthemums, two important plants to the autumn cutting garden, as though the unimaginative use often made of them makes them unfit for sophisticated gardens. It's the local dahlia and chrysanthemum clubs that may have the best displays.

Many annuals in the cutting garden are still flowering away as September arrives: cosmos, marigolds, emilia, eustoma, snapdragons, calendula, nicotiana, ageratum, celosia, castor bean, some hollyhocks, scabiosa, sunflowers, snow-on-the-mountain, zinnias, globe amaranth, hyacinth bean, nasturtiums, tithonia, China asters, and kiss-me-over-the-garden-gate. Keeping your plants in good condition through summer is important to a successful fall harvest. Don't neglect deadheading, which prevents them from entering the seed-production stage and ending bloom.

Some annuals will flower particularly well in fall when sown in early or mid summer, where climates allow. Cosmos is one that even highway departments sow for fall displays. You'll notice that a few sunflowers described in catalogs are especially suited for "late" sowings (in June or July here), because they are day-length neutral, meaning that they continue to bloom despite the shortening day, and may even bloom until frost. The colors of all sunflowers in shades of red, brown, and gold are ideal for harvest arrangements.

Some tender perennials grown as annuals, such as the salvias

S. farinacea and 'Indigo Spires' and *Asclepias curassavica* (blood-flower), are at full glory in fall, the cooler temperatures intensifying their color. Trachelium and snapdragons also go somewhat dormant midseason in areas of warm summers and rejuvenate after the heat has passed. Dahlias produce showy flowers essential to every fall cutting garden, beginning in August for some varieties planted in spring and up to a month later for the largest, but sensitive to the first frost. Gerberas, tuberoses, and nerines may also remain in bloom through September and even into October.

As the annuals finish from midsummer on, you can clear them away and prepare the soil for late summer and early fall sowings of hardy annuals and biennials such as nigella, poppies, and larkspur (and perennials like anthemis or feverfew, which bloom the first year) for flowering the coming spring. Now you'll want to plant out the young seedlings you may have begun indoors under lights, like Canterbury bells, or purchased, like pansies (see chapter 2 on biennials and chapter 3 on sowing seed in the fall garden). Remember to reserve an ample area for the spring sowings you'll want to do.

Among the summer-flowering hardy perennials and bulbs suitable for cutting that may still flower nicely past the end of August, what Allen Lacy calls the "lingerers" in his beautiful book *The Garden in Autumn*, are boltonia, pink obedient plant, balloon flowers, blanket flowers, garden verbena, Mexican hat, society garlic, golden aster, turtlehead, tall sedum, liriope, hardy begonia, gloriosa daisies, crocosmia, garlic chives, *Kalimeris pinnatifida*, *Calamintha nepeta*, *Aster* × *frikartii*, *Knautia macedonica*, *Malva* 'Zebrina', *Verbena bonariensis*, and many grasses, among them *Chasmanthium latifolium*. Pokeweed, or pokeberry *(Phytolacca americana)*, can be scavenged from neglected areas. Roses make a good show in fall, and some gardeners will want to have flowers to arrange with them.

Once summer passes, the Michaelmas daisies *(Aster novi-belgii* but commonly also *A. novae-angliae)* are the well-known shrubby asters of early fall, a little clumsy but good for bushy arrangements in many colors. There are also the finer *A. pringlei* 'Monte Cassino', with clouds of tiny white daisies, *A. laevis* 'Bluebird', and *A. tataricus*, splendid long-stemmed violet daisies appearing weeks later. *Salvia azurea* and less hardy *Caryopteris incana* throw lazy arching stems of glorious blue flowers that are perfect for September cutting with late sunflowers. I like masses of goldenrods for their fall feeling, excellent choices for arranging with seedheads and grasses. The pretty leaves of *Arum italicum* 'Pictum' appear in fall, and the leaves of bergenia become handsomely bronzed. If you're a gardener who is not bothered by the idea of irises in September, you can look for reblooming iris in nursery catalogs, as well as spring-flowering *I. foetidissima* for its autumn pods of red "berries."

Late in October the unusual all-weather *Ligularia tussilaginea* produces rubbery 22-inch cut stems with curious yellow daisies, and lastly, the little late-flowering yellow buttons and silver edged leaves of *Chrysanthemum pacificum* make a simple November bouquet for the dinner table. Arranging these later flowers becomes more difficult as the season progresses, as there are fewer and fewer flowers and you struggle to make companions of them. Massed arrangements of one type of flower are the easiest solution, along with fixing them in small vases again for the first time since early spring.

Some gardeners avoid chrysanthemums for cutting in fall because they're tainted by overuse the rest of the year. Much better, I think, to skirt florist chrysanthemums most of the year and revel in your own in autumn. Their scent is, in part, the smell of fall. They're valuable for their courage in the face of cold weather, flowering through October and into November, still good for cutting when little else is left, and coming in an enthralling variety of color and form. But planning and discretion are important with mums; it's better to build a thoughtful collection of attractive hardy specimens in spring than to attempt every fall the last-minute planting of mediocre mums from the grocery store or garden center.

Perennials that you often see listed for August, like Joe Pye weed and monkshood, may bloom in the fall cutting garden in the North, though some, like the later Japanese anemones, flower so late they're caught there by frost. Similarly, the fabulous tender perennial *Salvia leucantha* doesn't come into bloom until mid-September in my Zone 7 garden and so is not reliable for cut flowers too much further north. Another superb hardy perennial, *Helianthus angustifolius,* waits until mid-October to flower, and in some years it is blackened by frost before I've cut more than a few stems (northern gardeners should give *H. salicifolius* a try instead). But if you're a gardener with a longer growing season, you can select late-blooming cultivars of plants that might otherwise bloom earlier, such as *Solidago* 'Fireworks' rather than 'Peter Pan'.

Pinching is sometimes suggested to increase bushiness in chrysanthemums, to reduce the eventual height of a plant like chrysopsis, and to stimulate side growth, as for dahlias. It's a technique that may delay bloom until fall, desirably, but depending on where you garden, may also delay it past frost, in which case you might have no flowers. Use pinching judiciously for the fall cutting garden, usually stopping by midsummer.

Look over your wish list in summer and autumn if you're planning on choosing an oriental poppy, peony, bearded iris, or hardy bulbs, as they're commonly sold in the greatest variety for planting in fall. In the South, fall planting of perennials is often more successful than spring planting. Now is also the time to notice which asters or chrysanthemums you want to beg from friends in spring, and tag them if possible.

The leisure of the fall garden is a just reward after the frenetic pace of spring and the demands of summer, the garden world so serene that a seed order that takes weeks to arrive in spring now comes in just three days. After sowing seed for hardy annuals and setting out new plants, the last work in my garden includes weeding and removing the suffocating blankets of oak leaves. Pulling out finished plants spells the end, but if you have started young plants of English daisies or sweet William indoors during the summer, you'll be putting in new life, instead of just clearing up after the old.

6

Two Hundred Choice Plants
for Your Cutting Garden

The flowers described here are far from being the only possibilities for the cutting garden. Every year the catalogs arrive with new surprises, and while some sound ghastly—dwarfed varieties and unlooked-for color breaks—others are reintroduced cultivars from old gardens, long-ignored American natives, or genuinely worthwhile new species from Japan or Korea or other parts of the globe. Many of these forgotten plants aren't showy and for that reason make delightful everyday cut flowers or serve as companions for the more eye-catching material. Unfortunately, a "new" plant may have a limited area in which it grows successfully, but you can hope to be the gardener it pleases. Buy from the bulb suppliers, nurseries, and seed catalogs that pioneer introductions and bring back cultivars that others neglected.

Some garden plants, such as asters or primroses, come in forms and cultivars too numerous for most of us; choosing among them is what makes your garden different from mine or someone else's. What follows are descriptions of many individual plants that I've found successful for cutting, and others that should cut well in areas where they can be grown. And I hope those gardeners who don't wish to cut their flowers will still find ideas here on growing some fine ornamental plants, almost all suitable for the flower border.

ACANTHUS

In late spring and early summer, a fine stand of the intriguing mauve and white flowering spires of **bear's breeches** is an arresting sight in the garden, with some of the appeal of both monkshood and foxgloves. The huge flower spikes make a grand, though prickly, display with other long-stemmed showy flowers for a large arrangement, or alone in the vase—you won't need many stems. Choose stems with at least a few opened flowers for cutting, and consider searing the ends to prolong their life in water.

Many gardeners find it difficult to establish acanthus, particularly in the East; mine were not with me long enough to flower. It's not hardy in much of the United States, is little tolerant of heat and humidity, and requires a well-drained soil. It's also likely to be invasive, and possibly should have its own corner, though it's as likely that it won't live as that it will take over your garden. *Acanthus spinosus* may be hardy here in Zone 7a with excellent drainage and survives heat better than the less hardy *A. mollis*, especially under light shade, but it has more spines. I've seen *A. balcanicus (A. hungaricus)* form a pretty clump on a hillside nearby, and it's the one I'm planting to give it another go. Acanthus is only for the ample cutting garden, as these majestic perennials require a spacing of three or more feet, but any gardener who has the right conditions and the strength to cope ought to try them.

ACHILLEA

Every cutting garden should have at least one **yarrow**, as they're indispensable company for all kinds of daisies and coneflowers, and one of the best for coral bells, blanket flowers, *Salvia nemerosa, Emilia javanica,* and the bronzed seedpods of nigella. The unassuming yellow is the most familiar, but white, pink, and red cultivars are perennials commonly available from nurseries. Many seed catalogs offer tempting mixed color strains, such as 'Summer Pastels' (hybrids of *Achillea millefolium* and *A. taygetea*), which should bloom the first year in captivating hues of sandy yellow, cream, salmon, apricot, orange, red, lilac, or purple, a tapestry when several are used together. All are perfect for casual arrangements of country flowers. If you're planting mixed colors, set them at some distance so they don't run together; my pinks were rather assertive and took over the other colors.

I no longer plant any cultivars of *A. millefolium* in fall, as they're too aggressive in my good garden soil; a tiny slip of 'White Beauty' planted in September becomes a patch three foot square by spring, only to be done in by the heat. Since a white yarrow can be very useful, I could perhaps plant one in early spring and remove it after flowering in May. White *A. ptarmica* 'The Pearl' is frequently recommended as a cut flower in June and can be used instead of baby's breath, but here it's rather stiff and awkward, and the plants weedy. I once saw a design for a cutting garden that recommended nine plants of this cultivar, and I was rather surprised by the idea. But I was even more taken aback by 'The Pearl' in Scottish gardens, where bigger flowers and far better-looking foliage in that climate made it quite attractive.

Cultivars or hybrids of *A. filipendulina* are the top varieties for cutting listed by the Flower Council of Holland. 'Gold Plate' and the related hybrid 'Coronation Gold' stand up well, are noninvasive, and are widely available. Similar to 'Gold Plate' is 'Parker's Variety' (the seed appropriately from Park's), which is easy to grow, requiring a year to reach blooming size in early June. It has large flowers and long, straight stems, with one plant commonly holding as many as 50 stems of more than 25 inches in length. After a thorough cutting, by late July it may have a modest second crop of handy smaller flowers. The plant may need tying around once with string to keep it erect, but the stems don't become bent like 'Moonshine'. Soft lemon-yellow 'Moonshine' is one of the first to flower, in May, but it is floppy.

Don't cut your yarrow too early; wait until the flowers are fully open in each cluster. The foliage is so easy to strip off that children enjoy doing it, and it's pleasingly aromatic with the smell of a summer meadow. Since the foliage withers long before the flower, you may want to remove almost all the leaves up to the flowerhead. Begin with one plant of any kind, and be prepared to divide yearly.

ACONITUM

Like delphinium, aconitums are perennials known for the color blue, with fine ferny foliage and long stems, especially enticing to those of us who can't grow it. **Monkshood** grows happily at my Aunt Dorothy's house high in the mountains of Colorado, where it's in the 40s every morning in July, but many of us in the South can't keep it alive to bloom. Just a half hour out of town here, out of the "heat island" and near cooling forests, some gardeners are able to establish it, with the plants living several years.

You may want to avoid the deepest violets and blues as almost too dark to be visible in the house, and having even a sinister appearance, and instead look for the medium blues, the white with blue, and the occasional pink or yellow; cultivars listed under *Aconitum carmichaelii*, *A. napellus*, and *A.* × *bicolor* are good starting points (the ×, which is not pronounced, means it's a hybrid). Aconitums usually flower in the last half of summer, and in the North bloom into October. Start with one plant, giving light shade where summer nights are at all warm, and you may find it will tolerate damp soils. As the plants are poisonous, don't be careless indoors with material you trim from stems or falling petals and leaves. Monkshood is extremely hardy to Zone 2 or 3, and long lived where it's happy.

AGAPANTHUS

The splendid big flowers of **African lily** (or **lily of the Nile**) bloom for two months in summer on strong leafless stems ideal for arranging and loved for their shades of blue and violet and even white. Most are hardy only to Zone 8, but the hardiest strain is also one of the tallest, *Agapanthus* × 'Headbourne Hybrids', described occasionally as hardy to Zone 6 in a well-drained soil. Some gardeners plant them in spring in containers that can be brought into a frost-free area for the winter. My spring-planted 'Bressingham Blue', a good-sized potted plant, produced only three stems its first summer, superb stems though they were of 36 inches, long enough to peek out the sunroof when I set the bucket on the front seat of the car. Mercifully, it lived through a mild winter and gave me seven stems the next year. Bulb catalogs occasionally offer agapanthus for spring planting, and mail-order nurseries may list it with the perennials.

AGASTACHE

The flowers of agastache are often recommended for picking, a bit of a puzzle as they're rather rustic indoors, but they're loved for their pretty aromatic leaves, which are a pleasure to handle, and their green stems, which have an upright habit that doesn't fail in hot weather. Some new seed strains offer a nice range of colors in blue, pink, and white. It's difficult to discover much about these long-neglected plants, as the **hyssops** are ignored for the most part by garden books—relegated to herb books, where they're included with herbaceous perennials—yet the best public gardens in the country use agastaches for summer displays.

I found *Agastache foeniculum* interesting for cutting only at first, as

the flowers on the plant aged rapidly, and deadheading didn't seem
to produce new long stems. A better choice is 'Blue Fortune', a recent cross between *A. foeniculum* and *A. rugosa* (both **anise hyssops**),
a floriferous plant with heavenly scented foliage and the expected
lavender-blue bottle brushes that keep on going and going. Cut it
when it first blooms; afterward, when you cut in the heat of summer,
you'll have to groom your stems. Run your fingers along the raceme
to dislodge the old dried florets and pick off any that remain; this
only works if the flowers aren't wet from a sprinkling and if you're
indoors so the bees can't get you. The stems should last several days
and are a pleasure on the table, because the petals do not drop off
until the end. Cut the entire plant back in early August for fresh
stems. Seed catalogs promote the tender perennial *A. mexicana,* or
Mexican hyssop, as a cut flower grown as an annual from seed, flowering the first year, though I wasn't one to succeed with germinating
it. Some agastaches are hardy to Zone 6 or 7 and are good perform-
ers in the Southeast. You can look to herb nurseries such as Sandy
Mush for a large selection of plants from cuttings.

Another perennial with fragrant foliage and tiny white flowers
you can press into service for filler comes to mind here. Deliciously
minty-scented *Calamintha nepeta* ssp. *nepeta (C. nepetoides)* produces
stiff stems (cut about 15 inches) from summer to early fall. Because
you won't want much of it, keep **calamint** in the border or herb garden. Provide good drainage and a little relief from hot sun in the
South.

AGERATUM HOUSTONIANUM

You'll recognize the old-fashioned **flossflowers** from bedspreads and
wallpaper and old chintz. While a bouquet of the quiet blue flowers—with perhaps dill and a pastel globe amaranth—is lovely in
a bedroom or informal space, it's not a choice for a showy arrangement. The white isn't as popular with people who've grown both;
I rather like the new dark violet red. Be sure to let at least half the
flowers in a cluster open before cutting, or they may not develop further. Ageratum lasts a long time in water, but it's important to trim
off the lower foliage to prevent wilting.

Find seed of the tallest, *Ageratum houstonianum,* sometimes called
'Blue Horizon'. It should be described as around 30 inches tall; unfortunately, most garden centers sell only seed packets and market

packs (small plants) of the low bedding heights. A tender annual, it's sown directly in the garden after the last frost date (notice that light is required for germination) for flowers in July or August. The seed requires quite warm soil temperatures for germination, so you won't gain much by sowing early outdoors. Some people feel the wait is too long outside and start the seed indoors four to eight weeks early to get sturdy plants that amazingly seem to like transplanting and grow quite large and bloom in June. Three or four plants might be a good number to grow, in a little shade if you don't have full sun, and you can hope to pick flowers well into fall, even November, here.

I'd heard of the "ageratum effect" when photographing, but never knew sunglasses could produce the same phenomenon, until one day I picked a selection of flowers focused around my newly blooming plants, only to take off my sunglasses and remember the ageratum was blue, not pink!

AGROSTEMMA GITHAGO

Agrostemma githago, or **corn cockle,** is one of the sweetest flowers you'll have a chance to grow, in white or a deep pink, all with an exquisite tracery of dots and dashes. While it's captivating by itself in the vase, agrostemma looks very pretty with campanula, cornflowers, sweet rocket, and bupleurum in May from fall-sown plants, and may bloom at the same time as annual gypsophila also sown the previous fall. You can cut stems 16 to 24 inches long. Leave some flowers on the plant, and the seedpods with their perky-eared tips make attractive filler in June while they're still green.

For best results in the middle states and South, sow this hardy annual the preceding fall in September, or in very early spring, in a well-drained soil, because agrostemma is susceptible to rotting in wet winters. The soil shouldn't be rich. In the North, direct sow in early spring. Sow thinly, as it comes up well; under favorable conditions, six plants may be plenty. They remain evergreen all winter here and begin to grow strongly at the first hint of spring. If your new growth begins to flop, tie once around with string early on. In easy climates, you may be able to sow several crops a few weeks apart. The first agrostemma I ever grew was the best, one of those fortuitous aspects to being a beginner that keeps us going long enough to become experienced.

ALCEA ROSEA

The stately **hollyhocks,** *Alcea rosea,* are grand plants whose continuous show keeps the cutting garden looking good. Put them at the front to hide the mess behind. Gardeners often avoid hollyhocks for the house, because they wilt badly after cutting, but if the flowers are prepared properly by burning the stem ends, they last a very long time in water. Because the stems are so long and the flowers so prominent, it's difficult to use tall hollyhocks in the average mixed arrangement unless you have a lot of long-stemmed material, like delphinium and snow-on-the-mountain, though the stems can be shortened at either end, as is seen in the old master paintings, for use with garden flowers of moderate length and size. The buds continue to open, making the arrangement even more beautiful one or two days later.

Some mixed-color seed packets result in quite a jumble of uncooperative colors, particularly true of the doubles, but one year the most beautiful flower I grew was the mixed color 'Indian Spring' strain hollyhock in shades of pink, rose, and white. The flowers glowed with luminous color, some with darker rose centers, others with shell-pink centers, and all magnificent together in the vase. It's not hard to find these singles and semidoubles prettier for cutting than the heavily doubled **powder puffs,** so lacking in subtlety of color. Several seed companies offer their own singles selections by other names, some with yellow. The interesting 'Nigra' is described as "chocolate maroon" by Thompson & Morgan—not black at all but similar in color to the beautiful black tulips, handsome against green foliage, and suitable for a sophisticated display.

The 'Indian Spring' seed has reappeared in the catalogs after years of absence. As hollyhocks are extremely hardy (to Zone 3), they'll begin flowering in early June from a direct sowing the previous September, and after heavy June cutting, they will continue to produce into September. Some suppliers say 'Indian Spring' can be treated as annuals and sown in spring for midsummer bloom, but I find sowing the previous fall in situ produces the strongest plants with the most flowers. A few hollyhocks sown in the garden in fall, however, such as the double 'Chaters' or 'Nigra', may not flower at all the next year, and so might as well be sown in spring for the next year's bloom. While most are short-lived perennials best grown as hardy annuals, a few seed catalogs separate their hollyhocks into annual, biennial, and "perennial" varieties, which helps you to know what to expect.

I'd always viewed the dwarf hybrids, such as the unusual 'Majorette', with suspicion, but after my success with the new dwarf delphiniums, I decided to give them a try. The results: the wide, semi-double flowers, with their fringed petals, arrange easily with other garden flowers because of their reduced height, and the finer foliage doesn't require so much removal. As hollyhocks open from the bottom up, you can wait until the stem lengthens adequately, to say 16 or more inches, before cutting.

Hollyhocks are big plants, requiring a spacing of at least 18 inches, so in any great numbers they're best suited to the larger cutting garden. An excellent low-effort plant for full sun, you can leave it to persist as best it can, or shake its seed-set branches over a desired area in September, then water. The large seed starts easily and much more cheaply in place than purchased plants. Under lights, I have my best luck by using a lot of seed and by keeping it well ventilated and not too cool.

Select a variety of stems for cutting to have opened flowers high and low in the arrangement. Trim all except the smallest leaves from each stem and place them in water immediately; the stems can be 30 to 36 inches in length and thus require a tall vase or florist's bucket. In the house, sear the stem ends over a flame; a gas stove is the easiest. Older children like this job, and even a visiting aunt enjoyed preparing the flowers for her room. The bottom inch or two should be thoroughly blackened. Slightly wilted stems may even revive after this treatment, but glass vases are out because of the appearance of the stems. Pick off fading florets as the new buds open. Many hollyhocks branch heavily, so six or seven well-grown plants can produce a glorious massing of 20 stems.

ALCHEMILLA MOLLIS

Alchemilla mollis produces greenish-yellow sprays of tiny flowers and lovely pleated leaves in mid-to-late spring and is one of the most valuable perennials in the cutting garden. Used as a filler, **lady's mantle** makes a luxuriant froth of spring green for other flowers to emerge through. It's essential company for columbines and *Lychnis coronaria* and a good easy solution for early torch lilies. In fact, lady's mantle doctors almost any spring arrangement that is wanting.

Lady's mantle in the South never looks as wonderful as it does in English gardening books, and it only rarely self-sows. Here it's best in the lightly shaded cutting garden. In full sun it has a dreadful

apappearance midsummer, but kept alive with extra waterings, the
next spring it will look better than could have been thought possible.
Lady's mantle usually needs some simple support to keep the flowers
off the ground. That includes even the "improved" cultivars that are
supposed to be more self-supporting.

This is an extremely hardy and durable plant, as I discovered
when I left one uprooted and forgotten in a plastic supermarket bag
on the ground all one winter, a cold winter, and found new leaves
showing in spring. I replanted it immediately, as such fortitude deserved to be rewarded. One well-grown plant provides plenty of material, but you might like a second.

ALLIUM

Every cutting gardener should try a plant from the **flowering onions**. Although they're bulbs from the onion clan, there's little onion
smell, and almost all are suitable for cutting. They like full sun.
Look for *Allium siculum* in this book under its newer name of *Nectaroscordum siculum*.

Early *A. aflatunense* is a favorite of mine, as it flowers reliably the
first season and comes back for several years. It's one of the best alliums for cutting and isn't expensive. A taller cultivar, 'Purple Sensation', blooms at the end of April with the last of the tulips and generously bears two or even three long, straight, leafless stems to about
18 or 24 inches. The simple, dusky pink globes go nicely with such
elegant flowers as Iceland poppies, pale pink peonies, camassias, or
early irises. Flowers cut when just opening continue to open in the
vase. Begin with 6 to 10 bulbs for mixed arranging, or choose to
make a great show with many more.

I never got more than one flower from a planting of *A. caeruleum*,
but it's a gorgeous blue on a stem 18 inches long, supposed to be
easily grown and clump forming. Since it is native to central Asia, it's
likely our eastern climate is at fault. Try this allium in as dry and
warm a condition as possible. If it grows well in your garden, you'll
want it for late spring and early summer flowers.

Usually seen in vegetable gardens, vigorous *A. cepa* var. *proliferum*
is also called **topset onion, tree onion,** and **Egyptian onion.** Egyptian onions form interesting green bulblets like shallots, "offsets," in
the tops of thick, hollow stalks (usually without flowers) that can
be used alone or for filler in mixed arrangements. The offsets send
exotic sprouts curving upward while still on the stalk, appearing with

the bearded irises and making a good companion for them. You plant the offsets to get easily grown new plants. Look for this from a vegetable gardener, particularly at a community garden where interesting things are passed around, or from a specialty catalog aimed at herb and vegetable gardeners. Sandy Mush Herb Nursery and Nichols Garden Nursery have offsets listed in their fine mail-order catalogs.

A. christophii, **star of Persia,** is the largest of the allium flowers. It's similar to *A. aflatunense* in color and blooms only a few days later in early May, but it is cantaloupe size and shaped excitingly like a starburst. It's simple to use by itself in a vase; three flowers might even be enough. I have them in extremely good drainage and they've returned for several years, even though they're in medium shade (they prefer full sun). Cut stems are 21 inches and long lasting.

Flowering in late spring on long stems, *A. giganteum* is so large it's good only for bold statements in large rooms and is not easy to grow. I lost every one of the huge bulbs on my first effort in my sunny winter-wet garden, and given their cost, I declined to repeat it. Try the **giant onion** only in the best of drainage; I've seen them growing well on a slope. There are other big new hybrids of similar appearance, even more expensive, but a smaller white I'd love to own— 'Mt. Everest'—is no more costly.

A. neapolitanum, **Naples onion,** makes a good cutting companion for many plants blooming in mid to late spring. It produces pleasant small white flower clusters with fresh green centers on stems cut to about 12 inches long, longer on selected strains. It's much more reliable in my garden than most alliums, and the bulbs produce more flowers in successive years. The foliage will be gone by early summer, so mark the spot. Begin with at least a dozen, but more pleasure will be had from twice that many.

Long-lived *A. schoenoprasum* 'Forescate' is a variety of **chives** selected for its big flowers of good pink color. It blooms heavily in midspring on sturdy stems to 15 inches and affords excellent companion material for hesperis, painted daisies, and *Linaria maroccana.* The flowers are especially wonderful when cut just as they emerge from their papery sheaths, or even before. They continue opening in the vase and last fairly well. I found my plant in a perennial catalog, rather than a bulb or vegetable list. It has done beautifully in the cutting bed where other alliums succumbed, and the foliage, of course, persists longer than most and can be used for cooking.

A. sphaerocephalum produces a two-inch wide egg-shaped purple flower in a papery sheath on wiry 20- to 28-inch stems in mid-June. This very hardy and reliable bulb also persists better than some others, if you can give it an area of good drainage. The **drumstick allium** is wonderful with flowers of an informal nature such as white clusters of yarrow and *Lysimachia clethroides,* zoned red and gold gaillardia, the small yellow flowers of anthemis, and a gloriosa daisy like 'Double Gold', all in a large crock. Their deep color also looked terrific with my salmon gladiolus. The flowers develop slowly; pick any time after they show color. Plant a lot, because they're very inexpensive, and grow them in a clump to keep track of them.

My *A. senescens* proved to be as tall as I hoped, with lasting lavender-pink globes in mid-July through the end of August, though it can be variable as to size. The plant named *A. s.* var. *glaucum* is likely to be a short form, so look instead for one described as having 12- to 24-inch stems, and maybe you'll get a 25 incher like mine. **Mountain garlic** is a long-lived, reliable plant that flowers obligingly even in the worst hot dry weather.

A. tuberosum, or **garlic chives,** blooms in mid-August through early September here, a long-lasting white flower a little like the spring-blooming *A. neapolitanum,* on longer wiry 22-inch stems. You can mix it with annual scabiosa, globe amaranth, chrysopsis, and small sunflowers or dahlias, and it's ideal for a late summer bouquet of white flowers. The plant is perennial in my garden and flowers heavily even in drought, the foliage persisting and marking the location. As it volunteers all too easily, you'll want to prevent it from setting seed. Look for it from smaller specialty or herb nurseries, or from a vegetable gardener.

ALSTROEMERIA

Long-lasting alstroemeria are familiar to customers of florist shops, where they're imported from abroad. The striped and spotted flowers in beautiful shades of pink, red, orange, yellow, and white grow in large clusters on long, strong stems in late spring and early summer. Also known as **Peruvian lilies,** they combine handsomely with many elegant flowers from the cutting garden.

Alstroemeria's relatively low cost at the florist, as well as a reputation for wandering, difficult propagation, and poor cold hardiness, have led few gardeners to try them. Although several species have been developed for commercial cutting by cut-flower breeders, and are not easily available to gardeners, the more commonly seen Ligtu

hybrids are often suggested as the best for the garden and less likely
to be invasive. I had decided *Alstroemeria psittacina* 'Variegata' was
the one for me, with an odd flower not everyone would covet. But
I love streaks and spots and green in a flower, and Allan Armitage in
Herbaceous Perennial Plants says it's one of the best for the South,
which I believe. I set it in the garden in the spring before the worst
drought since Dust Bowl days, and I only saw it once or twice after
that. A fragrant new hybrid called 'Sweet Laura' is said to be hardy
to Zone 5 and tolerant of hot summers.

Allow one plant some space, avoid dividing or moving, and
mulch well for winter protection in Zone 6 and 7, the usual limits of
hardiness. Partial shade is a good idea in the South. Look for al-
stroemerias in a good bulb catalog like Brent and Becky's, or
a specialty nursery catalog like Plant Delights.

AMARANTHUS

Like planting celosia, choosing amaranthus for your garden leaves
you vulnerable to the wits and wags. You can't very well hide that
you are growing it. One remarked that my love-lies-bleeding looked
like a Chinese vegetable; another snorted "We called that a weed
back home" and marched me over to see where an invader not unlike
it was growing unwanted in someone's plot. Despite such carping,
amaranthus is a good choice for an annual to be sown late in spring
or early summer because it germinates readily in hot weather. And,
unlike liatris or Shirley poppies, which must be cut at the right time,
there's some leeway for cutting amaranthus, because the flowers develop slowly—a great advantage for people who are inattentive or go
in and out of town during the summer.

One of my favorites is **prince's feather,** which bears upright, deep
reddish-purple feathery spikes on stems cut about 24 to 30 inches
long, with dark purple-green or plain green leaves, and green or
purplish-red stems. 'Intense Purple' is one such selection, a masculine flower with deep red stems that are marvelous to see through
clear glass. Arrange it boldly by itself in a simple vase for a room
with lots of light. You can combine it with an ornamental grass, or
the pink wheat celosia 'Flamingo Feather', and it's exciting with
other strong flowers such as little sunflowers and mahogany-zoned
calliopsis. A small amount of the green-leaved type is also successful
in a mixed arrangement of pink flowers.

I first bought seed for prince's feather under the name *Amaranthus cruentus* 'Oeschberg', but it may be called *A. hypochondriacus* or *A. hybridus*, even *A. h.* var. *erythrostachys*. There are desirable golden-brown and wheat-colored versions, such as 'Golden Giant' and 'Hot Biscuits' (this last often listed under *A. paniculatus)*, fabulous for late summer and fall, though a little too much like mighty oaks, and I've not yet discovered whether pinching, or even crowding, will produce finer stems. You can't go wrong with 'Split Personality', wine red with touches of green. The names are dreadfully confused, but both prince's feather and love-lies-bleeding differ from the types of amaranthus bearing foliage in several colors, such as **Joseph's coat** *(A. tricolor)*. I saved my own seed for prince's feather for years, as I hadn't always seen it listed. Though some states have it classified as a weed, which is why many catalogs choose not to offer it, prince's feather self-sows only modestly in my garden. It has never been weedy, unlike some others I could mention that seem to be sold freely.

Prince's feather can be sown here as late as early June for flowers in August and September, and ready for cutting in 60 days. Space the plants well, avoiding too rich a soil, and it's best not to transplant. Each plant bears one main spike, so grow at least eight or nine, or more. The useful laterals that follow grow to as much as 25 inches on a large plant. Allow the stems to lengthen before cutting. Try always to cut newer flowers rather than huge developed plumes, and cut in the cool of the day. You may have to remove every leaf but the tiniest and stand the stems in a cool dark area to keep them from wilting. They last about three days.

The hulking *A. caudatus*, or **love-lies-bleeding,** is surprisingly elegant in water, especially the subtle 'Viridis' or 'Green Tails', though the red is more showy. It's a plant for the large garden. You can use the green dreadlocks as filler for big mixed arrangements in July for a cool effect in hot weather. The central stem of each plant carries the longest tassel, dangling to two feet easily, best not used unless you're adventurous and capable. The side stems sport excellent nine-inch tassels that are much easier to arrange and make an ideal subject for pedestal vases. One plant can supply enough material to fill quite a large vase, with cut stems 24 to 30 inches in length. Tall red and brown versions with similar, but marvelously upright, spikes have recently debuted in the seed catalogs; they look like they'd be excellent for exotic cutting, though green-flowered 'Green Thumb' failed to reach a cuttable height the only time I grew it, nor have I seen it perform acceptably elsewhere. In addition to removing all the lower foliage, trim some leaves around the tassel to prevent wilting and to emphasize the flower. If you cut in the heat of a hot day, it may wilt and not recover. I was disappointed to find I couldn't grow a fall crop of love-lies-bleeding by sowing in midsummer.

AMBROSIA MEXICANA

I never got to order *Ambrosia mexicana* 'Green Magic' from the Country Garden cutting-garden seed catalog before it went out of business, but I kept the catalog for reference and my eye out for the unusual items it mentioned. Years later to my delight, **Jerusalem oak** showed up in several seed lists. The Country Garden had recommended it for fresh or dried flowers, and as an aromatic that would be excellent for wreaths. It does have a strong scent of bayberry, but only when it's handled. The tiny flowers and small leaves, all green, make a nice filler, their fine texture pretty with sweet peas or veronica, and the stems have a gentle curve to their 16-inch length. This annual germinates readily sown direct in the spring in full sun, for about seven or eight plants, and you'll see why it's called Jerusalem *oak* when the curious leaves first appear. Some books have this plant listed as *Chenopodium botrys,* and all of them comment that it's a weed, so I wasn't going to be surprised when it volunteered, but it never did.

AMMI MAJUS

Ammi majus, **bishop's weed** or **false Queen Anne's lace,** is a half-hardy annual similar to Queen Anne's lace *(Daucus carota),* with large, upward-facing, flat flower clusters suitable for large arrangements, and with a very long vase life. To my eye, it's prettier than Queen Anne's lace, but not so easy to grow where it's hot. Ammi makes a wonderful companion for belladonna delphinium around the first of June, if it has been started early under lights, and it's an appropriate companion for ornamental grasses. The tiny, greenish-white flowers calm the strong colors of phlox or purple cleome better than the bright white of baby's breath or other white whites, and the result is a far more elegant arrangement. It's a tall, narrow plant with one magnificent main stem, and after cutting there are many smaller flowers left behind that are lovely for medium-sized arrangements. Ammi may require staking, but if some stems do become bent, they may be even more beautiful in the vase, because they will face out rather than up. A small tomato cage set over the plant when small works suitably.

Seed companies advise that it's best to sow outside in spring in full sun, an excellent proposition for cool summer areas, where repeat sowings are also possible. However, when I've sown direct in April, the coming heat has stunted the plants at only 18 inches tall; yet when started carefully in peat pots in mid-February and set out in earliest April, the plants have on occasion reached four and a half feet, blooming about two weeks before Queen Anne's lace. If the weather is dry, the plants burn after only a couple of hot days, and they are more sensitive to heat than poppies in my garden. The best ammi I ever grew was crowded in among other plants in full sun, the others providing shade and support. It's fairly frost tolerant and can be hardened off and planted out several weeks before the last frost date, but it won't live over winter here. In mild-winter areas, you might sow in fall for larger plants and heavier flowering in late spring. Ammi may even self-sow. Two or three plants will probably supply one large arrangement, but more won't take up much room.

ANCHUSA AZUREA

I find *Anchusa azurea* is better admired in the garden than the vase, as handling the prickly leaves and stems is most unpleasant, but the glorious blue color of **Italian bugloss** tempts some gardeners irresistibly. If you insist on arranging with it, cut the stems when fairly full in flower and give them support for a while in deep water. Nursery plants of 'Dropmore' or 'Loddon Royalist' are sometimes available from catalogs; I've also sown the easy seed for 'Dropmore' under lights in February. The seedlings grow large quickly for planting out in April, with flowering in May one year later. Keep mulches away and allow good ventilation, as rot is a problem. Keep this huge perennial in the border for a little cutting (where it may attract more comment than any other plant in your garden), or save it for a very large cutting garden.

ANEMONE

The silvery buds are almost more beautiful than the single pink flowers of the tall perennial *Anemone tomentosa* 'Robustissima' (sometimes listed under *A. vitifolia*). It may wilt badly after cutting unless you take a short stem 18 inches or less, and cut when the plant first blooms, mid-August in Zone 7. You can make a lovely bouquet from the shade garden with short stems of 'Robustissima' along with pink sedum and purple spikes of liriope. They drop their petals rather easily, but the tiny ball-shaped centers left behind are charming exposed. The least likely of the **Japanese anemones** to need staking, it requires moisture and shouldn't be planted in full sun in the South. It is also called **grapeleaf anemone**. One plant spreads slowly, eventually turning invasive and not suitable for small gardens. 'Robustissima' blooms about four weeks before the taller *A.* × *hybrida* cultivars, so fanciers of this flower can prolong the season by also selecting later hybrids such as the single white 'Honorine Jobert' or rose-colored double 'Pamina', though late varieties may bloom too late for the frost in northern gardens. The related *A. hupehensis* is said to tolerate heat better and blooms between the other two. These are all handsome plants that can be cut from the border rather than the cutting garden and last about four days in water.

A. coronaria is an ideal bulb for planting in autumn in the South (but really in any mild-winter area, especially with cool summers) in sun or preferably light shade, where it may flower very early with the daffodils. The original of this flower is thought to have been the biblical "lily of the field." The brilliant colors of red, rose pink, blue, and white and extremely long life in water make them popular florist stock. Some bulb catalogs offer separated colors of the single De Caen hybrid **poppy anemones** and the semidouble St. Brigid hybrid, the latter perhaps being slightly hardier. You may be able to find a bicolor mix with a white zone around the black center. Gardeners who are experienced with starting plants under lights may like the challenge of the longer-stemmed 'Mona Lisa' strain of seed—if they find room in their garden accounts, as it's not cheap—or tubers if you can locate them. Thompson & Morgan offered the seed most recently. Poppy anemones combine handsomely with euphorbias and with tulips, especially lily-flowered tulips: brilliant red and violet-rose anemones with bright pink tulips generate rich, rich color.

A. coronaria has never been so long stemmed in my garden as at the florist (whose flowers are probably greenhouse grown). I used to despair that my early stems stood so short, but by the end of April, they lengthen to 10 to 13 inches. Adequate moisture is often related to stem length in a flower, so you'll want to water generously in a dry spring. I've erred in the past in not soaking my corms overnight before planting in fall, which partly explains their erratic performance, but in the coldest part of Zone 7, we may also be at the upper range of their hardiness. Be sure to plant in a well-drained location and on their sides, which is usually easier to determine than which of their peculiar anatomy is top or bottom. They don't repeat well, but each corm can produce many flowers in its first year. In the North, you may need to start your plants in pots, keeping them quite cool, and plant out after frosts are over. My garden colleague, Mary Ellen K., reports that she got great results by soaking her corms for eight hours and planting them on their sides in full sun in October, in a well-dug spot adjacent to her manured sweet pea bed. They bloomed gloriously for two weeks beginning mid-April, with stems about 16 inches, and she notes that the next year, half came back. Test your garden with a dozen corms; thereafter plant more if you're successful.

If you don't have a little shade for *A. coronaria* in areas where it's necessary, *A.* ×*fulgens* supplies a similar brilliant red flower with a black center that can take more sun. **Scarlet windflower** is at its best as the daffodils are ending, so skip the red tulips with black centers, you won't need them; used in the vase with purple honesty, the color is royal. Each corm produces several flowers, and bloom ends by late spring. The corms are reputed to like hot summers and to be long lived in good situations, but they haven't come back for me. Smaller and earlier *A. blanda*, the blue or white **Grecian windflower**, is more reliable and lasts about six days in water, though the stems will reach only seven inches.

ANETHUM GRAVEOLENS

The sophisticated acid-green color and lacy shape of *Anethum graveolens* compliments almost any flower, from English garden pastels to warm American "tropicals" like bloodflower and nasturtiums, an essential flower for the cutting garden. This annual herb, better known as **dill**, is one of the best fillers in early June for both elegant and casual mixed arrangements, or used alone massed in a tall vase. A hard-to-find variety bred for cutting (most recently from Select Seeds and Nichols Garden), 'Vierling' grows to four feet with huge flower heads 10 inches across, a flower most likely to succeed in large arrangements. Or look for a seed supplier like Cook's Garden, which has offered a special strain described as "florist's dill." The common dill, better for medium-sized vases, grows to three feet, with seven-inch flowers. There's a slight smell of dill in the vase, which becomes stronger as the flower declines.

The recent periods of heat and drought have made dill difficult to grow, and self-sown plants had disappeared from my garden until the cool spring after the explosion of Mt. Pinatubo brought it back. Seedlings sown in spring in full sun here frequently fizzle in the early heat before they have time to bloom. It's more successful to sow in light shade, or among tall and lush flowering plants, for example Canterbury bells, hesperis, cornflowers, sweet peas, calliopsis, and Shirley poppies, which won't overwhelm the dill but will give it a little shelter from sun. In too much shade dill may have only one loose flower head.

In cool summer areas where dill thrives, there should be 11 or 12 big flowers per plant, blooming into August, and successive sowings from spring through midsummer prolong the season. An acquaintance who moved to Michigan heard from the neighbors later that she was supposed to have located her dill so that it seeded on its own side of the fence—there's good reason the label on the supermarket bottle says "Dill Weed." Plants that go to seed early enough may produce a second crop that year, flowering in fall; though when I've sown dill as late as August, it grows lushly through autumn but never flowers. And it doesn't survive the winter because it's only half hardy. You'll want at least four or five plants.

Lovers of dill flowers may like the biennial wild parsnip *(Pastinaca sativa);* fennel *(Foeniculum vulgare),* which can be obtained easily at an herb nursery; or parsley *(Petroselinum crispum),* a biennial that flowers the year after you've grown it in the vegetable garden.

ANGELICA ARCHANGELICA

Wild parsnip is one common name for *Angelica archangelica,* though it's a different plant from the true parsnip gone wild *(Pastinaca sativa),* also a good cut flower. Usually found in herb gardens, angelica is an umbellifer similar to fennel and true parsnip in its enormous head of greenish-white flowers on long, strong stems. The big flowers make forceful additions to large arrangements in summer, with the smaller side stems being more appropriate for medium-sized bouquets. The fantastic seedheads are also suitable for filler.

Efforts to grow angelica from purchased seed aren't always successful because the seed loses viability quickly, but you can find plants from a good herb nursery. It's a short-lived perennial, usually treated as a biennial, which self-sows well, perhaps too well; you'll be lengthening its life and reducing its spreading propensities by cutting the flowers. Angelica needs light shade and moist soil and possibly a patient owner, as my current plant has not bloomed yet in over two years. Expect it to die once it goes to seed. This big plant takes too much space for a small cutting garden.

ANGELONIA ANGUSTIFOLIA

I took a chance just recently on *Angelonia angustifolia;* it had the little scissors next to its name that signals a cut-flower, which always takes my eye, though with a little doubt. It's a tender perennial grown as an annual, with tiny purple snapdragon-like flowers with a little white lip to brighten their countenance and delightful faint whiffs of grape soda when you're cutting. The foliage is narrow, like a small toadflax or penstemon, its curving stems sprawling a bit here and there, about 16 inches long when cut and trailing casually from a small- to medium-sized bouquet. The stems look so alive the first couple of days, but they soon lose their fizz. Put the plant in the border (light shade will do), and cut occasionally from it there. Bloom should begin by June and continue over a long season in summer, even during hot weather.

ANTHEMIS TINCTORIA

Though **golden Marguerite** makes no pretense to long life in the Southeast, its masses of cheerful yellow daisies in June satisfy the requirements for a good beginner's "perennial." The supple stems bow out from the sides of the vase in a graceful curve, the sort of amiable flowers to just drop in water. Nursery plants under the name 'E. C. Buxton' are white.

After repeatedly losing mail-ordered plants to death after flowering, I found better results by growing from seed, usually *Anthemis tinctoria* 'Kelwayi', the tallest. The seed-grown plants are much larger, and certainly cheaper, than the mail-ordered ones. You can sow in place in September, or start the seed in July under lights—it germinates easily and grows strongly—setting out just one young plant in early September in a roomy spot. The plant should be quite full by November, and simply enormous by flowering time in late May, with cut stems easily 27 inches long, though plants grown in a warm, dry spring are considerably smaller. While flowering continues for six weeks, much longer where summers are cool, they're best harvested immediately; it's easiest to grasp many stems in the hand and cut them all at once. Golden Marguerite is somewhat floppy and needs to be tied around with string if the plant has grown large. It still dies by midsummer here, but anthemis self-sows strongly and even requires some hoeing away of extra seedlings. One large plant should provide plenty for mixed bouquets or for huge masses of daisies.

In cooler and less humid climates where anthemis thrives, such as the North and the Northwest in the United States, and in Great Britain, where they may reach five or six feet in height, the very hardy plants live longer and can be divided to keep them strong.

ANTIRRHINUM MAJUS

Antirrhinum majus is an impossible name for something as common as **snapdragons.** I look for starts of the familiar tall white 'Rocket' snapdragons at the garden center in spring, as they're lovely by themselves and so pretty with green and pastel flowers, with hollyhocks, late delphiniums, monarda, and snow-on-the-mountain. Large heads of summer phlox and garden snapdragons fill out a vase admirably, too. Cut when half the flowers have opened and pick off faded florets as the stems age in the vase.

Most seed catalogs have extensive offerings of snapdragons in their annual section, many of dwarf and intermediate height, in addition to the tallest, which are the ones wanted for the cutting garden. American seed catalogs usually have Rockets (traditional single, closed flowers) in separated colors, including an excellent shade of rose. Mixed colors never look good to me. A recent development in snapdragon hybrids are the "butterfly" snaps with a larger open flower, rather than closed dragon's mouth; they may be single or double, and they make a larger, showier spike. "But can they be worn as earrings?" my friend Mary Ellen K. asks. She likes to show children how to put them on their ears.

Your snaps aren't likely to be as spectacular as the long straight stems commercial growers produce, but don't let that deter you. One of the prettiest stems I ever saw was one I grew myself, Burpee's 'Plum Blossom', handsomely colored, with a faint but delicious fruity scent. Snapdragons do best in light, fertile soil and tolerate light shade. If you buy young plants at the garden center, be sure they're small and preferably haven't been pinched. Otherwise, start seed early under lights and set the plants out to harden off soon; as they're half hardy, snapdragons perform best in cool weather and slow their growth in warm, and they may be flowering by the first of June. If you garden in a hot summer area, you may not want to pinch back the young plants (as seed packets recommend) to increase bushiness and side branching. That may delay bloom, and stems grown in hot weather will likely be shorter and of lesser quality.

It's often a good idea to stake or provide a tomato cage, the small conical kind, before you discover your stems have grown too crooked for arranging, which happens as soon as you turn your mind to something else. In that event, try cutting back low but above a growing point or leaf, stake the plant well, and wait for better results.

Snapdragons usually produce new stems into fall when they're rejuvenated by cooler weather. They often seed little plants that winter over, and even established plants may bloom again the next year, as snapdragons are perennial where the climate allows; in fact, in Britain they're frequently grown as biennials.

AQUILEGIA

From the genus *Aquilegia* come the **columbines,** delicate airy flowers for mixed arrangements in spring, and almost never seen at the florist. One usually wants the taller plants for cutting, but smaller columbines make especially pretty little bouquets on the dining table. Some seed catalogs offer extensive selections, including spurred and spurless, long and short stemmed, doubles, species, and fancifully colored hybrids. The plants tend to be short-lived perennials, but they're easily started under lights (a rewarding choice for novices), and they often self-sow.

The well-known 'McKana's Giants', huge bicolors four inches across with spurs over two inches long, attract all eyes for big blowsy romantic arrangements. You'll find other new strains not dissimilar. A columbine that persisted particularly well in my garden for years is *A. vulgaris,* or **Granny's bonnet,** because it reseeds heavily. The neighbors brought it from the family homestead in Cleveland. The vigorous plants with the characteristically short-spurred flowers do surprisingly well in dryish shade, once established; in full sun where it's hot, they should have plenty of moisture. You'll find seed strains of these in pale pink, rose pink, and a rich violet blue, often with doubled flowers, which some of the opinionated can't say enough against.

The unusual pink and white 'Nora Barlow'—the "flower arranger's columbine"—sometimes must be cut into separate sections
to relieve the tight awkwardness of the stiff and clumsy stems. However, a single well-grown plant may carry as many as 13 blooming
stems at once, beautiful with tellima and lady's mantle or *Euphorbia
robbiae,* which also provide a screen for the long, embarrassingly
naked, columbine stems (up to 32 inches in length). Nora reseeds well
and true, sprinkling one portion of the garden here with her progeny.
You may also find packets of white and mixed colors in Nora-shaped
flowers. After 15 years of looking, I finally found a "clematis-flowered"
columbine at the Thomas Jefferson Center for Historic Plants, at
Monticello, and wasn't disappointed. It has a pale pink, largely spurless flower very much like a single or semidouble Nora but not any
longer lived than Nora.

Columbines are important choices for shady gardens, though
some can abide happily in full sun. They cross readily, which is why
one often sees interesting columbines in curious colors, even "black,"
in established gardens; certainly one of the charms of *Aquilegia* lies
in finding new versions growing in your garden. When the colors
lose their clarity, pull them up and put in new plants. One plant each
of any cultivar may be sufficient for use in mixed arrangements,
though you'll likely want several altogether. If you hope to encourage
them, allow them to go to seed, cut the dried stems in late summer
and shake the seed out where you'd like columbines next year.
They'll even come up in the cracks in pavement.

ARMERIA

One of the few armerias tall enough for cutting, *Armeria plantaginea*
'Bees Ruby', is a perennial **sea pink** or **thrift,** furnishing loads of hot-
pink globes on 15-inch stems. It makes a bright addition to arrangements of pinks and greens, especially using lady's mantle or the delicate and pale *Dianthus superbus* in bloom at the same time. Strains of
A. plantaginea and *A. pseudoarmeria* are apparently easy to grow from
seed (I haven't needed to try, as my first plant still lives with me),
with pink, rose, and white plants resulting from selections such as
'Bees Hybrids'. Mature plants flower heavily, one in its second year
producing fully 100 stems. They're simple to cut, as you can grasp
handfuls of stems and shear them off just above the basal foliage.
Provide excellent drainage for armeria; it makes good use of dry soil.

ARTEMISIA

Although there are several tall perennial **wormwoods** (or **mugworts**) suitable for cutting for their silvery foliage, I like the green-leaved *Artemisia lactiflora* for the thousands of tiny creamy buds dotting its stems. The stems are at their best when the swollen buds haven't yet opened (they open in late July or early August), developing slowly over several weeks for a long cutting season, and lasting a good while in water. You can combine the long stems (to 34 inches) with mixed green and white flowers for a subtle effect, or with *Eupatorium purpureum* for a voluminous roadside look, and you can add the shorter stems to smaller mixed arrangements of many kinds, especially helpful with difficult flowers such as tithonia. One plant grows quickly, but not invasively like some artemisias, though it may need tying around early on to keep it upright. *A. lactiflora* takes light shade and likes a moist soil.

You may like *A. ludoviciana* 'Silver King', or 'Silver Queen', with similar but cut-edged silvery gray leaves, for arranging, particularly with pink, white, or blue flowers. Like ferns, the mature foliage is less likely to wilt. They form fine clumps that prefer a dry, well-drained location, and they may become aggressive, especially in light soils, though they've joined the ranks of the deceased here with little complaint. 'Powis Castle' is a large plant some people swear by for arranging; it may do better in the South than the others. Good herb nurseries often offer unusual artemisias. Another gray foliage plant you can pick from occasionally for filler is *Nepeta fassenii* 'Six Hills Giant', with violet-blue flowers.

ARUM ITALICUM

The green, or green and white marbled, foliage of *Arum italicum,* so popular with arrangers and florists, makes a good perennial ground cover in the shady garden, where it spreads slowly. **Arum**'s upright showy leaves appear in late summer or fall on cut stems about 12 inches long (including the leaf) and persist through winter, disappearing after flowering in spring. Use them for greenery with the little flowers of spring ephemera. The plants produce a calla-like flower in spring and red berries for fall where they are hardy, to Zones 6 and 7. 'Pictum' is a superb variegated form. In some gardens I'm told you may find birds spread the seed, for young plants here and there.

ARUNCUS DIOICUS

It's a pleasure to catch *Aruncus dioicus* just opening, when most of the microscopic creamy-white flowers are still in bud, and the huge plumes quite green. The loose, feathery flowers make an important feature for big billowy arrangements, combining luxuriantly with so many garden flowers and foliage. As **goat's beard** is a dioecious perennial, many people believe the bloom of male plants to be showier, but I like mine just fine, whatever its gender, and in any case one isn't usually offered the choice on purchasing a plant. You can cut big arching, astilbe-like flowers on strong 30- to 40-inch stems in late May, but if they're not cut soon enough after blooming, the fuzzy brushes fill up with an amazing assortment of black bugs that can't be shaken out easily. If need be, I leave the stems in water on the porch overnight, when many of the insects kindly depart, and I pick the rest out the next morning.

Goat's beard must have reliable moisture, needs partial shade in the South, and dislikes heat; I finally got one settled in by buying it in a large pot at the garden center, as mail-ordered plants had never lived long. Once established, it's more tolerant of heat and drought and proves to be a choice for the big cutting garden. Goat's beard should be planted where you'll notice it has come into bloom, as its prime is so short.

ASCLEPIAS

The **milkweeds** contain a number of interesting plants. *Asclepias tuberosa* supplies one of the very best oranges for the cutting garden; it's modest despite its hue. Many people don't like orange in a flower, however, and might prefer the red, gold, or pink **butterfly weed** such as 'Gay Butterflies', which, though a perennial, blooms in its first year from seed started under lights. 'Hello Yellow' blooms a week or two earlier than the orange. One mature butterfly weed provides a nice bunch of flowers in June and has a second equally good flowering about six weeks after, when the summer palette is more cordial to orange. My cut stems were never long, sometimes only 11 inches grown in full sun, but I've seen marvelous taller plants (to three feet) in other gardens, partly shaded by neighboring plants. Cut the flowers when they're mostly opened and burn the stem ends. To use them for greenery, many gardeners may prefer the long pointed green seedpods held in clusters atop each stem and at their prime in late summer. To get these, of course, you have to forgo cutting the flowers. Good vase companions are difficult to find for orange flowers, but one is the green and white *Euphorbia marginata.* Keep your butterfly weed in dryish soil in a well-drained bed. Take heart when the plant doesn't reappear until late in the spring and is presumed dead.

A. incarnata, or **swamp milkweed,** also appears very late, just when you're about to plant something else in that spot. It's a choice plant for summer wildflower bouquets, with attractive narrow foliage, similar in appearance to *A. tuberosa* but for its greater height to four feet, white or dusky rose color, and ease of use with other flowers. The greenish-white 'Ice Ballet', with its cluster of pretty faceted buds in June and July, often shows up better than the pink in arrangements. It's helpful with many summer flowers like coreopsis and yarrow and produces an excellent second flush of bloom after the first harvest. Seed catalogs offer "improved" strains of swamp milkweed, which are recommended for cutting. If the stems wilt after cutting on a hot day, remove as much foliage as possible, right up to the flower head, wrap the stems in paper for support, and stand them in water to revive, but they're not long lasting in the vase unless you also sear the ends. For fresh seedpods, cut them while they're still green and lush, as by mid-August they begin to dry out and later burst open, when they are perfect for children to take to science for show and tell. One plant may provide enough material, including seedpods, but it increases only slowly in my garden and needs extra moisture and occasionally some support. In wet years, it may develop into quite a large plant and need to be tied up, not because it's weak stemmed, but to prevent its hogging too much space.

Occasionally showing up at the florist in early fall, **bloodflower,** *A. curassavica,* has similar flowers on long stems, each flower red and orange together and tropical in feel. It is excellent with warm-colored zinnias (especially the long-stemmed 'Old Mexico' type), peppers, nasturtiums, *Verbena bonariensis,* and the like; it also has fine green pods held upright in August. Bloodflower is much prettier than its common name. I once saw it called "sunset flower," which fits its appearance much better. A tender perennial, it's hardy only to Zone 8, but elsewhere you can treat it as an annual, blooming the first year in summer and fall, even self-sowing. Tolerant of heat and humidity, it's ideal for the Southeast, but my self-sown plants don't have a long enough season to reach a good size. Where it's not too cold, try to keep it alive over winter for a bushier plant the next year, growing to three feet or more.

All these milkweeds accept light shade and revel in warm summers. As they're tap rooters that resent transplanting, sow them direct or start the seed in large peat pots and plant out carefully. Or buy small plants. They're all tormented horribly by aphids.

ASTER

There are a number of hardy **asters** for cutting, all perennial and sun loving (find the annual China asters under *Callistephus chinensis*). The pretty cultivars of marvelously blue *Aster × frikartii* make desirable garden subjects for blue summer asters with large, long-rayed flowers. They should be attempted by cut-flower gardeners in Zones 5 through 8, though so many people, including myself, find them impossible. Mine rarely live through the winter and always need staking. The failure of the captivating but short-lived *A. tongo-lensis* 'Wartburg Star' was another blow to my hopes for blue summer asters; it has a delectable orange center, and it was painful to see it go.

But the fall asters, many of them natives (the above two are not), are so easy and prolific that it's even possible to cut from a plant in the border without spoiling the picture, though a particular plant may be wanted for the cutting garden—I should say the large cutting garden. The *A. novi-belgii* (**New York aster**) cultivars are usually recommended for cutting over the *A. novae-angliae* (**New England aster** or **Michaelmas daisy**), as they have smoother foliage and don't close their flowers at night; it's the species listed by the Flower Council of Holland. However, the *A. novae-angliae* asters count as their member the irresistible deep rose-pink 'Alma Potschke', which I love to cut and put with *Boltonia* 'Pink Beauty', closing blossoms or not. The *A. novae-angliae* also better tolerate damp soils. They are both fairly coarse. You can with good conscience cut from either species, and like many people, I call both of them Michaelmas daisies. A white aster from either group is a wonderful choice to combine with the yellow aster look-alike, *Chrysopsis villosa* 'Golden Sunshine', in bloom at the same time.

The Michaelmas daisies are woody and pose a challenge for arranging (they aren't first-rank cutting plants), but a few bushy stems make a very large bunch of flowers with an airy appeal. You can use

long stems of 20 inches, or you can cut the big clusters into shorter
sections for use on the dinner table, perhaps with a few flowers like
Malva 'Zebrina'. Faded flowers can be snipped out of the clusters.
The plants begin to bloom in mid-August or early September, not
reaching their prime for weeks and giving the arranger lots of opportunity for cutting. But don't be surprised if a new aster is discovered
to commence bloom in July, as they frequently do. Like chrysanthemums, neighbors often have marvelous asters from whom you can
beg a piece, and the plants respond well to yearly division. One is
usually enough.

A breeding parent of many *A. novi-belgii* cultivars is *A. laevis,*
smooth aster. The smooth feel to the foliage gives it the name, and
it is indeed more pleasant to strip the leaves from the pretty cultivar
'Bluebird' than many other rough-skinned asters. The tall plant is
nicely erect (though you need to tie it around once), and its long-
stemmed narrow clusters of one-inch lavender-blue flowers are
easier to arrange than the wide bushy heads of the Michaelmas daisies. I liked the rustic look of this aster in September arranged with
the goldenrod 'Fireworks' and gloriously blue *Salvia azurea.* The
buds continue opening in water.

I hoped *A. ericoides* 'Monte Cassino', **heath aster,** would be the
small fine-rayed blue or white daisy I see at the florist (where it's
called **September flower** or **September aster**), but the stems my first
plant produced were far too coarse. The next one I bought (from Allen Bush's sadly now-gone nursery, Holbrook Farm) under the name
A. pringlei 'Monte Cassino', bloomed profusely in clouds of tiny
white daisies in mid-September and was much more what I wanted,
though it requires thinning of its abundant stems and needs staking
early in the season. Stake it loosely with tiers of easily untied cloth
strips or lengths of twine, which allow you to release the plant temporarily in order to tease out the stems after cutting, rather than
break the stems from dragging them through a string corset or tomato cage. You can cut the rather stiff stems as long as 22 inches,
making luxurious long-lasting sprays for large arrangements, or cut
them into sections for smaller bouquets. The buds open slowly over
a long period in the vase. My plant has self-sown modestly, and one
wet summer it reached an astonishing four feet.

A somewhat coarse aster to keep in the border for the handsome
dark purple coloring of its foliage through spring and summer is
A. lateriflorus, **calico aster.** I have 'Prince', the darkest. In his *Garden-*

er's *Guide to Growing Asters,* Paul Picton suggests 'Lady in Black',
a more upright version of 'Prince', as one of the best cultivars for cutting, and I found it listed in a number of catalogs offering more
than the commonly listed and almost-tiresome **Frikart's aster.** By
flowering time, the purple has changed to dark green, and the tiny,
quarter-inch white flowers on brushy stems make a rustic bunch
that seems as deserving of the name "heath aster" as *E. ericoides.*
The stems are about 18 inches cut (choose the finer stems). Not for
everyone.

 A. tataricus didn't bloom the first year I planted it, and it put out
such huge ungainly leaves that it was an act of faith not to believe it
was some gigantic mislabeled vegetable. But the next September
strong stems to six feet rose up with sizeable loose clusters of small
lavender daisies. The stems can be cut as long as 30 inches, with attractive stem foliage smaller than the basal. A shorter version is 'Jin
Dai', or make your own shorter version by pinching the plant back in
early summer. **Tatarian aster** comes slowly into bloom, taking a little
shade, if necessary, and is useful over a long period in late September
and October, still going strong when the Michaelmas daisies are
finishing. This is a prime choice for massing in a large vase. The
flowers are extremely long lasting in water. You can use short stems
with the last zinnias and smaller dahlias and with other asters or
chrysopsis for fall arrangements. Give one plant plenty of room, as it
spreads.

 An interesting aster relative for cutting is the half-hardy annual
Tahoka daisy, *Machaeranthera tanacetifolia.* Its pale blue yellow-
centered daisies are native to cool, dry areas of the North American
West, where it can be grown more easily than in the East. Sow direct
in spring.

ASTILBE

The popular **astilbes** (or **false spireas** in older garden books) take
a central position as perennials for the damp shady cutting garden.
The bright magentas and watermelon pinks, such as 'Cattleya' or
'Federsee', bunch eye-catchingly for simple massed arrangements in
June. All astilbes offer opportunities for innovative color combinations, but true reds and those with bronzed foliage may be difficult
to combine with others. I like the quite tall astilbes with arching
stems, like the fragrant pink *Astilbe* × *thunbergii* 'Ostrich Plume'—
the plumes are airy and loose, and it's a simple matter to cut 30-inch

stems for the vase. You'll need two, perhaps three, plants, if they're in a good bit of shade. The shorter spikes of other cultivars in pastel colors, such as pale pink 'Finale' and 'Peach Blossom', are pretty with belladonna delphinium and *Nicotiana* 'Lime Green'. Astilbes from *A.* × *arendsii, A.* × *japonica,* and *A.* × *hybrida* should produce pretty feathery spikes, while the *A. taquetii* and *A. chinensis* flowers stand a bit stiffer and less graceful though sometimes longer stemmed (the symbol × in these names indicates that they are inter*species* hybrids, and you don't pronounce it).

Pick stems when they're showing a great deal of color, as the buds may not open in the vase. Remove extra foliage to prevent wilting; then stand them in hot water. They flower more heavily with less shade, but in that case, they require more moisture. Divide every few years, fertilize them well, and keep them watered for the best stems.

ASTRANTIA

Almost all the **masterworts** are desirable for cutting. Their color ranges from greenish white to dusky red, with a charming ruff of stiff bracts surrounding a pincushion center. The flowers last longer if you allow them to develop well before cutting. Begin with a white like *Astrantia major* or 'Margery Fish' (the delicate flowers are lovely with roses in place of the old baby's breath) and add a pink like 'Rose Symphony', the larger *A. maxima,* or a deeper red. Astrantia is difficult to establish in areas of hot summers, and I've seen the proof at Green Spring Gardens Park in Alexandria that it's possible to grow here, but I won't be trying again in my own garden. Every gardener is crushed that some perennial won't bloom, or even live, for him or her, and this is one of mine. They require consistently moist soil and partial shade, and under good conditions one plant spreads to form a good colony, flowering prolifically.

ATRIPLEX HORTENSIS

The lovely foliage is the real interest of **mountain spinach** (a much nicer name than **orach**), so you should pick while the flowers still appear to be in bud and the delicate leaves in good condition; don't allow it to pass its prime in early July while waiting for the buds to change. *Atriplex hortensis* 'Green Plume' grew to six feet in my garden, tall and narrow and standing up beautifully, with tiny, barely discernible white flowers. The reds, by names like 'Rubra', 'Cupreata', or 'Crimson Plume', have handsome bronze or gray-green leaves, with bronze or beet-red stems, making a sophisticated foliage display with greens, and especially pink flowers, but also splendid with difficult prospects like the orange *Gomphrena haageana*—the thin red stems contrast in the best way with bright green stems through clear glass, making what goes on below the waterline as interesting as above. Atriplex does fairly well in a hot, dry summer with watering. In August, you can cut from plants that have gone to seed, as the little wine-red disks are more long lasting than the flowers. With autumn approaching, the disorderly seed clusters make great company for amaranths in harvest colors, with some strappy leaves of liriope and a few cones (without the petals) of purple coneflower. This annual is not much for germinating indoors, preferring to be sown direct, but once established in good conditions, it volunteers. Sow a four- or five-foot row. J. L. Hudson offers several selections in the specialty vegetable section, even one he says is "bred for the European florist trade."

AURINIA SAXATILIS

I'm always disappointed when my **basket-of-gold** dies, as its rich color is so wonderful in spring. *Aurinia saxatilis* needs excellent drainage and does not thrive in our warm climate. I've enjoyed its short (about eight-inch) stems with the small green flowers of *Helleborus foetidus* and the dainty miniature daffodil 'Segovia' in mid-April. Choose either lemon or golden-yellow cultivars. Although it's a perennial, you could plant it every fall in a raised bed for spring flowering, as you would a biennial, and you can also grow it from seed, but I haven't tried it. It's scraggly out of flower, and twice I've unintentionally weeded plants out of the garden. Cut it back after flowering, and keep a name tag with it. You'll only need one plant. You may also see basket-of-gold under the name *Alyssum saxatile*.

BALLOTA PSEUDODICTAMNUS

The soft, wooly, gray-green foliage of perennial *Ballota pseudodictamnus* is a lovely companion in late spring and early summer for many smaller flowers, especially a small table iris like 'Violet Rose' or 'Sand Princess', and with nigella or lychnis, which often need a green filler. Give it excellent drainage. One plant forms a fine little clump, and it surprised me by being hardy in my Zone 7a garden.

BAPTISIA

The elegant blue pea flowers of **false indigo** offer some slight solace in late spring, because I've failed with lupines and so often with sweet peas, too. You might locate this handsome vase-shaped perennial in a flower border rather than cutting garden, as its blue-green foliage is so beautiful. The strong stems cut to 18 inches, even more, and in water the tips of the stems turn up prettily to the light. Add *Baptisia australis* to casual country bouquets, as well as to large formal arrangements of long-stemmed flowers like irises, Egyptian onion, *Nectaroscordum siculum,* and wild parsnip. The flowers are long lasting, though you should remove most of the stem foliage to prevent wilting. Some arrangers use the foliage for filler.

You'll find big baptisia is better off in an ample cutting garden, because it forms an extensive system of thick roots that make it almost impossible to move, or even to locate other plants nearby. Decide carefully where to plant it. Deadheading the heavy seedpods may help the plant stand more erect for the rest of the summer, as will tying it once around or even cutting it back. Baptisia is slow to establish—I often thought it was dead the first year or two—but it is worth the wait.

The small-flowered yellow baptisia, *B. perfoliata,* has long arching stems of eucalyptus-like gray-green leaves, which look like they must be marvelous for green filler, though I'm still getting a plant going. The almost inconsequential flowers become round green pods. It's happy in dry soil in full sun, but it's hardy only to Zone 7.

BEGONIA GRANDIS

Its late August bloom making it doubly useful, exotic *Begonia grandis* (until recently *B. evansiana,* but better known to gardeners as **hardy begonia**), is an ideal perennial for the shady cutting garden. Pale pink or white flowers stand from branching stems 18 to 20 inches long when cut, and intriguing triangular pink pods turning to green dangle below the flowers. The green stems shift to red at the leaf nodes and leaf stems, and the green leaves are veined so strongly with red on the reverse that they appear bronze. This unusual coloring may make hardy begonia a poor mixer with other garden flowers, but it's exciting arranged by itself in a plain glass vase so the colored stems can be seen through the water. For a wide-mouth container, be sure to save some of the large leaves you trim off in arranging, and place them in the vase so you can see the handsome veining on the back.

Hardy to Zone 6, hardy begonia is an easy plant to grow, despite its omission from many gardening books and nursery lists. It's extremely late to appear, not making an entrance until early summer, almost the latest of any of my plants, and self-sows nicely, even too generously. If you have room in your shady garden, develop a nice sweep of *Begonia grandis* with hosta or ferns, as it looks better out of the border. An attractive plant for tired August gardens.

BELLIS PERENNIS

While short stemmed, the little **English daisies** of *Bellis perennis* in red, rose, and white, are so welcome when they bloom early in the year, gathered into a sweet bunch with *Helleborus foetidus* and a miniature daffodil like 'Rip van Winkle' if you have it. They exude the pleasant scent of warm foliage on a summer's day. Four to five plants bloom prolifically, and you need a tiny vase to show them off well, perhaps with those inevitably short stems of *Anemone coronaria*, Johnny-jump-ups, dianthus, and wallflowers. The stems were only about three inches long one March 15, but 10 days later were five inches, seven inches by April 18, and nine inches by May 4th. As English daisies are quite weatherproof, you can delay picking for weeks until you need them. Reach your fingers deep into the tight foliage and pluck the stem as low as possible. They're easily grown biennials to sow in late summer under lights and plant out in fall, for bloom beginning during quite poor winter weather. They hit their prime when warmer weather appears in March. Another option is to sow in the garden in September, for somewhat smaller plants blooming here two weeks before the last frost date of April 15, through May, and into June when the month is cool. In areas with mild summers, English daisies bloom all season. They may self-sow.

BERGENIA

The sturdy wide leaves of **bergenia** are handy most of the year for adding green to arrangements, become bronzed in the fall, and may still be in good condition going into early winter. The showy flowers aren't as ugly as some people say, but may be limited in number. Cultivars of *B. crassifolia* and *B. cordifolia* are the best choices for cutting, the latter possibly taller by a few inches. While it's often said that bergenia is a good perennial plant for dry shade, in my shady garden it grew little, never flowered, and became a victim of neglect. In sun, or maybe the lightest shade, deep soil, and plenty of moisture, it performs much better and flowers in spring with stems as long as 15 inches. One bergenia will form a large clump, and in cool moist climates where the plants grow lushly, it's splendid for the general landscape. To see this plant growing in Britain is to understand its possibilities.

BOLTONIA ASTEROIDES

Boltonia asteroides is an outstanding perennial for the sunny late summer and early fall cutting garden. 'Snowbank' and 'Pink Beauty' furnish masses of lasting long-stemmed white or pink daisies, with thin rays and foliage like asters. The pink generally flowers before the white. 'Snowbank' makes a lively companion for *Salvia azurea* and small sunflowers, but for cutting purposes it has a short bloom period, in full glory in early September here. **Boltonia** can be massed alone in a vase with a narrow neck and allowed to billow out like a cloud of small pink or white daisies, or combined with other asters and chrysopsis. You may find boltonia easier to arrange in a mixed bouquet if a green twist-tie is used on each stem to bunch tighter the loose panicles, about 12 to 14 inches below the uppermost flowers; the twist-tie will go unnoticed. Snip out any flowers past their prime.

I sometimes read that boltonia falls down in the rain if not staked, but I've never experienced this with the white, and the stems are exceptionally sturdy. It's the magnificent 'Pink Beauty' that has been leaning over at the ankles in my garden. You'll be able to harvest stems even though it may be in a glorious state of collapse, but it really should be staked, and staked early, to prevent the stems becoming bent and awkward. Boltonia grows rapidly in good soil and definitely needs division in the second or third year, so that one plant is more than adequate.

BRASSICA

You can scavenge the yellow flowers of wild **mustard** by the waysides in early spring and also grow it as a crop by sowing mustard greens, *Brassica juncea,* in the cutting garden or vegetable patch, eating from it while you're waiting. Stems of mustard make a flattering filler for country flowers like Queen Anne's lace, larkspur, and even delphinium, and complement white flowers especially well, showing off the beauty of a bowl of white larkspur or white peony-flowered tulips. Plants sown the previous spring or summer bloom in early spring, with long-stemmed clusters of yellow flowers, which are particularly useful because of their stem length to 24 inches, and thus are good for tulips. Seed I've sown in March blooms in June, but the flower clusters are much smaller though the long stems grow speedily. Once I sowed seed in September for wintering over, and it must have been sown too late for the seedlings to survive, but I had all the flowers I could cut from mustard sown the previous spring by vegetable gardeners at my community garden.

Large fragrant moonlight-yellow flowers are copiously produced by wintered-over **collard greens**, *B. oleracea*, in early to mid-April here. The long stems, 20 to 24 inches when cut, are one of the longest stems around at that time for arranging, the soft color pretty with tulips, Spanish bluebells, and late daffodils. The flowers are usually seen in the spring in vegetable gardens, where they were sown mid to late summer for a fall crop of greens, as they're almost always winter hardy here. Mature plants may be more frost tolerant than seedlings. You can sow your own in the cutting garden, eat from them that fall, cut the flowers in the spring, and allow some to set seed for sowing again the next July or August. Like mustard, spring-sown collards go to flower quickly, but aren't as floriferous.

BUPLEURUM

Bupleurum's splendid little yellow-green flowers and pretty leaves for filler or foliage are relatively new in popularity. A hardy annual similar to euphorbia in flower and color, **thoroughwax** takes a marvelous loose, picturesque form that makes it one of the most sought-after flowers for the cutting garden. Fall-sown plants flower in early May here (with baptisia and sweet William); those sown indoors in winter under lights bloom a few weeks later, providing handsome company for all the prettiest flowers of late spring. You may see it offered as *Bupleurum griffithii* or *B. rotundifolium*. The seed catalogs are effusive with praise.

It's difficult to find advice on how to grow the best bupleurum, beyond the admonition to treat it like its relative, parsley. If you haven't grown parsley, this isn't much help. The natural form of bupleurum seems to be one slim stalk, with well-spaced laterals, that

may require a stake in shade. I cut the entire plant when in full
flower and then into stems of about 15 inches, as any remaining plant
often dies after cutting; for similar reasons, it doesn't work to pinch
to encourage branching, either. The stems may wilt when cut midday, but they will revive after standing in deep water. My plants don't
like full sun, becoming scorched in warm weather; light shade, with
plenty of water, is its ideal situation in the South.

Sow only in a row in a well-weeded bed in spring or fall, as the
seed germinates erratically and the young sprouts look like grass
seedlings. Wait to weed until the seedlings have two or three pairs of
leaves and can be more easily identified. Sowing under lights is usually the safest way to start plants for a shady patch. Sow in market
packs in early February to set out in late March after hardening off.
One well-grown plant can supply enough for a mixed arrangement.

This isn't an easy plant, though it volunteers when the conditions
are right. My gardening friend, Gail B., called me once to come over
to her mother's garden and see the self-sown bupleurum from the
one plant I'd given her. It had been an unusually cool, wet spring,
and the many sturdy plants reached to four feet. My own volunteers
are usually small and not so valuable.

Another even more rarely seen parsley relative for filler is *Smyrnium perfoliatum*, with pretty lime-green leaves like euphorbias, tiny
yellow-green flowers, and growing in deciduous shade for cutting in
mid to late spring. It's summer dormant, and monocarpic, meaning
it dies after flowering. I sowed it in my rather disorderly shady garden and then was stymied by Christopher Lloyd's description in
Garden Flowers from Seed of the year's wait for the single pair of
cotyledons, which disappear, another year for a little foliage, which
disappears, and then finally the flowers arrive the following year.
I never did hunt through the tangle for the cotyledons. It apparently
self-sows happily, in Britain anyway, so if you can get it from friends,
you'll save a lot of bother.

CALENDULA OFFICINALIS

The bright little **calendulas,** or **pot marigolds,** warm the garden.
One favorite of mine is the radiant simple original, *Calendula officinalis*, single or double, with either a greenish-yellow or brown center,
depending on the seed supplier. I much prefer the light center for
spring. This is the golden-yellow English marigold, a half-hardy an-

nual excellent for a mixed bouquet from the herb garden, and so right with tropical colors and foliage like nasturtiums, bloodflower, and green nicotianas. It's a good breakfast table flower, as the stems for me are rarely over 12 inches, while the flower is a good size, despite the fact they close partially a few hours after dark. The plants perform best in cool seasons, though in my garden they're more heat tolerant than many other plants that dislike summer. The 'Pacific Beauties' are reputed to withstand high temperatures better. Plants kept alive over the summer will be rejuvenated by the cool fall and produce better flowers; I've had 'Pacific Beauties' in autumn like little gerberas. Colors are yellow, orange, and apricot.

I treasure calendulas because they bloom after the chrysanthemums have finished, even after Thanksgiving. They're like pansies in that you can still pick a few when everything else is dead. You can cut unopened buds showing color and they'll open in the house. I've cut flowers in early December when a nearby bucket of water was crusted with ice; there won't be many, and they'll be small, but they extend the growing year. The plants haven't been winter hardy here, but they may be where they receive snow cover.

Germination is easy, indoors or out, and the seedlings transplant well, in sun or light shade, for bloom about 60 days later. I sometimes start them early to get a jump on the cool season, but my efforts to start them in summer especially for fall weren't so successful. Grow at least four plants of the Pacifics or other tall strains, avoiding the dwarfs, but one plant of *C. officinalis* may do. Keep up with the deadheading. If you're so fortunate as to have your calendulas come in from the garden with an inchworm, as we once were, you can watch it measuring your marigolds.

CALLISTEPHUS CHINENSIS

Each year I'd forget how much I appreciated **China asters**, *Callistephus chinensis*, until they bloomed in August and September when so little else was coming on. Now I know to be sure to sow one of the many types of China asters in late spring. They're tender annuals that almost always are listed under "asters" in the seed catalogs. Some, like Stokes, almost make a specialty of them. They're popular for country bouquets and are loved by people whom they remind of their grandmother's garden. In the vase, they remain in good condition for at least 10 days.

You'll especially like the tall daisy-like singles—sometimes called **Marguerite asters**—if you've lost your painted daisies or haven't yet chosen your perennial asters and chrysanthemums for cutting in early fall. With cut stems of about 16 inches, they come in shades of pink, red, blue, lilac, and white; I once ordered seed for just white Marguerites, and while they were useful, I found I missed all the wonderful colors. Semidoubles with wide yellow centers like the 'Matsumoto' strain are also among my favorites; in pastel colors they can look quite elegant.

The **powder puffs** are double China asters, also called **bouquet asters**. Those with the yellow petals at the center are most charming and old-fashioned in appearance. The individual flower stems may be too short to cut separately, and the narrow, upright plant usually comes into bloom all at once, so the idea is that the entire plant can be pulled up (or cut just above the ground), with the soil washed off in the garden, and casually put in water for the easiest arranging imaginable. Four to seven small plants handled this way make a long-lasting bouquet about 18 inches high, but sow many more so you'll have enough plants ready to cut at the same time. Each plant should have at least six or seven opened flowers plus buds when picked.

The shaggy 'Crego', or **ostrich-feather aster,** is a larger, looser plant with branching stems you can cut as the big flowers open. I enjoy these, especially the useful whites, but the purples are a little crude.

Seed for China asters should be sown direct in place in spring, my preference, or carefully started early under lights, with as little root disturbance as possible. The seed germinates readily in the garden once the soil warms up, and it can be sown later than many other plants, as late as early June for flowers in early September. Sowing late requires you to be meticulous in watering the seedbed, however. Like annual blanket flowers, the plants are small for so long you think they're never going to be worth the space they're taking up. They bloom about three months from sowing and generally have one main cutting, as few produce new stems of any appreciable quality. They're obliging plants that even like a hot, dry location, performing well enough with light shade. Although China asters are famous for being disease prone, I've never experienced this problem. Grow them in a new location each time, just in case.

CAMASSIA

The long, strong leafless stems of camassia, or **quamash,** as long as 25 inches when cut, are valuable for large spring arrangements with flowers like irises, tulips, and old-fashioned bleeding heart. Cut the stems a little less long for handsome company with the shorter spring phlox, hesperis, cornflowers, chives, and *Linaria maroccana.* Although camassia isn't long lasting when it blooms in midspring, as each floret lasts only a day (and all the varieties should be cut when first opening), a few stems from my stand of *C. cusickii* in a narrow vase make a beautiful, starry pale blue or white display. The large budding head of *C. leichtlinii* 'Blue Danube' is especially attractive, and there are several species to choose among altogether. In the vase, trim withered florets from the stem as more buds open.

While suited to sun, this is a good bulb for the lightly shaded garden. It needs reliable moisture and isn't bothered by poor drainage as my tulips and lilies are; in fact, the stems are longest in a wet spring. The ungainly foliage is clumsy in the border (though it does disappear in July), so the cutting garden is an excellent spot for it. Begin with at least six bulbs, which increase obligingly. The bulb was a food staple for the Native American people of the Northwest, and Lewis and Clark recorded in their journals encountering wide fields of flowers of shimmering blue that from a distance they took to be water. They had been living on a heavy diet of meat, and the "camas" the Indians fed them gave them bellyaches for days.

CAMPANULA

The **bellflowers** of the genus *Campanula* include some of the prettiest flowers for the cutting garden. *C. glomerata* 'Joan Elliott' (or the taller 'Superba') blooms heavily in spring before *C. persicifolia,* with vibrant violet blue or purple clusters for mixed arranging. The strong color is especially complemented by euphorbia. The white I have, *C. g. alba,* isn't as long stemmed as I'd like in full sun (often only nine inches when cut), and more chary of bloom, but it makes a useful big bunch of white flowers for a contrast of size in a little vase with smaller flowers like English daisies, dianthus, and wallflowers. Plenty of moisture and light shade, even that cast by a neighboring plant like hesperis, lengthens the stems to as much as 15 inches.

C. glomerata has been the only campanula for cutting I've found easy to grow in full sun in our hot summers. Stems of 'Joan Elliott' cut to about 12 inches, and while many flop on the ground, there are usually enough that do not. You'll need to burn the stem ends to prevent wilting. One plant is adequate, and even vigorous to the point of invasiveness in the North.

C. persicifolia is always recommended highly for masses of the color "blue," though it doesn't live long where summers are hot. My neighbors with a little light shade are able to keep the **peachleaved bellflower** alive more than one year; further north and in the West plants live many years. They are beautiful white or periwinkle-blue bells in late May for exquisite bunches with penstemons, sweet rocket, agrostemma, poppies, bupleurum, nigella, and cornflowers. Cut the stems when they first bloom, and the buds continue to open. The first stems are the longest (about 26 inches) as the plants exhaust themselves with continued flowering, producing shorter and shorter stems. *C. persicifolia* is so productive, however, that it may be worth the expense to put in a new plant each year. Where it lives through the summer, gardeners may also want to try *C. lactiflora,* as it's sometimes suggested for cutting.

Most people in this part of the country do not know the biennial **Canterbury bells,** *C. medium,* and are captivated on encountering them. They're delightful old-fashioned flowers that go on and on in the vase, blooming in late spring and early summer here, longer and fantastically where summer days and nights remain cool, such as in the mountains. The white, pink, and purple colors are outstanding and the individual flowers are enormous, appearing as singles and double **cup-and-saucers.** A few stems make quite a show. The first time I grew them I was surprised by the coarse hairy stems and leaves, despite the charm of the flowers.

The seed must be sown by midsummer or earlier, and as it can be hot then, I start them indoors in my cool basement and plant out in September in what I hope will be a well-drained area. I set out 8 to 12 plants so that if I lose a third or half by flowering time, I won't be crushed. If they aren't started early, they may not be large enough the next spring to flower decently. Canterbury bells grown by my neighbor, Gail B., in a considerably raised bed with light soil and part shade performed particularly well. One year I lost all my seedlings by allowing them to be stressed by heat while hardening off at the end of summer. A little shade can be a big help here.

A vigorous plant will have many stems, each so laden with huge buds that it may topple. Watering at the base will help prevent them going over, but it's handy to have a tomato cage to set over a plant at the first sign of leaning. Cut stems are 20 to 24 inches long. The flowers should last longer if they're cut when they first open, but I usually cut them when I want them; burning the stem ends will prolong their life. In the vase, snip off florets as they finish. An "annual" Canterbury bells I tried was a bust.

The long spires of biennial *C. pyramidalis* are sold by florists on occasion. **Chimney bellflower** is also grown from seed and comes in mixed colors. Cut it just as the first flower is ready to open, as pollination by bees causes it to go rapidly to seed. It must bloom quite a bit later than *C. medium,* as my big, fine-looking plants all died in the swelter by mid-July without ever flowering. They clearly were more sensitive to heat than Canterbury bells.

CAPSICUM

The "ornamental" **peppers** aren't usually tall enough for picking, as they're intended for bedding, but many of the long-stemmed vegetable varieties are no less attractive. Both sweet and hot peppers are hybrids of the annual *Capsicum annuum* and tender perennial *C. frutescens,* though all are usually grown as annuals. For arranging, they're attractive for a fairly long period with exotics and warm-colored heat-loving summer flowers like hyacinth bean, bloodflower, zinnias, and marigolds, and greenery like swamp milkweed pods. Any long-stemmed cultivar that displays its peppers upright at the stem ends is a possibility for cutting. Also try cutting from those plants that hold their fruit in an evident fashion in the foliage along the stem rather than deep within the plant (you'll see that many don't hold their peppers where they can be easily seen). And you'll have a few extra for cooking.

Of late, the better seed catalogs catering to cooks, like Shepherd's or Cook's, offer the most intriguing pepper selections, with notes as to their ornamental value. 'Mirasol' is one I've grown that has big pointed peppers in erect clutches at the stem tips, changing from green to bright red in short order. I cut stems only 12 or 13 inches long in order to have more of them (grow more plants if you want long stems), and remove most of the long narrow leaves. Sara C., a friend from Guatemala, says these are also perfect for *pico de gallo* sauce when green. 'Firecracker' bears tiny fat purple peppers all along the branching stems, changing quickly to orange and then red as they mature, with a 16-inch stem holding the three colors in exciting proximity. While the peppers are smaller than 'Mirasol', there are many more of them, and the branching stems are attractive for the abundant purplish green foliage. You'll need to trim away the larger leaves that obscure the fruits. Very hot, they're excellent for a range of dishes. Sara says in Guatemala these are called *Cobanero* peppers, as they are grown in Coban. I've seen 'Friesdorfer', with upright pointed red peppers marching up the stem, recommended for cutting, but I was never able to find seed and my other peppers probably did just as well.

Start your peppers indoors under lights about six weeks before the last frost. Plant them in four-inch pots so you won't have to repot, and in a warm spot or using a heat mat, as they need 80 to 85 degrees Fahrenheit to germinate. Aside from the requirement for warmth, they're easy to grow. Plant out only when the weather has warmed up, as they're heat lovers, and always in full sun and not crowded by other plants. You'll be cutting by mid-August for colorful peppers, earlier for green.

CARTHAMUS TINCTORIUS

From the seed of *Carthamus tinctorius*, the annual **safflower,** comes our cooking oil. The flower is a coarse orange or cream thistle in appearance, though soft to the touch, on a stiff stem set with moderately spiny leaves, most of which need to be removed after cutting. It's commonly dried for an everlasting, but you may like it fresh in summer for an unusual display in a modern container. Safflower dislikes root disturbance, so it must be sown directly in the spring garden and only in light soil. As my soil is fairly ponderous, even after many improvements, it hasn't been possible to produce more than stunted stems six inches high, despite seed catalog assurances that safflower is easy to grow. This isn't a flower that breaks my heart to give up on, though I can love almost anything that grows with gusto.

CARYOPTERIS

The common cultivars of *Caryopteris* don't fit neatly into any category of garden plant. Frequently termed subshrubs (and called **blue** spirea or **bluebeard**), they're woody at the base but usually die back in winter, exhibiting some of the behavior of perennials. Their long wands in several shades of blue are welcome in late summer and fall and bring long-lasting elegance to bouquets of casual flowers like goldenrods and China asters or the more dignified dahlias.

Though it's hardy only to Zone 8, *C. incana,* or bluebeard, is always said to be the first choice for cutting. Its tiers of tiny flowers set above neat pairs of trim green leaves restore faith in the cutting garden at the end of August. In gardens where bluebeard must be replanted each year, the cut stems may be only 16 inches long, but where the plants live through winter and grow large enough to be suitable only for a roomy garden, the stems are much longer. The foliage strips off easily. You can grow it from seed (it may also be listed as *C. × bungei*), or it may be simpler to search out a new plant each year at a garden center or from a mail-order nursery that likes to offer something different, though my first-year plants never grew big enough to cut much. It may accept partial shade in the South.

Blue mist spirea, *C. × clandonensis,* is hardier to Zone 5, and not as showy, but it seems to me its greater mass and longer stems north of Zone 8 compensate fully. Catalogs are more likely to have this one of the two. It usually needs to be cut back hard in spring, and it also grows large. Cut both of these when they first bloom and buds should open in water.

CATANANCHE

The heavenly blue flowers of *Catananche caerulea* and the white *C. bicolor* are enormously appealing in late spring and early summer, with splendid wiry stems and much of the charm of cornflowers for a mixed bouquet. Seed-grown plants should bloom the first year and are an inexpensive way to experiment, though **Cupid's dart** doesn't easily survive the heat and humidity of the East, even the Northeast, and seems to resent transplanting. Sown in mid-January under lights, the seed germinates easily, and the plants grow quickly. Don't overwater; allow the seedlings to look a little dry. Raised beds and light soil with plenty of sand are key, with just a little shade to make it perfect, as it must be in my colleague Joanne H.'s terraced beds, proof that a glorious plant can be grown around Washington, D. C.

It is possible that container growing is another solution for these temperamental plants.

CELOSIA

The many varieties of *Celosia argentea* are easy heat-loving plants to have coming on in August, a good choice for beginning gardeners, so reliable that roadside growers almost always have them. Because celosia is a tender annual that prefers not to be sown in cool weather, that usually means a sowing date in May here, for picking about three months later. The stems are excellent for cutting for several weeks, as the flower heads mature quite slowly. Your vases will need frequent topping up. Beware of low-growing bedding types.

Look for the **feathered celosia** (also called **Prince of Wales feather**) *C. a.* var. *plumosa* 'Sparkler' or 'Century' series, in separated colors from Stokes, especially tall for cut-flower purposes. ("Var." in the following names is short for "variety," which indicates a subspecies that is slightly different from others of the species, and generally comes true from seed.) Also look for the old-fashioned feathery and much the best 'Pampas Plume' from Burpee and Select Seeds' delightful antique variety they call 'Thompsonii'. You can neglect these last two for a month and still produce an armload of excellent stems for cutting. I like to mass it by itself, but good companions for arranging are other exotics, like colorful amaranthus and hyacinth bean, even small torch lilies. 'Pampas Plume' is so candyfloss pretty that it can accompany snapdragons, China asters, and even dahlias without causing these more conventional flowers to shrink away in horror. Then there's a celosia like 'Wine Sparkler', almost all parts a vivid red, which looks wonderful in a clear glass vase to reveal stems almost as interesting as the flowers. When feathered celosia is sown thickly, there is one long main stem cut to about 20 or 24 inches, with slender laterals or sometimes none at all. The finer-stemmed later flowers are as useful as the first show, continuing into September. This celosia lasts for only about three or four days in water, which is not as long as the following.

I enjoy cutting the **cockscomb** or "brainflower," *C. a.* var. *cristata*, before it becomes a huge brain, when only two to four inches across. Its undulating forms in glowing colors look like creatures from the ocean floor or jewels set into gorgeous ruffs of pointed green leaves.

These are quite long-lasting flowers, and since at first you can leave on much of the foliage just below the flower, the effect is luxuriant in the vase. After a few days, the foliage goes into a rapid decline and must be removed. You need at least 12 to 15 plants to cut at this stage of smaller bloom. If you allow the brains to become large and bulbous, a big arrangement will make a spectacular exhibit and not require as many stems. A massing of red flowers like 'Fireglow' is particularly handsome, and if you can find the old 'Toreador'—Twilley has it now—its bizarre fan-shaped flowers are just the thing to surprise your guests. My celosia adviser, Stanley Mehr, grows 'Toreador' for his roadside cut-flower business and says it's one of the easiest and most productive. The excellent 'Chief' strain produces quite tall plants; 'Rose Chief' is really almost attractive.

I like to grow mixed colors of the varieties *cristata* and *plumosa* at the same time, as they'll bloom together. They're good for outrageous combinations, using *Amaranthus cruentus* 'Prince's Feather' too, if I have it (amaranthus needs to be sown a month later than celosia, because it flowers so much sooner), along with any bright gomphrena. The glowing purple, scarlet, salmon, orange, rose, and cream in their remarkable flower forms combine fantastically. These flowers could be called masculine, and certainly there are many people who don't find them at all pretty. They're not what you think of when you think flower.

The **wheat celosia**, *C. a.* var. *spicata* 'Flamingo Feather', looks, as a member of this household says, like an extruded clover. It blooms about nine weeks from sowing, sooner than other celosias. It is ideal as a "country" flower, because it resembles a grass. The bottle-brush flowers may be creamy at first, aging to light pink in a few weeks; there's also a dark rose version. Trim the cut stems of immature laterals and leaves, separating longer laterals, if necessary, to prevent wilting. Cut out the oldest finished flowers if there are any. Wheat celosia is the best mixer of the celosias: excellent with cosmos, annual scabiosa, snow-on-the-mountain, and many others.

Stokes says to plant celosia closely for the strongest stems, and you can indeed thin to just six inches apart; you'll also get more flowers per foot of planting, though the flowers may be a little smaller, actually a good thing for some of these strains. You can scatter the seed over the bed, or sow it in rows, as I do, and harvest as the flower head and stem length reach the size you wish; Stanley

Mehr starts all his under lights. Wait until days and nights are warm before sowing in the garden, in good soil with adequate moisture. Sow a lot to enjoy it in abundance. There will be several harvests, though by September and October the flowers and stems will be thinner and more delicate and will not grow so tall. Most celosias self-sow, though they won't always come true.

CENTAUREA

You can so easily have masses of **cornflowers** in spring that it's a shame to miss them. You'll find separated colors of *Centaurea cyanus* (also known as **bachelor's button**) in white, blue, and pastel pink available from almost all seed catalogs, and as the flower is so strongly associated with the color blue, the pink and splendid snowy white flowers are an unexpected delight, lovely in late May with any of the prettiest flowers of the cutting garden. The astonishing 'Black Ball' is another surprise, a good foil for blue or pink flowers, and interesting for massing. The usual packets are doubles with singles sprinkled in, but there is a hard-to-find selection of a blue single, 'Emperor William'. Look carefully for taller selections, not bedding heights. They occasionally need some support.

The first year I grew cornflowers for cutting, I bought four small plants in October at a garden shop, where the proprietor had thoughtfully brought in the started plants. By late April, the immense plants were a willowy four feet tall and a gorgeous dark blue, and I got two huge armfuls of 24-inch stems for myself and another for a friend. I didn't know I should save the seed for this unusually good strain, and I never had such plants again from seed I've sown myself. But even the most commonplace flowers are a pleasure in spring.

In most hot summer areas, sow in September in full sun for flowers the following year. The plants will be enormously larger and more floriferous than spring-sown seed or plants started indoors— cornflowers don't like transplanting in spring, as far as my experience goes. Unless the winter is severe, fall-sown plants become quite large even by January, when they may have a spread of basal foliage 10 inches across. In those lucky places where gardens are not stressed by early heat, you may be able to make two sowings in spring. After flowering begins, deadhead all the plants thoroughly at one time, and three days later you should have dozens of newly opened blooms for cutting. The stems are brittle, and you must move among them

with care as you cut, but when packed into a vase, they billow outward gracefully like a fountain. When the flowers are done, in June
here because of the heat, pull the plants up to make way for early
summer sowings of tender annuals. *C. cyanus* self-sows nicely if you
aren't too severe with your hoe.

The tall, thistle-like annual **basket flower**, *C. americana*, with
larger and more interesting flowers, blooms mid-June from a spring
sowing in place. It's not hardy enough for fall planting here. The
bud is a large woven basket in appearance for several weeks, resembling an everlasting and even causing you to wonder if you somehow
missed its blooming, until the top magically opens and the feathery,
soft pink outer ray petals emerge. The big flowers reach almost four
inches across, on cut stems 12 to 16 inches long, attractive with astilbe and larkspur, and with greens such as sedum, dill, and *Euphorbia robbiae*. The fine outer petals don't survive cutting very well
when the flower is developed, so cut when it first opens. *C. americana* isn't easy to grow, and I get few plants from a sowing; light
shade may help here.

Where *C. americana* is difficult, similar easier plants for cutting
are perennials *C. hypoleuca* 'John Coutts' and *C. dealbata* 'Sternber-
gii', though neither are as long lasting in water as I would like. I also
like to cut the April-flowering **mountain bluet**, perennial *C. montana*, handy for a big, three-inch-wide, single cornflower (especially
if you don't sow the annuals) with a pretty green "basket" to hold the
petals, and fewer flowers on shorter stems, but it's frequently invasive
in the North. It blooms with thermopsis, myosotis, and *Veronica gentianoides* and lasts only a couple of days.

Sweet sultan, *C. moschata*, is a fragrant annual nice for cutting,
but difficult, because it's not as hardy as *C. cyanus* and so can't be sown
in fall. Yet it burns to a crisp here in Virginia when sown in spring.
Another cornflower relative, perennial *C. macrocephala*, or **Armenian
basket flower**, also does poorly in the Southeast unless given light
shade, light soil, and excellent drainage. Joanne H. has done it
justice here in the same raised bed with the living-and-breathing
Cupid's dart, but it should please with less fuss in the North or West,
where the robust plants grow to four feet with a good spread. It's an
unusual long-legged, stout-stemmed yellow thistle, something like
safflower but with one large coarse flower per stem, which you occasionally see at the florist. It can easily be grown from seed, if you
have difficulty finding a plant.

CENTRANTHUS RUBER

I don't often see the large heads of pretty red, rose, or white flowers of *Centranthus ruber* used for cutting, but I rather like them in water in late spring. 'Albus' flowers on long strong stems with good foliage, excellent as white filler for a fairly large mixed arrangement, with hesperis for example. My attempts to sow **red valerian** outdoors went nowhere, though a purchased plant will reseed well enough once established. As they're short-lived perennials, they've often died on me in midsummer, so the seeding tendencies are welcome; young plants should flower their first year. Centranthus accepts poor soil, and if your soil is acidic, you might try a careful sprinkling of lime.

CEPHALARIA GIGANTEA

Cephalaria was once included in the genus *Scabiosa,* so fanciers of that flower form may like it particularly. I always found *Cephalaria gigantea* an appropriate plant for a spacious cutting garden, not only because you must allow it at least three feet to grow in, but also because the long-stemmed flowers aren't particularly big and so look better in mixed arrangements with other long-legged flowers like delphinium, ammi, or Queen Anne's lace, with plenty of filler to mask the naked 24-inch stems. The pretty flowers are most like the annual scabiosa in size and shape, and are a lovely pale greenish yellow like *Scabiosa ochroleuca* in color, though plants I've seen in Britain since mine departed the garden (on account of dry heat) bore much larger two-inch flowers. This perennial isn't simple to replace, because few nurseries carry it. But it grows easily in full sun if not allowed to dry out.

CHEIRANTHUS

The biennial **wallflowers,** *Cheiranthus cheiri,* and *C.* × *allionii,* bloom in early spring. Their lively little yellow, orange, and buff-colored flowers make welcome long-lasting additions to the pastels of April and May; use them with dianthus, forget-me-nots, English daisies, and larkspur. Allow the stems to lengthen a bit before cutting, but if they're short, pack them into a low vase to bring their curious scent indoors. These are very popular plants in Great Britain, where they grow to two bushy feet in height and even live another year; English seed catalogs, such as Thompson & Morgan, have extensive selections. *C.* × *allionii,* the **Siberian wallflower,** is the more cold tolerant of the group. You may find this last, or even all wallflowers, in books and catalogs under *Erysimum*. All the wall-flower names are terribly confusing.

Wallflowers need cool conditions and sharp drainage to flower well, and definitely put them in a limed corner if your soil tends to be acid. They'll self-sow where they're happy. Give a little shade where muggy days come early, though from seed sown in early September I get only 11 or 12 inches before the heat sets in and ends the show. For the biggest plants where climates allow, sow direct in late spring for the next year's bloom. My friend, Terry R., whose father brought her his own seeds from England, fearing (wrongly) that he'd be arrested as he went through customs, starts them in spring under lights in individual pots, which she keeps outside in constant light shade through summer. In fall, she plants the nice big wallflowers in the garden for fabulous stems of burnt orange the next spring. She lives among low hills in the warmer part of Zone 6, so summer nights are probably cooler.

CHELONE

Chelone's odd looks inspired the name **turtlehead.** Its liking for a wet spot provides a good opportunity for the owner of a damp garden. *Chelone lyonii* in my dry shady soil never amounted to more than a few stems, blooming agreeably in mid-August. But in a moist soil with sun or light shade, it can form a prolific stand of pink flowers that will never leave you. *C. obliqua* is the species illustrated in the Dutch Council of Growers guide used by the wholesale flower marketers in the United States; it's a perennial suited to wet soils and bogs, blooming somewhat later in September. It has a white form, 'Alba'. Give one turtlehead plenty of room, and expect it to be invasive.

CHRYSANTHEMUM

Many plants from the genus *Chrysanthemum* have received new botanical names and then gone back to old ones in the past few years. **Painted daisies,** one of my favorite midspring flowers for casual display, familiar to many gardeners under the old name *Pyrethrum roseum* and even recently *Tanacetum coccineum,* has returned to the fold as *C. coccineum.* Painted daisies bloom in pink, red, and white in early May here, two or three weeks after the last frost date. The flowers are useful by themselves or in large, romantic mixed bouquets with sweet rocket, columbine, camassia, tellima, and Solomon's seal. They're the first long-stemmed perennial daisy of the year, followed a week later by *C. leucanthemum,* the white ox-eye daisy, and several weeks later by the Shastas. Painted daisies flower heavily. One year in my garden a plant produced almost 60 stems at one time, with a smaller flush of flowers later. Stems are about 21 inches in length, and are long lasting.

The short-lived plants can be started easily from seed under lights, my preference, as the seed-grown don't die as expensively as the mail-ordered ones do. Plant more than you want; only occasionally will I have a painted daisy live many years. I like to use packets of mixed colors for variety, especially those selections that promise to contain doubles, as they're particularly winning, some with crested centers. You do get more malformed flowers when you grow them from seed, but you can remove those plants.

Of the various locations I've tried painted daisies, they succeed best in a lightly shaded spot at the edge of a raised bed. Grown in light, fertile, deep soil, they're much more floriferous, and worth the effort of digging the spot well before planting. I don't try to move or divide them; just plant more every few years as they disappear. (I don't think they like the heat.) You can also start them in summer to set out in early fall. Plan for two plants—but perhaps plant four— to provide material for mixed bouquets, more if you fancy them a great deal.

C. leucanthemum 'May Queen', or **ox-eye daisy,** has big white single daisies similar to the Shasta daisies, but it blooms weeks before in early May, and does not die right off as some Shastas seem to do. Or rather, it dies after producing a handy replacement for itself. It's a welcome bridge plant between tulips and the rush of bloom to follow, a good companion flower for many late-spring plants. There have been times when I've thought it had an odd smell indoors, largely from flowers with developed centers, but you can avoid this by not using great bushels of them. Ox-eye daisy frequently needs tying around once, or it may sprawl and the stems become crooked and useless. Stem lengths are 16 inches and more, but handle them carefully, as they're liable to bending. My plant was wrongly described by the nursery as a version that didn't stray; however, it keeps young plants about. Begin with one.

Pleasant single white daisies in loose clusters on branching stems, the individual flowers of *C. corymbosum* are considerably smaller than ox-eye or Shasta daisies. It's especially enchanting for its contrast in size with larger flowers like painted daisies in mid-May. Cut shortish stems, up to 18 inches, because it sometimes wilts. One plant grows to a good size, but the gardener who loves masses of these white daisies in a wide container may want a second plant. Unfortunately, it's hardy only to Zone 6.

Shasta daisies, *C.* × *superbum* (or *C. maximum*), are the familiar white daisies everyone loves so well, singles and doubles, a few with crested centers. Some gardeners feel strongly that only the old-fashioned single white daisy will do, while others enjoy the more exuberant hybrids. Be careful to select a Shasta of adequate height. Among the taller are 'Becky' (reputed to be especially heat tolerant), 'Aglaya', 'Polaris', and 'Marconi', this last a superb plant with long arching stems of big frilly flowers with high centers in early to mid-June. Flowers that follow the first cutting will be smaller and lighter stemmed and easier to work into smaller arrangements. Shasta flowers that are cut before they're half open usually won't open fully.

Shastas may require division every year in spring for best performance. They tolerate light shade. You often hear gardeners complaining that their daisies have died, meaning their Shastas, and it's likely that the culprit is disease. I've begun growing them from seed as a cost-effective method, rather than replacing nursery plants with more nursery plants. The 'Starburst' Shastas are supposed to flower the first year from an early sowing under lights, but for me they grew very large the first year and waited until the following June to bloom heavily, with single flowers as large as four inches across on 18-inch cut stems. Mixed packets of singles and semidoubles are also available from seed suppliers.

If you want large white daisies at other times of the year, look for the occasional white painted daisy, China asters, and single fall garden mums. *Anthemis tinctoria* 'E. C. Buxton' is a good daisy that is frequently white, rather than the expected yellow, though short lived here. There are also small white daisies from fall asters and *Boltonia* 'Snowbank'.

It's handy to have a nice white **feverfew,** *C. parthenium,* for filler in mixed country-style arrangements. There are single and semidouble tiny white daisies, which I like so much, and button types like 'White Wonder'. There usually is more of a selection in seed catalogs than at nurseries, but divisions or self-sown plants are easily had from neighbors. The seed for feverfew is sometimes found under *Matricaria,* even when the catalog has a separate *Chrysanthemum* section; read carefully to choose the tall types. Sow the easy seed direct in fall or spring. You can also start seedlings indoors in late winter, perhaps February. Start them in larger pots, as they grow big quickly. Transplant around the last frost date, in sun or light shade, for heavy bloom the first year in June. You should probably divide feverfew every spring. One plant will do, as too much seems unimaginative and it bears a strong odor of chrysanthemum. If you like this plant, you might also enjoy the small doubled daisies of perennial *Kalimeris pinnatifida.*

Two cultivars of *C.* × *rubellum* (sometimes listed under *Dendranthema*) should be mentioned for summer cut flowers here, and for late summer and early fall in the North. I ripped out my 'Clara Curtis', because its single pink flowers appeared to me too saccharine. I regret I was so hasty with this popular flower, and would like to see it again, if only to confirm the impression. The less well-known straw-colored 'Mary Stoker' is infrequently offered; the color is appealing, but I've not had one that lived to flower.

October is the month for garden **mums,** *C.* × *morifolium,* blooming as many asters and chrysopsis have finished. Dahlias and only a few others remain, such as *Helianthus angustifolius* and *Aster tataricus.* While the season begins about the second week of October here, many chrysanthemums will have only just begun to bloom in the last week of the month and will bloom until the hard frosts of November. They provide the long-season value at the end of the year that daffodils provided in the first. Although their stems aren't as straight or as long, garden mums are much more natural than store-bought mums for casual arranging and are extremely long lasting in water.

Most people select flowering plants in spring and give less thought to the end of the garden year; it's only after several, sometimes many, years that a thoughtful collection of fall bloomers is put together. For your cutting garden, buy the taller garden or border mums, described in catalogs as hardy mums or perennials, rather than the bred-for-container plants seen in abundance at grocery stores and garden centers in September. Many such sellers can't truthfully tell you if their plants are hardy because they don't know. The plants are often of inadequate height for cutting, won't live through the winter, and the flowers may not hold up to weather as well as they should. Respected garden centers in your area may have made the effort to offer suitable hardy plants, and while autumn is not the perfect time, you can often plant them successfully. However, some of the super-hardy mums offered by far-North mail-order nurseries may flower earlier than is wanted in the South (you can try pinching these to delay bloom).

A better opportunity than garden centers may be neighbors who would share at division time in spring. Most people don't divide their chrysanthemums as often as they should and might welcome assistance in spring in exchange for a few divisions. (People who don't know they should divide their mums every year or two can be informed of this, but don't expect them to take it well.) A lovely one circulating in my neighborhood is pink with a crested center and short outer rays, single and charming. It came from an elderly resident's garden and is useful to contrast with showier cultivars. A neighbor gave me a division from 'Sheffield' one fall, and I hope never to be without it: a long-stemmed single salmon pink, like a painted daisy with its narrow pointed petals, looking as good in the vase almost two weeks later as the day it was cut.

Local chrysanthemum societies are an excellent source for distinctive hardy mums. In autumn, they put on shows of enormous, ghastly flowers from disbudded plants with a few untampered garden flowers thrown in, and you must view each variety as to whether you'd like it at one half the size. But in May, their garden sales are a tremendous opportunity to acquire interesting plants from people with direct knowledge as to their hardiness in your area. From my gardening colleague, Bessie S., who shops regularly at these sales, I discovered 'Helen Brant', an intriguing dark pink of "anemone" form, reminiscent of a scabious, and 'Kelvin Tatoo', a small bronzed-gold pompon excellent for contrast in that color range. Both of these bloom quite late. Another interesting division in chrysanthemums is Brush and Thistle, but you have to arrive early at the sales to get one. 'Red Saga' is a "brush" with dark red deeply cut flowers, handsome in the garden and splendid in the vase. 'Wisp of Pink' bears wonderfully delicate light pink "thistles" that unfortunately shrivel up in warm dry fall weather, so you should cut this one in bud to open in the house.

Specialist chrysanthemum mail-order nurseries like King's offer many fine cultivars, but generally they can't assure that the plant will be hardy in your area. However, the little cuttings are inexpensive and flower heavily enough in fall that you can afford to get new plants each year if some don't pull through. Good general nursery catalogs like Niche Gardens or Andre Viette will have a few, but only a few, hardy selections. Or join a society so you can order from their list.

In selecting cultivars, three to five different plants in the white-yellow-gold-butterscotch-bronze-wine range make wonderful mixed bouquets in October. If you prefer pinks, lavenders, and deep roses, an entirely different scheme can be created. Variety of flower shape is essential, so don't base your choice on color alone. Pick a button, a spoon, a daisy, a spider, a double, a large and a small, and so on, avoiding a preponderance of the mushy medium-sized doubles favored for fall bedding and pots. If you have room, grow six or seven, or happily more. You can cut from a large collection in the border successfully without spoiling its appearance.

There's usually no need to pinch plants, except to make a particular plant flower later if desired. Don't pinch past the middle of summer, or flowering may be delayed past the first frosts. For plants grown in a little shade, pinching may help prevent sprawling.

The first hard frost puts an end to the bloom of most chrysanthemums, but some continue to flower untouched. Tall 'Venus' is one, a single late-flowering pink that is very hardy and appears to self-sow. Take notice in nursery catalogs if plants are described as late blooming and tolerant of frosts, especially if the nursery is located in your part of the country. Watch for them in neighbors' gardens and beg a piece; often such a plant will not have a name, only its good reputation.

While short stemmed, *C. pacificum (Ajania pacifica)* is a valuable plant for table decoration in autumn (October and November here), alone or with other late bloomers. It is one of the very last plants of the year to flower. The silver-edged leaf is so handsome, stems can be used before the buds open fully to the diminutive yellow buttons. **Silver and gold chrysanthemum** shows its stuff best in its second year, when it has formed a good-sized clump; allow it to grow large for ground cover in an ornamental spot about the garden. Cut stems are about nine inches long in full sun, longer in light shade, but are likely to be woody and barelegged. It may be thought dead until very late spring, when the rosettes begin to show.

All the annual chrysanthemums are charming in the garden if grown well, but they need cool weather. In mild winter areas, sow them in the fall. One of the earliest to flower in this big family is the tall, edible **spring chrysanthemum,** or *shungiku,* grown as an herb in Japan. It is *C. coronarium,* a hardy annual we call **crown daisy,** with yellow, or yellow-and-white, single daisies on long lithe stems. Bailey's *Manual of Cultivated Plants* says it's "to be looked for among the Chinese," though *Hortus* notes that it's in Japan that the flowers are eaten. Seeds of Change catalog has offered it. My gardening neighbor, Michiko M., sows *shungiku* sometimes in early spring for spring eating, but when she sows in September for greens earlier in spring, the pretty flowers following are a delight. Michiko gave me some seeds safely tucked into a marvelous little paper tea bag with *shungiku* written across in pen. She says you buy these bags in packs in Japan and fill them with tea yourself, but you can get them here in Japanese or Korean markets.

Years ago I grew a relative of *C. coronarium,* crossed with *C. segetum,* called 'Cecilia', which I got from the now-gone Country Garden seed catalog, though they termed it *C.* × *spectabile.* The cheerful single white daisies, with their rings of yellow livened up bowls of flowers, charming with calliopsis and yarrow. It has thick, fleshy stems and odd rubbery foliage. If the seed ever reappears, start it early by about six weeks, as 'Cecilia' appreciates cool growing weather, but plant out soon without crowding on your average last frost date, as the plants grow large quickly. Pinch back once to encourage branching; they may need some simple support. Like most chrysanthemums, 'Cecilia' accepts very light shade and also seems to appreciate moisture. The plants begin to fail with the appearance of hot weather but should have already flowered heavily if started early enough. Put in three or four plants. The Country Garden also had a double white named 'Annette' I never got to try.

C. carinatum, the annual **tricolor daisy,** with its rings of lively color, hasn't grown even passably for me, with sparse flowering and a remarkable number of deformed flowers. It also needs cool growing conditions. Another family member I had hopes for, *C. nipponicum,* has a strange barelegged, thick-stemmed growth habit in its second year, making it difficult to cut. These are welcome white daisies in late September, growing several to a shorter stem 10 inches long. They're perfect for the dining table and long lasting in water. For better stems, it's vital to cut it back to the ground every fall.

C. frutescens (Argyranthemum frutescens), or **Marguerite daisy,** is a tender perennial with a woody base usually found potted and already in bloom at good garden centers in spring. Our garden center here calls them **Boston daisies** and in France they were called **Paris daisies**. The small casual white, sometimes light pink or yellow, single daisies make delightful additions to late spring and summer bouquets, with several flowers to a thin wiry stem cut about 12 inches long. They're dependent on light shade here, but once the heat appears, the flowers become tiny and few, the pink fading to white, and the plants eventually dying. Forget about it in the South.

CHRYSOPSIS VILLOSA

An essential fall cutting perennial coming into bloom at the end of August and frequently assumed to be an aster, *Chrysopsis villosa* 'Golden Sunshine' bridges the gap between the mildewing zinnias and the unarrived chrysanthemums. **Golden aster** looks wonderful with *Allium tuberosum,* simply ravishing with the boltonias, white and especially pink, and picks out the yellow centers of white fall asters.

My plant surprised me by growing to six feet, but even with its added height it hasn't required staking in some years. In other years, it begins to list at the base. You can pinch it back once in late spring or early summer to get shorter and better stems that don't lean over. The stems cut conveniently at about 16 inches, or longer to 26 inches, if need be. Golden aster is simpler to cut from than the Michaelmas daisies, with slimmer stems and leaves that strip off with ease. One plant grows rapidly and withstands heat and drought remarkably. You may infrequently find it called *Heterotheca villosa*.

CIRSIUM JAPONICUM

The cornflower shape and "pins" of the bright raspberry-colored **plumed thistle**, *Cirsium japonicum,* charm just about everyone in May and June. Some seed selections include a lighter pink. Use the flower as an accent with snapdragons and verbascums, among others, so not many are needed. That way you won't have to handle many of the thorny plants; the stems are free of prickles, but the leaves are sharp. As it blooms into fall, you'll find plumed thistle useful with China asters and caryopteris. Depending on what authority you accept, this is a perennial hardy to Zone 5, or a biennial that blooms the first year from seed started early under lights (easily done). My plants sometimes return the next year, but I've not had much success with direct sowing. As it prefers cool weather, I imagine seedlings could be planted in the fall for earlier bloom the next year, and might even perform better than spring-sown seed. Plumed thistle takes light shade.

CLEMATIS INTEGRIFOLIA

A small nonclimbing **bush clematis,** *Clematis integrifolia* bears nodding single bells in mid-May. The unusual four-petaled blue flower reminds me more of campanula than clematis. You can cut stiff, almost woody, stems of 15 or 16 inches for use with painted daisies, iris, coral bells, and hesperis, among others. By June, the fascinating swirling seedpods begin to form, and for weeks you can cut both flowers and silvery seedpods on the same stem. The plant flops considerably, but the stems stay stiffly straight if the plant is staked early on. A small cage set around it, made from the low green wire fencing sold in rolls for edging flower beds—parents or in-laws always have some of this in the garage—works admirably. You can also cut gorgeous flowers from the vining types of clematis, held on a shorter stem of about seven inches. These may also have showy seedheads.

CLEOME HASSLERIANA

I remember the first time I saw *Cleome hassleriana (C. spinosa),* at the U.S. Botanic Garden in Washington, D.C., and had to ask about it. It amuses me now to remember not knowing **spider flower,** an excellent pick for the cutting garden. The white cleome 'Helen Campbell', like white phlox, looks marvelous with almost everything; the purple and pinks are magnificent even as the petals are falling to the table top. Just one stem of cleome adds a significant dimension to a mixed bouquet.

Sow seed outdoors several weeks before the last frost date, as it likes a cold period before germinating, to produce flowers for cutting in July. I found it impossible to germinate indoors, even using the refrigerator as directed. Cleome is occasionally available in the spring in market packs, which produce blooms long before self-sown plants, but the direct-sown plants really do best. Since mature plants are enormous and spreading, cutting will allow you to grow them closer together than usual, perhaps 15 inches apart. Cleome does best here, with fuller flowers, in light shade; when grown in too much shade it may have only one flower head. It doesn't mind the ordinary hot summer.

Wait until the plant branches a little before cutting to get the maximum number of flowers on good stems, but cut before they go strongly to seed. You may want to trim off most of the seed-filled "whiskers" before arranging. In full sun, the petals may roll up during the heat of the day, so cut in the evening or early morning, as the petals will not unroll after cutting and the flowers won't be as long lasting. The stems are sticky and spiny, and the flower occasionally even stinky. I'd never experienced malodorous cleome until a friend remarked that she didn't care for cleome because it smelled so bad. I didn't believe it. Later that summer, I was weeding and wondering where someone's encounter with a skunk had occurred the previous night, when lo—there stood the cleome. The puzzle is why it sometimes smells and sometimes doesn't. Use only a few flowers, or leave the windows open, and observe that many people can't smell it.

Cleome self-sows amply, and unwanted seedlings are easily hoed away. In most years, plants I've grown near a vegetable garden have become magnets for bugs in midsummer; harvesting the flowers as soon as they're ready is a good solution. Two or three plants may be enough, and you'll find they bloom into September.

CONSOLIDA

Sometimes called **annual delphinium** (never mind that you can also grow true delphinium as an annual), *Consolida ajacis* or *C. ambigua* (or *Delphinium consolida*) is much better known, and less confusingly so, by the name **larkspur.** These are beautiful flowers, similar to delphinium though relatively smaller and shorter, with more finely cut leaves, and covering the same glorious range of colors: pink, salmon, blue, lavender, violet, and white, some bicolored like the glorious 'Frosted Skies'. The colors, particularly the purples, are so rich they look as though they'd dye cloth. Good seed catalogs have selected and mixed colors, though there's never enough of the white tinged with green. I like to sow a mixed packet and a selected color packet to get more of a color I'm in the mood for. The new 'Earl Grey' is an intriguing color, more the mauve my grandmother loved than gray, and a very long-lasting flower.

There are larkspurs that are roughly analogous to the several major types of garden delphinium, and while the nomenclature is terribly confusing, larkspur by any of these names will be sweet. "Branching larkspur," the best known being the 'Imperial' strain, is much like the elegant loose-flowered branching delphiniums such as the belladonnas and 'Connecticut Yankees'. The larkspurs that are nonbranching, with usually one thickly set, dense-flowered spike and called "hyacinth-flowered" or "rocket" larkspur, easily remind me of the big 'Pacific Giants' type delphinium; the 'Earlibird' series is among this type. I've been thrilled that *C. regalis* 'Blue Cloud' has reappeared in the catalogs after years away. This is a small-spurred blue flower in a cloud of airy foliage, quite different from other larkspurs, and most like the small-flowered Chinese delphinium, *D. grandiflorum.* Its vivid violet blue is ravishing with the hot pinks of Shirley poppies or annual *Penstemon* 'Rondo'. You can cut when only the first few flowers open, as the multitude of tiny green buds makes delightful filler. There's also a 'White Cloud', which may need staking. Like the various delphiniums, all forms of larkspur look wonderful arranged together.

After several years of failed spring and late winter sowings in the garden, even the comical sowing on snow, I began to sow in September to much better results. The robust little plants appreciate the longer season of cold to grow large and strong before blooming at the end of May. The first two larkspurs rarely reach the promised height here, however, and because the arriving heat stunts the plants and burns the lower foliage, I have to content myself with a range of cut stem lengths averaging about 18 inches. (It is important to cut your stems when no more than one third of the flowers have opened to give them the longest vase life.) In the North and areas with cool summers, the plants should bloom for weeks and reach four to five feet. 'Blue Cloud' blooms for a longer period and seems to be more heat tolerant than other strains; those plants that survive the summer here may continue to bloom in fall. It self-sows particularly well, at four feet growing much taller than transplants, with cut stems easily as long as 25 inches. All the larkspurs will self-sow, even in light shade. Give them a good soil.

Larkspur sown indoors under lights in spring germinates like crazy and grows along happily—'Blue Cloud' grows particularly rapidly—but the plants are poor shadows of those sown in place and are likely to need staking. Market packs I've seen at the garden centers are the same, one thin stalk and little basal foliage, while those sown in the garden have many stems, some as thick as a finger. Larkspur seed doesn't have a long shelf life, so I always sow the entire packet. If for some reason my fall larkspur sowing fails, I make plans to sow delphinium in late winter under lights to replace it. Put your seed packets in the refrigerator immediately upon receipt, as the seed needs about two weeks chilling before sowing.

Larkspurs are very long lasting in the vase, but once they begin to shed petals, you'll want to shake the stems every morning and clear up the mess. (The seeds and plants are poisonous.)

CONVALLARIA MAJALIS

I'm happy that it's my neighbors, and not me, growing **lily-of-the-valley**, and though my share has certainly crossed under the fence, I keep pushing it back. *Convallaria majalis* is an invasive (and poisonous) plant, but it's also a solution as ground cover for shady areas and heavy clay, far away from anything precious. Its little white bells are undeniably sweet smelling in a small vase in late April, in large bunches along with its upright leaves or mixed with other spring flowers, the stems about 9 to 10 inches long. Very rarely you'll see a pink offered, for an arm and a leg, expensive like lily-of-the-valley from the florist, but the white is best. It's popular for wedding bouquets. One plant will certainly get you started, or buy a few of the deceptively harmless-sounding "pips" from a bulb supplier.

COREOPSIS

Tickseed is an essential country flower for casual arrangements, cut mostly from cultivars of *Coreopsis grandiflora*. I love the taller (to three feet) single-flowered golden-yellow coreopsis, despite their tendency to flop on the ground in too-good soil. The single daisies have large, pleasingly flat golden centers that make them look just opened, with wonderful wiry, leafless stems. Seed for 'Mayfield Giant' germinates decently sown in September, for flowers the next June. The plants become very large their first year and don't need staking. The sturdy double grandifloras that can be grown from seed, 'Sun Ray' and 'Early Sunrise', are shorter perennials acceptable for cutting, but the stem lengths, at only about 11 to 13 inches, might disappoint some gardeners. One plant flowers heavily in full sun over a period of at least five weeks and has later flowers quite as good as the first.

The perky little flowers of **calliopsis**, the long-lasting hardy annual *C. tinctoria*, appear in golden yellow or mahogany, or the more usual wonderful yellow zoned with reddish brown. In my garden, it has pleased me by consorting wildly with Queen Anne's lace, and even offering shade to a few suffering neighbors. It's important to cut this airy plant when it first blooms, because it becomes untidy rapidly and is almost impossible to deadhead. Buds open in the vase. Two or three plants produce enough easily arranged flowers for casual mixed bouquets. Eight to twelve yield a fantastic billowing mass of calliopsis and assure a full range of colors.

You can start calliopsis under lights in early spring if you need early flowers, but sowing outdoors in spring produces flowers later in summer when fewer plants are blooming. In cooler areas and the North, June sowings may produce excellent plants for fall flowers. I prefer sowing seed in September for the tallest, most vigorous plants; they'll be flowering in June the following year, and every year thereafter.

Be sure to get seed for the tall types. The plants are narrow and can be spaced closely in rows. Sow seed very, very thinly, as nothing germinates better than calliopsis, and once growing strongly, the seedlings can be impossible to thin; I've had to slash at mats of calliopsis in late fall to open up areas between plants, though it's said they flower best when crowded. Mine are always crowded, because they come up themselves between other plants. While calliopsis seeds heavily and may require some timely hoeing, you wouldn't really call it invasive. Self-sown plants growing through winter in my garden become five feet tall, with cut stems around 36 inches. One usually reads that calliopsis requires good drainage, but these plants have often grown best in the trenches between my raised beds.

COSMOS

Cosmos is one of the easiest annual cut flowers to sow directly in the garden; the fine fields of cosmos sown by highway departments are proof. It's especially suitable for careless arranging and keeps good vase company with a great many summer flowers. *Cosmos bipinnatus* is the best for cutting, because *C. sulphureus*, of the orange and gold flowers, doesn't last as long in water. *C. bipinnatus* blooms largely in shades of crimson, rose, pink, and white; some are zoned with a darker pink such as 'Daydream' and others with curiously scrolled petals or crested centers. The old 'Sensation Mixed' and the new 'Versailles', in mixed or separated colors, are the types that most often come in market packs from the garden center. The ordinary pink is still delightful with its enormous flowers; I love it with dill. White cosmos is essential for any white flower collection; 'Purity' has produced strong stems 30 inches and longer, with huge flowers making a surprising impact for a white flower. I was happy to find a packet of a rarely seen pale yellow named 'Yellow Garden' just recently.

Cosmos blooms most prolifically the last half of summer and late into fall. It is a tender annual, liking warm soil, which makes it ideal for sowing somewhat late even in hot weather (as late as early July) in the place of something that finished or failed. It's a good choice for the person who got started late in the season, and the new earlier-flowering varieties such as 'Early Wonder' should produce flowers sooner for late sowings. You may start seedlings under lights if you wish, but cosmos is a snap to sow in the cutting garden, as few as two plants, or as many as 10 or 12. If you sow just after the last frost date, it should bloom in only 60 days. Instead of tedious deadheading, you may elect to cut back the entire plant periodically to revive its flowering.

Cosmos prefers poor soil. Rich soil causes the plants to grow enormous, a forest of heavy foliage that may never bloom or not bloom until fall. If your plants do become big, they may need to be staked before they topple. The best cosmos I ever grew flowered in the year I foolishly tilled under in spring a massive amount of shredded leaves that hadn't composted properly; the disastrous result was a poor, dry soil for the entire summer, but the cosmos was amazing. If your plants don't do well in one spot, try another situation.

CRASPEDIA GLOBOSA

Craspedia globosa 'Drumstick' bears the finest little yellow globes just an inch across, called **Billy buttons** in its native Australia, on long wiry leafless stems about 18 inches in length. I imagined them to be much larger flowers before I grew them. They last forever in water and are outstanding for casual arrangements, but my plants flower so sparsely. The seed is small and there's not much in the packet. I've been unlucky sowing outside, so I prefer to start them indoors. The seedlings transplant nicely to the garden, but they die over the winter, because they're hardy only to Zone 9. Where climates are mild, with low humidity, this is an excellent cutting plant that will grow to a good size and bloom over a long season. It has also just received a horrible new name, *Pycnosorus globosus*.

CROCOSMIA

The wiry stems of **crocosmia** take the same arching posture of free-sia, with sword-leaved foliage and seedpods you can also use for ar-ranging. This attractive garden subject was known as *Montbretia*. The vivid red flowers of the popular 'Lucifer', a big plant ubiquitous in British gardens, stud the strong stems and combine excitingly with the robust yellows of meadow flowers like the rudbeckias, yarrow, and blanket flower. But any crocosmia is superb by itself in water, a perfect choice for outstanding summer color. While 'Lucifer' be-gins bloom in the upper South in June, in the North it may wait until August and prove to be a valuable plant into fall. The stems should be cut as soon as the first flower opens, and are usually about 24 inches in length.

Crocosmia needs a moister soil when in full sun than I could offer it, so its leaves were brown tipped and the flowers frizzled prema-turely in my garden; give it some light shade in the South. I made a present of this plant to my neighbor, Augie S., who has morning shade, and it's beautiful there. For some reason, the orange and yel-low cultivars aren't seen as often in the catalogs. One example is the smaller, later-flowering (July here), apricot 'George Davidson', with dainty flowers a little spidery on more erect cut stems about 17 inches long. Another is the pretty yellow 'Citronella', which is also less ag-gressive in hue than 'Lucifer'. 'Lucifer' forms a large clump that doesn't need to be lifted for the winter here, but it may need to be lifted north of Zone 5; other cultivars are hardy only to Zone 6. Divide these easy plants every few years to keep them blooming strongly. Look for crocosmia in bulb catalogs as well as nursery list-ings. You should only need one plant.

CROCUS

The tiny **crocus** are disarming in earliest spring in the smallest of vases, placed where they'll be noticed on the dining table or night-stand. My favorite spot to see small flowers often is on the window-sill behind the kitchen sink. As Henry Mitchell so amusingly ob-served—see his *Essential Earthman*—small children love to pick crocus. Perhaps it's because they're so noticeable after the long winter absence of flowers. If you've planted crocus for cutting, you can ask a young neighbor to help you pick them, a small act of kindness that might keep you a lifetime in someone's memory.

Some years it seems the species crocus put on the best show, other years it's the larger *Crocus vernus* Dutch hybrids like 'Pickwick' or 'Remembrance', as the result perhaps of variable weather in the spring. Generally, the species bloom two to three weeks before the hybrids, which come into bloom in that anxious week before the first daffodils and may last as long as three weeks. The hybrids can be very large—in my garden it has been the pure whites that are the largest—with stems fully six inches when picked; their longer stems make them easier to arrange. Crocus flowers usually close on cold cloudy days, but indoors they open widely in the vase, even at night, the big ones as wide as three inches. They last only a few days.

Since you'll need so few, crocus can be tucked into odd spots if there's little space, even the lawn, though there only the early species should be used so that the foliage ripens before mowing is necessary. Mixtures of named forms of the species *C. chrysanthus* are commonly sold and bloom at the same time, as do mixes of the large-flowering Dutch crocus. Under good conditions, crocus multiply rapidly. Begin with at least 18 to 24 corms.

CYNOGLOSSUM AMABILE

Cynoglossum amabile is one of the several plants bearing forget-me-nots (see also *Myosotis*), sweet with chives and globeflowers, or various pinks. **Chinese forget-me-not**'s lovely little blue flowers, occasionally white or pink, without the white eye of the other species but with a violet eye in the case of the pink, make a short-lived bouquet of intense color in early summer on stems of about 14 inches. It's a biennial that may bloom the same year from an early sowing, so where winters are quite cold and summers pleasant, gardeners start it early indoors under lights, or sow outdoors in spring for bloom all summer. In areas of moderately cold winters and hot summers, cynoglossum needs to be sown under lights in midsummer for fall planting in order to grow sufficiently before cold weather arrives, with profuse bloom the next year in early May. Allow them to self-sow, but hold the finished plants at arm's length when disposing of them, because the barbed seeds hook onto shoelaces and socks and it's a job to remove them. You will want at least two or three plants.

DAHLIA

Some years my **dahlias** bloom so wonderfully for so many weeks that I forget to cut the chrysanthemums. Dahlias offer an exciting color range, particularly in ravishing purples, cherry reds, and watermelon pinks. Their arresting forms, such as the incurved cactuses, make a dramatic, even masculine, show. It's true there are many gaudy dahlias, and too many perfect pompons, but you'll find others to adore.

A good dahlia catalog will describe the various classes and sizes, which vary enormously, and often mention those with good cutting stems. I sometimes choose the up-to-four-inch "miniature" class dahlias (not the same as dwarf) and the four-to-six-inch BB size for mixing with other flowers. The larger dahlia flowers to eight inches across (B size) are splendid in water, but it's less likely they'll work into a mixed arrangement of garden flowers, unless they're mixed dahlias—and mixed dahlias are a great favorite of mine in September and October. The very largest flowers, 9- and 10-inch "dinnerplates" (A and AA size), may also be "floated" in a shallow bowl and make an excellent dinner table arrangement.

I've grown to enjoy the big flowers best, especially the shaggier and less formal varieties known as informal decoratives. Massed in a vase, these easily arranged giant dahlias are the peonies of fall; apart from sunflowers, they're the most sizeable flowers commonly grown in the garden. The largest dahlias are frequently considered to be exhibition varieties, and for cutting they're heads above the awful hulking exhibition chrysanthemums, while not being too top-heavy for vases. For some reason, dahlia suppliers assume these are the last flowers you'd want for cutting and are always packing their "cutting collections" with pompons. The only trouble with the big ones is the plants don't always produce many flowers.

Catalogs offer mostly cactus and formal decorative types, but with some searching, you'll find informal decoratives with twisted and irregularly placed petals such as 'Walter Hardisty'; orchid forms such as dainty and useful 'Star Child'; and collarettes, which are frilly singles, such as the wonderful 'Cherubino'. Elegant water-lily-class dahlias like 'Keith H' and 'Red Velvet' will not disappoint; this class contains many of the prettiest forms. Every listing of dahlias seems to have an almost completely different selection of names (some of them atrocious), which means that dahlias are like hostas in the number of offerings.

You can easily make successful mixed dahlia arrangements by choosing three or four cultivars of varying sizes and forms around a color focus like pinks and salmon, or purples and rose, or shades of autumn gold. 'Michele Mignot' furnishes big salmon-pink beauties, pretty with smaller 'By Golly', a gorgeous watermelon pink that blooms prolifically. Magnificent 'Purple Taiheijo' also combines well with a rosy dahlia like 'Gunyuu'. An incurved cactus in a pastel pink, 'Curly Que' provides a contrast of form and color for richer pinks. If you like a pale lemon-ice color, 'Cynthia Louise' produces enormous yellow cabbage-rose flowers; add a big white like 'Walter Hardisty' for a sublime lemon-cream result. Orange and bronze dahlias like 'Hamari Gold' and 'Clyde's Choice' and salmon like the marvelous 'Touche' are most attractive for fall color; I only wish it stayed warm enough here to grow them closer to Thanksgiving.

While I don't much care for loud bicolors, I'm drawn to the pink or white dahlias described as variegated, like 'Pop Talk', 'Bristol Stripe', and 'Vernon Rose', flowers streaked and flecked with crimson that bring to mind other old favorites like *Rosa* 'Mundi' and tulips such as 'Shirley' or 'Ice Follies'. If you do want a bold flower to draw all eyes, try 'Jessica' or 'Santa Claus'.

The wonderfully strong stems cut easily to 16 inches and longer and should be put in hot tap water after cutting, but I only recently trained myself to do this, and it seemed they did acceptably without it. While dahlias are long lasting, the singles and collarettes must be handled carefully or their petals may snap off. If the faces of the largest flowers hang down in the vase, put them into a narrow straight-sided vase to stand the stems up better; they look good in glass vases, because the water stays crystal clear and there's relatively little stem compared to the mass of flower. The beautiful buds won't open, but don't trim them off unless they're in the way. The lush foliage makes its own filler.

Dahlias flower three to four months after planting, so you can plan their bloom to correspond with the slow time before garden chrysanthemums bloom in mid-October. A May planting will likely produce flowers for August through October. I usually plant at least six different dahlias each year, particularly if they're the largest-flowered kinds, as often one or two don't grow well for one reason or another, and because bloom times vary somewhat. Dahlias planted at the same time may bloom more than a month apart. The largest-flowered plants produce fewer flowers than the smaller, and usually bloom later. If you have space, a second tuber of any particular kind will allow you to arrange more flowers on longer stems. They tolerate light shade; I've seen them do excellently in afternoon sun only. Remember to fertilize.

Seed catalogs offer mixed color seed for growing dahlias, which will bloom the first year and produce tubers by fall, but these have never tempted me. It's a cheaper way to acquire dahlias, but with little of the sublimity of color and form, and the tubers themselves are inexpensive.

The appearance of cool weather deepens colors remarkably, but dahlias can't be counted on for prolonged fall bloom, as the first real cold, the kind that blackens the basil but spares the tomato vines, puts an end to their performance that year, leaving cosmos, calendula, gaillardia, and, of course, all the chrysanthemums flowering away. If you're able to protect them from the first light frost, say by throwing bedsheets over them, they may last another week or two before the next drop in temperature.

When I've neglected to stake, the plants have indeed fallen down, and when I've not pinched the main stem once, it's been October before I've had more than three flowers at a time. If you don't stake at planting, place the label where you know it'll be safe later to drive in the stake. For large plants, the stake should be a strong one, such as a fence picket. Find the kind of strong stake you'd use to anchor a tomato cage. In fact, you can grow large plants in a tomato cage, anchored of course. Or grow them tied to a fence.

I rarely dig up my dahlias in fall, as I have little luck keeping tubers healthy indoors, and when we have the occasional mild winter, even in upper Zone 7, they may sprout again the following spring (and bloom as early as June). Dahlias shouldn't be planted out too early, as the soil (not the air) needs to be at least 55 degrees for tubers to break dormancy, and in good drainage (not near a spot you'll be watering), as the tubers may rot before sprouting. I learned this by sowing seed one spring next to a row of dahlias. Another May, and once in June, in my not-so-well drained garden, we had prolonged cold rain after I planted my tubers, and not a one came up. None had returned from the year before, either. For this kind of disaster, you can call specialist nurseries that may have potted dahlias, already showing growth, to ship. But to avoid this situation, and for bloom as much as six weeks earlier, you can pot up your tubers indoors in mid-March and plant out around Mother's Day in early May. Amusing practical descriptions of propagating dahlias are included in Henry Mitchell's *Essential Earthman* and Eleanor Perenyi's *Green Thoughts*, which are worth the read.

DAUCUS CAROTA

The large flowers of biennial **Queen Anne's lace,** or **wild carrot,** *Daucus carota,* are prized for both formal and country arrangements. I might like the very similar *Ammi majus* better if I could grow it at all well, but my patch of Queen Anne's lace serves me handily over a lengthy period in summer. The stems are long, to 24 inches and more, or you can cut suitable lengths to go with shorter stems of gloriosa daisies and coneflowers. The biggest flowers come early; later in their two months of bloom the flowers become much smaller on shorter stems, and they are completely finished by mid-August.

For my first attempt, I sowed seed in August in a fairly wide area, and the seed germinated promptly. The plants grew lustily through fall, but hefty white carrot-like roots stood out of the ground prominently by late October and were somewhat alarming. Should these roots be mulched? Would they survive the winter? Some of the carrots were as much as four inches out of the ground. I left them alone. They flowered beautifully in early June and sowed themselves thereafter. Yet when I started plants early under lights, Queen Anne's lace would not bloom the first year and became a woody old thing that died without flowering.

Cut down most of the plants as they go to seed and dispose of the detritus carefully to reduce the seed spreading about, as *D. carota* can be a pest (some people become very exercised about this plant). If a thick patch of seedlings results in the fall and spring, thin it thoroughly at least once; however, you get the best flowers from a fresh sowing in a new spot. If you no longer want it around, it's easily removed.

You can also cut the flowers of true carrots from the vegetable garden. In some English garden books, the name "Queen Anne's lace" is used loosely for *Ammi majus* or other airy roadside flowers or weeds of a similar appearance, and *D. carota* is referred to as "carrot." Even American books may use "Queen Anne's lace" for *Anthriscus sylvestris* (cow parsley). These common names are unfortunately imprecise and, as is always the trouble with common names, in some places refer to different plants. Many, many garden books do not include *D. carota* at all, or refer to it only in passing, reflecting its usual status as a weed (you wonder how certain other plants, like violets for instance, get included). Very few seed catalogs list it either, but you can often obtain seed from Select Seeds or the delightfully subversive J. L. Hudson.

DELPHINIUM

Delphinium sets the standard for the color blue. Few other flowers bloom so truly blue without a hint of purple. It's one of my favorites, up there on the list with daffodils, though I saw only expensive failure on my first attempts with nursery plants. Until I discovered you can easily raise delphinium as annuals from seed started under lights in winter, I thought I'd never have them with our heat and heavy soil. I can grow them now in quantities without worrying whether they persist, and if they die or fail to flower properly, all that will have been lost is the minor cost of seed packets.

Most of the major seed catalogs offer a nice selection of the well-known 'Pacific Giants' in mixed and separated colors and may also offer newer dwarf versions of the Pacifics, such as 'Magic Fountains'. The tall *D. × elatum* hybrids are often doubles and frequently have a contrasting "bee" at the flower center. These are moderately easy delphiniums to start under lights, but they should be expected to be short lived in the East, even in parts of New England. They haven't needed the famous required staking in my garden, both because they don't grow so tall or so grand and because I cut them fairly soon after flowering. When purchased from the florist, the long stems and majestic flower heads can be difficult to arrange, but the smaller home-grown Pacifics cut from the garden add beautifully to casual arrangements of garden flowers like *Dianthus superbus,* Queen Anne's lace, globe thistle, and veronica. And the lovely dwarf versions have shorter, though not short, stems, which you can work easily into elegant medium-sized bouquets.

From my spring-planted Pacifics (the seed started in January), I generally get only one stem per plant, but a very nice stem to be sure, blooming in latest May or early June. Since the stems don't mature all at once, it's wise to have planted at least 10, and even 16 plants. From the rare plant that survives into its second year, I may get a taller stem and more impressive flower, but still only one. Yet where delphinium thrives, their many stems require thinning, and a second flush of bloom may even follow the first cutting, an idea verging on horticultural fantasy for some of us. It's always possible, though, that I never fertilized them enough and that the soil needs liming.

Less showy but even easier to grow from seed are the heavenly blue *D. × belladonna* hybrids and their relatives, the 'Connecticut Yankees' or 'Steichen Strain'. These single to semidouble flowers,

more widely spaced on the stems, make for a less majestic, though
still very elegant, look. 'Bellamosum' is a rich, out-of-this-world
blue, darker than the pretty lighter blue 'Belladonna', and both combine splendidly with a wide range of flowers the gardener can grow
easily; one year I particularly enjoyed the belladonnas with the pale
pink *Astilbe × arendsii* 'Finale' and *Nicotiana* 'Lime Green'. They
usually are the best delphinium to attempt first, as you may be
able to grow them fully as nice as the ones you get from the florist.
D. × belladonna stems are shorter than the Pacifics, and the cut-and-
come-again plants may branch nicely and flower heavily. Bloom begins in early June for new plants (about four months after sowing),
and three weeks earlier for plants that wintered over into a second
year. Mature plants, of course, produce many more stems. Nine
young plants started early under lights allowed me to cut as many as
12 stems at a time one spring, with cutting continuing into mid-July.
The stems were about 18 inches long, and to 26 inches on a plant in
its second year. It's my observation that these plants withstand the
heat longer than the Pacifics (though the nine plants in full sun became five by the end of summer, and two by November).

The more difficult (and short-lived) *D. grandiflorum (D. chinense),*
or Chinese delphinium, reminds me strongly of the larkspur 'Blue
Cloud'; the selection I grew recently was called 'Blue Butterflies' and
flowered through July. This seed may be hard to find. It's a shorter
plant with many slender branches of small, airy, incredibly rich violet-
blue flowers on stems cut to about 11 inches in my garden but much
longer in cool-summer areas. These fine stems can be used in small
bunches with lavatera, snapdragons, small pink alliums, scabiosa,
and *Dianthus superbus.*

All three of these delphinium types are wonderful together in the
same mixed arrangements, sufficiently different to add greatly to
each other. Cut the stems when about a third of the flowers are
open. Like larkspur, delphiniums are petal shedders in water. Once
the petals begin to drop, shake the vase every morning and clear up
the mess; as the plants are poisonous, be sure to remove fallen petals
from the floor for the sake of pets and children.

I've tried sowing seed of belladonnas and Pacifics outside in ordinary garden soil in September, and while it germinated, the plants
scarcely grew at all. The seedlings I started under lights in summer
and planted out in September also remained small and produced
only one stem. Starting seed in cell packs in January is more success-

ful for me. Harden the young plants off outdoors (and put them in a cold frame if you have one) as soon as they're big enough, as these very hardy plants grow best under cool conditions and should have a period of cold for the best bloom. Delphinium seed requires two weeks of chilling before sowing and darkness to germinate. The plants need a lot of water, rich light soil, and lots of fertilizer (always my oversight). In the West, or any cool climate of low humidity, delphiniums that receive persistent care (they must be deadheaded, watered, and fertilized regularly) will be true perennials.

A little shade is so helpful to delphinium here; one year I set mine back by weeding out the self-sown calliopsis that I thought was in the way. It turned out to have been shading the delphinium, and they began to decline. My few acquaintances who can regularly keep plants alive for a second season have them in light shade.

DIANTHUS

Long lasting in water, *Dianthus* offers many choices for cutting. The long-stemmed florist's **carnations** aren't usually grown in the home garden, as they're a year-round greenhouse flower, but for the cutting gardener, the garden dianthus are far worthier of attention, with great variety in size, doubling, and coloration.

Sweet William, *D. barbatus,* is a biennial usually sown in spring for bloom the next year. They're luxuriant plants for the late-spring garden in shades of red, pink, and white, with spreading clusters of flowers with characteristic fringed petals and contrasting "auricula" eyes. As they're so prolific, you can cut from large plants located in a display border without spoiling the show, and the fully opened flower heads provide glorious spots of color for mixed arrangements.

When buying seed, be certain you're getting a tall type. It germinates easily indoors in spring under lights in my cool basement, more so than in summer when the basement is warmer. The tiny grasslike seedlings are lank at first, but they grow strongly. In the garden, good spacing is imperative, as the plants grow very large their first summer. If you're able to germinate sweet William indoors by midsummer, planting out in fall should be successful, but plants sown directly in the garden in September here don't attain full size by bloom time the next year and flower only sporadically. You need only one or two plants, but you might want more for variety of color from a mixed seed packet. I discovered I get much more variety of color and eyes sowing in the garden; presumably, I inadvertently

select similar plants when thinning under lights, probably from
choosing early sprouters.

The flowers open slowly in the garden over a period of many days,
and the sturdy stems lengthen (to about 14 to 17 inches) as the heads
open fully. While sweet William in cool summer areas may live
several years and bloom all summer, my plants little like the hot
weather and often die by fall. But they sometimes leave behind volunteers. Be careful how you weed, and mulch lightly around your
sweet William, if you'd like them to self-sow. They accept light
shade.

Modern and old-fashioned perennial **pinks** such as the big flowers of the popular salmon-pink *D.* × *allwoodii* 'Doris' or 'Helen'
and the smaller (on 12-inch stems) heat-tolerant pale pink 'Mountain Mist' are also good choices for cutting, some even in the South
where they bloom in late spring. I was slow to catch on that a few
dianthus can be grown successfully where summers are hot and humid. Like the primroses, many of the pinks have faces and markings
to delight in, and the bewitching flowers inspire the impulse to collect—you may enjoy choosing a treasure like 'Laced Romeo' in
bloom at a good garden center. Most bloom so prolifically you can
almost grasp bunches in the hand to cut, and the charming angular
branching stems make arranging a simple matter of dropping
a bunch into the vase. And of course, the short-stemmed varieties
are always good for corsages.

So many of the dianthus family aren't long stemmed enough for
medium-sized bouquets, but a good perennial candidate is *D. superbus,* the **lilac pink,** or **lace pink,** with charming narrow buds, and
deeply cut pale pink or white petals producing so lacy an impression
that it may be used rather like a baby's breath. It can be so transpar-
ent that the gardener only just notices it has bloomed, valuable for its
light effect arranged with delphinium, globe thistle, veronica, spider
flower, Queen Anne's lace, and many other summer flowers. You can
cut stems to 18 inches long, each with many flowers held loosely.
Snip out any individual flowers that have finished from a spray, and
arrange them in bunches.

This taller species has been easy to grow and withstands heat better than you might expect from a dianthus. You can get plants from
a nursery, or start them from seed. Park's and Twilley have offered
seed for *D. s.* 'Prima Donna', described as an annual, perfect for
a January or February midwinter sowing under lights. The seedlings

grow quickly, and after planting out are flowering heavily by the end of June, through the summer and into October, when they're rejuvenated by cool weather to flower lushly. *D. superbus* only blooms again for another year or two before disappearing, as it's short lived.

DICENTRA

Dicentra spectabilis, old-fashioned (or common) **bleeding heart,** produces arching stems laden with the popular bright pink or white hearts and soft gray-green leaves in early April. The generous length of the stems (22 inches when cut) makes it a valuable companion for tall tulips, late daffodils, honesty, and the yellow flowers of mustard greens. Because of the gentle curve to the stems, bleeding heart arranges easily and looks good by itself, though the pink fades after one or two days in the vase. The useful white form isn't as vigorous, but short stems of it make all the difference to a little spring bouquet. One or two bleeding hearts should supply plenty of material, even in the considerable shade of deciduous trees. Don't be surprised when the foliage disappears in summer.

'Luxuriant' (find it under *D. eximia* or *D. formosa*) is a much smaller bleeding heart, coming into bloom at the same time, in the same shade, but continuing happily through summer. The stems in early spring stand about 9 inches, and up to 14 inches later, though in wet springs a full 16 inches. This is a delightful plant for small spring posies of delicate flowers and, with its leafless stem, easy to work in with a host of good friends, including primroses, merrybells, *Phlox divaricata,* and *Euphorbia polychroma.* You can take these small arrangements of spring flowers from the ornamental garden with little damage to its appearance. One or two plants will provide quite a few flowers in deciduous shade, but you might want three for a spring border.

DICTAMNUS ALBUS

The perennial **gas plant,** *Dictamnus albus,* glories in the early summer of cool climates, its long-stemmed fresh flowers and green seedpods a joy in the cutting garden. Gas plant's shrubby appearance suggests it's a serious, not a trifling, plant, a plant that deserves a place in the border, too. The colors are white, rose pink, and purple, with the flowers of some cultivars veined with purple. Gas plant doesn't like disturbance, nor hot and humid summer nights, though it's extremely hardy to Zone 2. Mail-order plants have always died promptly for me, and sowing seed requires too many patient months. Potted plants offer more chance at success—it worked for a colleague whose several-years-old plant finally bore three fine stems—but few garden centers like to sell gas plant where summers are hot. If you do get one going, it may be slow to establish, but it should be long lived and carefree, thankfully requiring no division. (Choose the location carefully.) The plants are poisonous and a skin irritant to some people.

DIGITALIS

Foxgloves are a favorite flower of mine in late spring and early summer for the lightly shaded cutting garden. Growing some of the unusual versions is a pleasure for the connoisseur. Among the many species and varieties available from seed (the best choice comes from British catalogs), there are lovely separated colors of white, pink, and apricot. I particularly admire their spotted throats. For the whitest white, *Digitalis purpurea* 'Alba' is a selection without spots. You'll notice that some foxgloves, like the showy 'Excelsior' hybrids, produce flowers densely packed around the tall spike, while others like the species *D. purpurea* (still available in bright pink from Thompson & Morgan) and yellow *D. grandiflora* have a simple chain of flowers down one side of the stem. Some people hold strong feelings about which they prefer—one is grander and the other more natural.

D. purpurea strains are fantastic flowers, what most of us think of when we hear "foxglove." They bear one majestic central stem and develop new smaller stems from the base after cutting. I like to grow the "annual" common foxglove, *D. purpurea* 'Foxy', for cutting, as it's so much easier to manage in the vase than the towering biennial sorts. 'Foxy' grows only about 30 inches tall and will probably be shorter when you cut it, a surprise to gardeners used to the tall foxgloves. But it's a delight to arrange foxgloves easily with garden flowers such as poppies, Russell lupines, *Erigeron* 'Pink Jewel', and green honesty seedpods. The familiar colors and spots are all there. The shorter flowering stems that follow the cutting of the main spike delight just about everyone when they are displayed in a smaller vase.

'Foxy' is a great foxglove for beginners to sow: it germinates like mad, grows quickly, and blooms in just five months from seed, the self-sown ones sometimes disconcertingly bloom in fall. They don't fall down with wind or rain, and so they require no staking. I worried that early summer heat would spoil spring-planted Foxies, but they take it fairly well. You may see Foxies already flowering in large pots at the garden center, or even herb nursery, in spring, but I'd buy them for the cutting garden only with the hope that they may subsequently self-sow, because they come at a relatively high cost compared to the ease of growing them yourself. Give preference to young not-yet-flowering plants in small pots, if you must buy them.

Foxglove seed is very small and requires light to germinate, so sowing indoors under lights is a good idea. I've had no luck with outdoor sowings, though foxgloves self-sow well, particularly liking to appear adjacent to paving stones and tops of retaining walls. In areas of hot summers, self-sown plants that appear after blooming (usually around midsummer) are often too small to survive the dog days and can't always be relied on. The young seedlings establish most easily when set out in spring; light shade is best for them, and a moist, organic soil. Foxgloves for cutting need to be planted under similar conditions, not spotted about here and there, so tempting because of their narrow and upright growth. I once began 24 plants and got only a few decent flowers at one time, because I had planted them in wildly different, even stupid, locations. I also thought it wise one year to set out 'Foxy' seedlings in autumn for flowering the following spring; the wretched squirrels uprooted all but two of the dozen plants, but it might otherwise have been successful.

D. grandiflora (D. ambigua) bears light lemon-yellow flowers on many arching stems not as grand as the common foxglove, and it flowers later, which makes it excellent for mixed arranging with *Campanula persicifolia,* nigella, and larkspur, all in bloom at the same time. Rose-colored *D.* × *mertonensis,* the **strawberry foxglove,** also flowers after the common. These two very hardy plants are usually available from mail-order nurseries and good garden centers and are supposed to be more perennial, though they never perform as well for me as the common kind, and frequently don't flower at all.

Foxgloves don't need their stem ends plugged with cotton wool as you may read. But if you wish, you can hold the hollow stem upside down and fill it with water, and keeping a finger over the end, place the stem under deep water in the vase. This will introduce more water than would otherwise enter the stem because of the air lock. If the lower florets on the spike appear faded at the time you cut, pull them off; the flowers will continue to open in the vase, and the stem

may even angle to the light gracefully. All parts of the plant are
poisonous.

DIPSACUS FULLONUM

You may want to try growing common **teasel**, *Dipsacus fullonum*, for
its dramatic and unusual green cones, set off by spidery, pointed
green bracts on long, thorny stems. The large thistles can be used
with strong material like sunflowers and prince's feather amaranthus,
and the smaller, finer laterals with more delicate material like summer phlox and *Veronicastrum virginicum*. Long stems are good for
greenery in ample arrangements, where the graceful outward curve
will be an asset.

The thistles are good for cutting while green for about two weeks
before they bloom the last days of June or early July. This is one of
the few times I wear gloves in the garden, as the thorns are considerable in number and sharpness. The flowers open in a band around
the center of the cone, opening toward the top and bottom—odd,
and not good for arranging while in bloom. The stems often wilt after cutting, so supply lots of water and a cool dark place to recover
in. If you like the teasels quite straight stemmed, support them in
a tall container or wrap them in stiff paper and condition in deep
water. The cone quickly takes on a brownish tint after flowering and
can be cut for dried material.

I sow teasel directly in the garden in fall, as it's a biennial, where
the seed sprouts easily (find it from J. L. Hudson). They grow to
be whopping big plants six feet tall, so space them at least two feet
apart. One or two are plenty, more become something of a disposal
problem because of thorns. I'm careful not to allow it to self-sow, but
I still occasionally find a huge seedling. One June I decided I didn't
want a teasel that year after all and asked my teenager to remove it.
He surveyed it with horror and exclaimed, "It's too late!"

DORONICUM ORIENTALE

Although *Doronicum orientale* strongly reminds many people of
a dandelion in flower and will make many cutting gardeners think
twice, its well-behaved single yellow daisies give a lift to spring arrangements and are appealing with the yellow green of *Euphorbia polychroma*. I rather like dandelions, and having already discovered that
the soft-stemmed dandies wilt irrecoverably after cutting, I'm just as

pleased with the several good cultivars of **leopard's bane** like 'Magnificum' and 'Miss Mason'. The stems should be about 15 inches when cut. Give one plant plenty of moisture and light shade. It's a perennial that detests hot, dry summers and often goes dormant with the heat, or dies, though it may self-sow. Few catalogs, particularly in the South, seem to offer doronicums.

ECHINACEA PURPUREA

The newer cultivars of *Echinacea purpurea,* such as 'Bright Star' or 'Crimson Star' (both of these **purple coneflowers** are strongly pink), are more likely to have petals held horizontally, rather than the drooping petals common to the species that suggest wilting to the eye—not a desirable attribute in a cut flower. The white, such as 'White Lustre', is especially beautiful when in its young green cone stage, but the flowers still hold up fairly well when cut after the cone grows brown. The flowers only open a few at a time on these plants, though they last a long while. As the flowers pass their prime in the garden, certainly by mid-August, you can still make use of them by pulling off the petals (children might clamor for this job, as may lovers) and arranging the long-lived greenish and olive-brown cones as filler. They have the same bristly departure of shape, which makes globe thistle so valuable in the cutting garden. Once the cones are fully brown, I call them a dried flower, though.

Other people's coneflowers always seem to have more flowers than mine, but I keep one plant to contribute to mixed "meadow-flower" arrangements in July, giving it the lightest of shade. Thankfully, echinacea tolerates dryish soil. One plant of each color will probably suffice for mixed arranging unless you particularly need more flowers. The flowers attract butterflies and draw goldfinches to your garden in August if you allow them to go to seed.

ECHINOPS RITRO

Every cutting garden needs a thistle. The steely blue balls of *Echinops ritro* are surprisingly versatile in romantic mixed bouquets with pink flowers like balloon flowers, *Dianthus superbus,* or *Malva* 'Zebrina' in mid to late June. **Globe thistle** is also outstanding for its contrast of form with other strong flowers, like orange sunflowers. With red zinnias and white *Veronicastrum virginicum,* the exploding spheres also make a droll July Fourth display for a picnic. The blue color deepens as the balls mature, so those cut early will be somewhat green; wait until they're about three-quarters open for the best color. *E. ritro* 'Vietch's Blue' brandishes smaller thistles than other selections. The stems are up to 20 inches in length and are long lasting in water. Although it's extremely hardy (Zone 3), I've had trouble keeping globe thistle alive in my imperfectly drained sunny garden. A neighbor with a good clump has it growing vigorously in a high raised bed, even in the morning shade thrown by her house. One such happy plant may grow very large, and in cooler climates, the globes seem bigger too.

EMILIA JAVANICA

Emilia javanica's charming tiny tassels in red or orange, several to a long thin pliant stem, bring interest and scale to arrangements. An annual, **tassel flower** comes up readily from seed sown outside in spring for full flowering in July and August, performing beautifully in hot summers. I grow emilia along with a wide selection of other plants, as it's really only useful in mixed bouquets. Sow a fair number of plants to make a good bunch of flowers: try a four-foot row thinned to about eight inches apart. Emilia begins to bloom when quite a little thing, the stems growing long enough as each plant matures. The flowers need to be cut promptly, however, as the plants go to seed quickly and their progeny can be in bloom again by October. You wouldn't call it invasive, though, because the seedlings can be sent on their way easily. When the plants begin to look ratty, chop back all the stems to just above the basal foliage; new flowers will appear and seed setting will be delayed.

EPIMEDIUM

If you delight in the miniature, the tiny flowers of **barrenwort** make an excellent spring posy in a very small vase, with delicate flowers like the trout lily, *Erythronium* 'Pagoda', or white grape hyacinths, *Muscari botryoides* var. *album*. There are many epimediums to choose from, with pink, yellow, or white flowers on stems about eight to twelve inches in length; the named cultivars may have the biggest flowers. *Epimedium grandiflorum* 'Rose Queen' bears larger flowers than some others, but you may like to choose your epimedium while it's in bloom. If your plant holds the foliage above the flowers, cut the branch carrying the foliage off the flowering stem (to leave the flower the longest stem possible), and use the foliage in the arrangement as needed, as the leaves are so beautiful. One plant grows wide slowly in shade, and while most are used as elegant ground cover, the larger may be used as specimens in the border or woodland garden.

EREMURUS

One of the most imposing flowers at the florist, *Eremurus* blooms on fantastically long strong stems that are ideal for stately arrangements, such as church decorations, that need to be seen at a distance. Maria C., who grows flowers for her church in our community garden, would like them, but her plot is too wet. Also called **desert candle** or **foxtail lily,** the stems range in height from three to nine feet in the garden. Almost all the species and hybrids are good for cutting, but the shorter-stemmed flowers can be handled more easily. The mixed colors of the *E.* × *isabellinus* hybrids commonly offered by bulb catalogs include the Shelford and Ruiter hybrids, which make excellent choices. Later-flowering *E. stenophyllus* (also called *E. bungei*) is the shortest yellow flower; early *E. himalaicus* is a four-foot white flower. Foxtail lilies bloom early for such huge flowers, in May and June. Remove the individual flowers as they fade, while the buds continue opening.

Foxtail lilies require excellent drainage and full sun. Heavy clay needs to be lightened. After failure with the quite expensive crowns in my winter morass, I considered trying to grow the Shelford hybrids from seed, but they take five years to reach flowering size. That seemed a long time to coddle something of questionable survival, so I stop in at florist shops to admire them.

ERIGERON

Erigeron bears aster-like flowers (earlier in the summer than the true asters) in violet, blue, pink, and white. There are a number of perennial hybrids (of *E. speciosus* or *E.* × *hybridus*) from 18 to 24 inches that are good for cutting, but the **fleabanes** rarely appear in nursery catalogs, and most perform better out of the South. 'Pink Jewel' is a fluffy pink flower with a multitude of closely packed fine petals, the flowers grouped in a cluster of as many as six at the top of the stem,

coming into bloom in late May. One plant makes a useful addition
to mixed bouquets of very late spring flowers such as sweet William,
Iceland poppies, and agrostemma. The flowers last a long time in
water, and buds continue opening.

'Pink Jewel' can be grown readily from seed. You may be able to
find packets of mixed colors, though I've not been able to start the
blue 'Azure Beauty' successfully. The seedlings grow slowly and
shouldn't be overwatered. My plants suffer my clay soil for a year or
two before disappearing, but they appreciate lighter soil as well as
more moisture and a little shade where it's hot. Although a neighbor
unaccountably has the idea that this erigeron is invasive and won't
try it, 'Pink Jewel' is finely behaved.

ERYNGIUM

The **sea hollies,** almost all of them perennials, produce long-lasting
thistlelike flowers of great personality, marvelous arranged loosely
in a modern style in glass vases (the water stays clear). Or you can
add them as "green" filler to expansive bouquets of mixed garden
flowers.

Eryngium planum gives me six or seven cut stems of small flowers
about 18 to 20 inches in length in mid-June. At times I cut when
there's only a little blue to be seen, as now and then I prefer greenish
thistles, and as the mature flowers sometimes have an odd smell.
One plant has always supplied enough for a vase, and I've never
wanted more in any one year; yet it's always a flower I look forward
to bringing indoors. A particularly good companion is stokesia, perhaps not surprisingly, as they both have a maritime look. This hasn't
been a robust grower in my heavy soil, but the following very hardy
(to Zone 2) sea holly does much better, and even roams, or seeds,
about. *E. amethystinum* is a quite similar flower on a thoroughly
branched plant, with cut stems about 15 inches in length. Use the
dainty thistles a few stems at a time in bouquets of casually elegant
flowers such as verbascum, lychnis, summer phlox, and salvia. Both
of the above carry smaller flowers than the very blue *E. alpinum,*
the largest flower of the sea hollies, the most beautiful in my estima-
tion, but one that I haven't been able to establish. It blooms in July,
so showy it doesn't require any companion material. The bristly
looking, but soft, bracts invite your touch. Nor could I grow **Miss
Wilmot's ghost,** the biennial *E. giganteum,* from seed or purchased
plants, but it's probably only for the largest cutting garden in any

case. You can try buying a plant to get you started, as it self-sows. Sea hollies need good drainage and prefer light, even sandy, soil.

ERYTHRONIUM REVOLUTUM

The **trout lilies** are excellent little flowers on short stems. Only two cultivars tall enough for cutting (and still only to about 12 inches) are also affordable and commonly available, *Erythronium revolutum* 'White Beauty' and the yellow 'Pagoda', their reflexed petals so pretty midspring in a little vase with other small flowers. Both should be located in the shady border or woodland garden (always with reliable moisture) rather than the cutting garden, to enjoy their mottled foliage. They do quite well in the Southeast, except that in my garden the foliage disappears in summer. You usually find trout lilies in bulb listings.

EUPATORIUM

You can cut particularly long stems from the six-foot *Eupatorium purpureum*, but 32 inches have always seemed a good proportion for the huge trusses of tiny, slightly fragrant, dusky-rose flowers. Remarkably long lasting in water, its subtle character is decidedly rural without being at all inelegant. Trim the very largest leaves away before arranging. Tall stems of the creamy flowers of *Artemisia lactiflora* make a lovely companion for the vase—the large vase. After cutting, the plant will produce a few smaller flowers for use in October. **Joe Pye weed,** as it's popularly known, is found in abundance along American roadsides in August, but you can get cultivars without stopping your car, shovel in hand, from many of the smaller mail-order nurseries. It's far superior for cutting to *E. coelestinum,* which resembles blue annual ageratum and is known as **hardy ageratum,** but which is invasive and weedy and not always upright. *E. purpureum* performs well in medium shade without requiring staking, or in full sun with plenty of water (it's one of the first plants to signal dryness in my garden). It grows rapidly in damp soils, so placing it in a drier area will check its ramble. One plant increases to a mighty stand, extremely late to appear in spring, and is best for a garden of considerable scope. *E. fistulosum* 'Bartered Bride' (surely not 'Battered Bride', as I hear some people say) bears similar big clusters of white flowers in mid-July; a good keeper and beautiful as filler. Cut just as the first flower opens, because like many white flowers, and like gardeners out too long in the sun, its age begins to show.

EUPHORBIA

The **spurges,** with their green or yellow-green flowers and pretty foliage, are indispensable plants for the cutting garden. Like *Alchemilla mollis* and *Bupleurum griffithii,* euphorbias add immeasurably to almost any arrangement, without ever seeming an afterthought. All of the following, except the last, are perennials.

Euphorbia amygdaloides var. *robbiae* has a great flower for everyday arranging and is easy to grow, standing up well to heat and dry shade. The large clusters of airy spring green and yellow flowers (or bracts) appear very early with the daffodils in March, three to four weeks before *E. polychroma,* and are still useful for long-lasting filler through June and July. The first flowers are ideal for cutting with big hybrid crocus, small early daffodils, and the hyacinths, and later they're spectacular as a companion for tulips and old-fashioned bleeding heart. As the weeks pass, the stems lengthen so that you may cut up to 18 inches eventually, the bracts gradually opening wider in the manner of a hellebore, with small round green seedpods, a pretty lighter green against the darker green. The flowers go on so long that the vase becomes dusty before the stems are finished. The plants spread widely—invasively—by underground rhizomes, coming up even between brick pavers, though in poor soil not so quickly that you can't control it by division. Friends will be glad to have the pieces. It is a superb ground cover and remains green throughout winter in Zone 7.

E. polychroma (E. epithymoides) is another superb filler for sun or light shade in early spring, before lady's mantle comes on the scene. Its yellow-green flowers and bracts are outstanding with smaller bulbs such as Spanish bluebells and with soft colors such as white primroses and small pink dicentras. They also do the difficult job of complimenting strong colors, such as black tulips. A must-have plant. **Cushion spurge** is cuttable for green filler for about 10 days before its full glory of brightest color, and it finishes in early May. It self-sows, never in a problematic way, for occasional new plants that garden visitors enjoy taking home.

Cushion spurge requires light shade here but accepts more sun further north. When it first blooms, the cut stems may be only six inches long, best for the small vase, but as a week or two passes, lengthen to about 14 inches. The flowers may wilt badly if they aren't given a long cool period in water, such as in a basement overnight.

Following that, they're long lasting in the vase. One plant should suffice, but as with lady's mantle, a second might prove useful.

E. palustris is a gorgeous plant, with a larger flower cluster similar to *E. polychroma* though not as hardy, perhaps only to Zone 5 or 6. It's taller and tolerates more shade and more moisture, and it has a longer, sturdier stem. But it simply must be staked if it's grown in medium shade. You can cut stems at least 15 inches long when first flowering. It's at its best for cutting a week or two later than *E. polychroma,* making both desirable, and after flowering has a very pretty "seedhead" of tiny, neat green bracts. All these spring euphorbias can be arranged together for a superb green display, even of their seedheads, in early summer.

Our native euphorbia, *E. corollata,* carries loose clusters of tiny white flowers from late June into September and can be used as a kind of baby's breath. While my plant never flowered heavily, it produced wiry stems cut about 17 or 18 inches long before it disappeared. It's useful in almost any mixed arrangement, a nice contribution to a grouping of green and whites. It may accept more sun than other euphorbias. *E. dulcis* 'Chameleon' is another small but longer-lived spurge, with purple-green leaves and a wiry stem that makes a good filler for smaller bouquets in early spring.

At the height of summer when the plants are the snowiest, a generous bowl of the annual green and white **snow-on-the-mountain** is cool and refreshing. *E. marginata* looks especially handsome in the vase with other white or green flowers, like white zinnias and the green zinnia 'Envy', white cleome and white cosmos, *Veronicastrum virginicum,* and perhaps the sunflower 'Italian White' for surprise. This versatile plant also provides good company for difficult flowers like tithonia or the orange butterfly weed; it's exquisite with the pastels of hollyhocks, monarda, or snapdragons and arranges prettily with other grassy plants like wheat celosia and solidaster. You'll probably be able to grow florist-quality stems in your own garden.

Snow-on-the-mountain makes a great choice for a beginning gardener, as the obliging seed is sown outdoors, in full sun in spring, for cutting in early July. Plants sown six weeks early under lights bloom in late May, good for cutting for many weeks through the summer. Don't start them too early, however, because the stems quickly become tall and lanky; if this happens, bury the stems deeply when planting. They'll self-sow heavily and return for years, but never invasively; friends will want to take some off your hands. Just two or three large plants may be ample for cutting, with cut stems up to 24 inches in length.

You can char the stem ends at the gas burner to prevent wilting if you wish (try this on all the euphorbias), and thereafter the flowers should be long lasting; wilting stems may also just recover overnight in plenty of water in a cool, dark place. Avoid getting the white milk on your skin, as some people are allergic to it. Like hollyhocks, snow-on-the-mountain makes an effective screen to hide a messy cutting garden.

EUSTOMA GRANDIFLORUM

Ravishing *Eustoma grandiflorum*, until recently known as *Lisianthus*, bears single and double flowers with wonderful soft blue-green foliage and has wiry stems averaging 14 inches when cut. The exquisite buds are long and narrow and beautifully furled. Colors are white, pink, and a very deep "blue" that might not show well in a dark room. **Prairie gentians** always remind me of campanula, but they're vastly more suited to a torrid climate and are especially valuable at the end of summer. If you're having trouble growing campanulas, try eustoma as a tonic: it needs heat to flower well. The flowers last an amazingly long time in water, as much as two weeks, and the buds open slowly.

You'll notice stems from the florist can be surprisingly long and heavy with buds. I imagine these are from growers able to sow direct or to acquire tiny seedlings. You rarely see eustoma well situated in borders or bedding; it often looks sprawling and stunted, perhaps from root disturbance. The cutting garden is a good place for it, planted carefully.

Look for this annual in market packs at your garden center, as it's difficult to grow from seed and requires seven months to flower. But avoid the dwarf plants they'll have for bedding and the full-grown already flowering plants in large containers. You want young plants, as with snapdragons. They might be hard to find. For several years I grew no eustoma, as it's very popular and I never got to the garden center in time. But just lately I mail-ordered seedlings with reasonable success from a seed company. Set them out in spring in a well-drained location to get flowers as early as June, but be careful when planting, as eustoma doesn't like its roots disturbed. Where it's hot, gardeners with light shade are able to grow it just as well as those with full sun, perhaps better. Six plants will do, and they should flower into September.

FOENICULUM VULGARE

Green or bronzed **fennel**, *Foeniculum vulgare,* is another hardy perennial (Zone 6) from the herb garden that is popular now for the border and also is useful for cutting. Its green or acid-yellow long-stemmed flowers are similar to dill and wild parsnip, though it blooms later, in midsummer and into fall. Use the flowers as a filler for other, showier blooms. You can find fennel from an herb nursery or garden center or, as it's often grown as an annual, start it quickly from seed sown in situ spring or fall. It's much more heat tolerant than dill. I have heard from a friend that you can also sow midsummer for fall flowers, though I have not done it myself. Allow at least two feet per plant, as they're large at maturity. One plant supplies a host of flowers and may self-sow abundantly.

FRITILLARIA

The **fritillaries** are among the most interesting clans of spring bulbs, though I don't believe they are widely grown. Among the smaller species are the exotic spring bells of *Fritillaria meleagris.* For some reason they always seem larger to me in the garden than they appear in catalog pictures. The usual "checkered" plum color makes a refined match for the greenish plum *Helleborus orientalis,* and both the plum and white **checkered lilies** (or **guinea hen flower**) are charming with little bunches of primulas, pansies, muscari, and cushion spurge. There may be two flowers to a stem, the cut stems about six or seven inches in my garden in deciduous shade. (Be sure you leave foliage behind to replenish the bulb.) Start with a dozen of the skittish bulbs in a moist organic soil (plant as soon as you can after receipt) and see how well they come back. I have one that has been returning for years—some people find theirs never flower at all—and discovering it blooming is one of the delights of spring.

F. persica, the **Persian fritillary,** bears a fascinating dark plum-purple spike of bells to as much as three feet. I was anxious to have this flower, but my garden proved to be unreceptive, probably because it was a little too shady and not reliably moist. I wasn't able to bring myself to cut the magnificent **crown imperials,** *F. imperialis,* the only year I had them (in an extremely well-drained shady terraced border) and did not have any at all the second year. They might have liked more sun and even moisture, and I didn't plant them on their sides like I should have. You also can't expect them to like a hot summer. It's a bit of a puzzle to see them in the elaborate vase paintings of the old masters, as when they're cut, their musky smell accompanies them indoors. They are still sold today as cut flowers, and the odor bothers some people not at all. It might be better to enjoy the crown imperial outdoors; it's an expensive here-today-gone-tomorrow guest in the garden anyway.

GAILLARDIA

My appreciation for gaillardia grows each year when I'm able to pick flowers well into fall. **Blanket flowers** are essential to a meadow-flower bouquet. They range in color from yellow to wine red, the red with yellow tips being the best known; I quite like the plain yellows, as they're so rarely seen. I also adore the color contrast of the perennial *Gaillardia* x *grandiflora* 'Burgundy' with a gloriosa daisy like 'Double Gold'. Like the rudbeckias, the first flower is often the best and should be cut and savored.

These are sprawling plants that are almost better suited to wild gardens, but they do not necessarily need to be staked. You can raise blanket flowers easily from seed, though among my 'Burgundy' grown from seed, some were more burgundy than others. Seed started in early March under lights blooms around the end of June, becoming large plants in their first year. The seed needs light to germinate. Gaillardia shouldn't get soggy at any season, and keep mulches away from the crown and leaves. Don't fertilize and avoid rich soil if possible; they aren't likely to be long lived but persist best in light soils. They frequently self-sow. Try one or two plants of different colors to begin.

The annual blanket flowers, *G. pulchella,* are satisfactory for mixed bouquets. Sown direct in spring, they may be thought barely alive through much of summer, but by September they reach full size and bloom heavily. Started early under lights, they flower by midsummer. There are singles or doubles, but only evil is said of the raggedy doubles. The doubles aren't really that bad when they are used sparingly, though a large bunch would hold no candle to a posy of singles; cut the doubles early when their centers are tight.

GALANTHUS

Snowdrop is the exciting first word of spring in my garden each year. It's when I go out to see the snowdrops that I realize it's time to pick up the boards and rocks left about by the children and uncover the pale splayed foliage of the other coming bulbs. The little white dangling flowers, surprisingly fragrant, bunch happily in a tiny colorful container. *Galanthus elwesii* is the largest of the snowdrops, and the earliest; *G. nivalis* is the more common bulb used for naturalizing. It has an eye-catching double, 'Flore Pleno', though none of the latter I planted were ever seen by anyone. Snowdrops are extremely weatherproof and give you a couple of weeks to decide when to cut. The stem lengths vary from four to five inches when first opening, and to seven inches after several weeks; indoors in warmth, the petals open widely to reveal the curious green inner markings. They're extremely hardy and inexpensive bulbs for planting in fall—plant them as soon as they arrive—forming large colonies in moist, even heavy, soil, and accepting medium shade. I don't have nearly enough to cut freely, and always mean to get more. Locate the cutting plants out of sight, so you won't be stealing from your only glimpse of spring in the garden.

GALAX URCEOLATA

With a leathery rounded leaf not unlike bergenia, *Galax urceolata* is used by florists for foliage; you can see the shiny bronzed green leaves on short stems at the wholesale florist markets, bound together in large bunches. It's a native North American perennial for ground cover in considerable shade, home to mountainous areas of the South, with a white flower that appears in late spring. But it may not be easy to establish. In cooler areas (to Zone 5), **galax** should tolerate more sun. Like hosta leaves, after cutting, submerge your fresh cut galax leaves in cool water for an hour or two to firm them up.

GAURA LINDHEIMERI

In early June, *Gaura lindheimeri*'s loose cloud of pink, white, and green is light and grassy. As the small white flowers finish, they turn a rose color and remain dangling on the stem behind the newly opened flowers, like pink chaff. I happen to love it and have used it in a big vase along with dill and artemisia, or sea lavender and sal-

vias. The cut stems may be as long as 40 inches and arch out gracefully from the sides of the container. **Gaura** must not be cut in the
heat of the day, as it may wilt badly. The plant leans out in every
direction in the garden and takes a good bit of space, but it never
requires staking. One will do, situated in full sun. Gaura doesn't always stay around reliably in Zone 7, though it's an excellent choice
for southern gardens and may self-sow.

GERBERA JAMESONII

The most spectacular of all daisies, the **Transvaal daisy,** or *Gerbera
jamesonii,* is a tender perennial usually grown as an annual. Most florists carry exotic cultivars in delicious colors grown abroad (some too
showy for mixed arranging), which make you want to grow your
own. But neither the very expensive seed nor pot plants took in my
garden. This isn't surprising, as gerberas dislike root disturbance and
few of the wonderful South African species do well here. Occasionally, I've seen a pot plant make the move smoothly into a neighbor's
garden, blooming into fall. Gerberas should have rich, moist, well-
drained, very light soil with lots of sand worked in; a raised bed
might be a good idea, with a little shade. They bloom over a long
season in Zones 8 through 10. Don't cut them too soon after the petals open, wait until the center just begins to develop.

Another South African difficult in the East, *Venidium fastuosum,*
the annual **Cape daisy,** requires cool summer nights to flower properly. They are large single daisies in wonderful colors that make me
think of gerberas and gazanias, orange with black, or the outstanding
white with black 'Zulu Prince'. They make fine cut flowers, though
they close at night. I could not start plants indoors or out. I've been
able to grow a few plants of the related and sublimely colored *Arctotis
stoechadifolia,* **African daisy,** perennials grown in most places as annuals, but they also closed their flowers at night and didn't grow as
tall for me as they might where it's cooler. They're so pretty, they can
be excused for that, though they're not long lasting in the vase.

GEUM

The Chilean geums, *Geum quellyon* or *G. chiloense,* bloom enticingly
on long 18-inch stems. But they aren't likely to be long lived in many
gardens, because **avens** are hardy only to Zone 5 and despise summer
heat. The yellow, orange, or red semidouble flowers, like little roses,

are so enchanting, however, that they seem worth replacing every now and then. 'Mrs. Bradshaw' has fine red flowers, and 'Lady Stratheden' is well known for pretty yellow flowers. Where the weather is cool, they flower heavily in early to midsummer. You can try them from seed.

The best geum to grow for cutting where summers are hot, *G.* × *borisii* or **Boris avens,** bears charming orange flowers, also like small single roses, on shorter 9-to-14-inch stems. It is perfect for bright accents to small mixed arrangements in April and one of the sweetest flowers in the color orange. My plants have never flowered heavily, so two plants seem more useful than one. All geums prefer good drainage, moist soil, and light shade where temperatures reach the heights. I killed my last one by thoughtlessly removing the weeds that were shading it.

GILIA CAPITATA

The light blue flowers of *Gilia capitata* go by the name of **Queen Anne's thimble.** It's a country or wild garden annual with fine foliage and round pincushiony flowers, pretty in the vase with unsophisticated flowers in May. Cut stems are about 15 inches in length and have many branches; they often need some support, because they become quite tangled. Gardeners in cooler areas can sow these flowers outdoors midspring. I've grown *G. capitata* from plants purchased in April, but I've been meaning for years to see if it might perform better from seed sown in the fall. Gilia can benefit from a little shade to increase stem length and from extra water to prolong its life, as it goes into decline with hot weather.

GLADIOLUS

The **gladiolus** clan contains some of the more easily grown spring-planted bulbs (corms, actually) for summer bloom. One of the most familiar florist flowers, hybrid *G.* × *hortulanus,* holds little interest for me. The stiff stems and huge flowers are so showy and formal, and suggest funerals to so many people, that they're difficult to use with garden flowers, though the remarkable colors certainly have something for everyone.

That said, I do keep a clump of a pretty salmon gladiolus, with smaller and almost completely unruffled flowers on long, more limber, stems, the benefit of admiring it in a neighbor's garden (unfortunately, he couldn't remember where he got it). Perhaps it's what gladiolus looked like before the hybridizers got to it. Pictures of old gardens with gladiolus crowded in great patches don't look as bad as one might think, but those were not modern hybrids. For casual arranging from the garden, choose the smaller-flowered and less ruffled "glads" when possible. (See also *G. × colvillei* below.) Cut when a few flowers are opening, as the rest will open in water, and keep the stems upright after cutting so they don't become bent. Nancy Hugo in her book *Earth Works* describes a technique for cutting the stems of the big glads into two pieces: cut just above the lowest flower for a long-stemmed single flower for use low in arrangements, and use the rest of the stem (you'll have to remove some of the lower flowers) as a "miniature" gladiolus.

Instructions for hybrid gladiolus almost always propose planting at weekly intervals for several months to have flowers all summer, but little is more depressing than the sight of one gladiolus flowering friendless in the cutting garden from the too-literal application of such a suggestion. You'll need to decide for yourself whether you'd like a big bunch at one time, or several smaller batches maturing weeks apart. Plant after the last frost—they can be put quite close together—for bloom in about 100 days. Once I was given a dug-up "camassia," which I tended carefully. It turned out fire-engine red: a gladiolus! They're not supposed to winter over in Zone 7 but commonly do, confusing everyone. The corms are easily lifted after the foliage yellows, if you want to save them for the next year. And they keep perfectly well in a paper bag under ordinary household conditions, like on the kitchen counter, much more reliably than the contrary dahlia tuber.

Easy *G. callianthus* will also be found in books and bulb catalogs under the old name *Acidanthera bicolor*. The soft white flower with its plum-colored throat is a charmer with phlox, sidalcea, and ammi. The flowers, as many as nine per stem, generally open one at a time, so with some discretion you can delay cutting until they're needed. The slender cut stems are about 21 inches long, unless you have extremely well-grown plants, which can be as tall as four feet.

If you've been keeping your soil well dug, you can place the corms into slots made with your shovel. Corms planted here in May flower in late July through August. *G. callianthus* is one of the summer bulbs that must be dug and stored for the winter here and further north, or not, as you can suit yourself, since the cost isn't outrageous. Two dozen can be had for the price of one amaryllis bulb.

The smaller bright pink flowers of the hardy (to about Zone 5) species *G. byzantinus* look much less affected than the large hybrids. The stems behave prettily in the vase, quite like freesia in their arching display of the flowers, and though they combine well with other late-spring flowers, they look fine massed by themselves. (Freesia can be grown in the garden only in frost-free areas that remain cool, which is very little of the United States and which is the reason it's a greenhouse crop.) I cut the stems to leave as much foliage as possible, usually about 16 inches. Cut when the first flower has opened, and the others will open in water; twist off the lower flowers as they fade. They aren't so bothered by poor winter drainage as tulips, and they appreciate light shade where summers are hot. This bulb passes that important question here of "Will it come back next year?" It does increase slowly, but I'd still begin with 18 or 24 bulbs, as they aren't expensive.

Gladiolus × *colvillei*, also known as *G. nanus*, is hardy to Zone 7. The smaller 12-to-20-inch flowering stem is similar to the larger gladiolus, blooming in early summer in white, rose, and salmon pink, some with pink markings. They're often available in bulb and seed catalogs for planting in fall.

GODETIA AMOENA

Since I was well warned that godetia won't grow in hot weather and resents transplanting, my first attempt was to sow **satin flower** in autumn, but the plants didn't survive the winter. The next year, sown in the coolest spring in 20 years—how did I have the foresight?—they grew well slowly, with cut stems about 12 inches long, but they would have been cut down before flowering by the usual heat, not blooming until the last days of June. When the heat did come, they expired. The flowers were exquisite, with a take-your-breath-away loveliness and long vase life. *Godetia amoena* is the botanical name for these annuals. (You find them often as not listed as *Clarkia* in books and seed catalogs.) They come in shimmering pink, salmon, red, purple, and white, in separated colors and tall cutting heights. (Watch out for the dwarf bedders.) A related plant I've never seen, with small double flowers in similar colors, is *Clarkia unguiculata (C. elegans),* or **mountain garland,** also suggested for cutting. If you

live in the Pacific Northwest, it will be at home. All these godetias
and clarkias—call them what you will—tolerate cold weather well,
so if you have the cool nights they need, you should grow them. The
plants may need staking, and must be sown directly in the garden.
Two other plants recommended for occasional cutting that need
a similar climate and that I hope to grow someday, though having
grown godetia here, I know better than to try them more than once,
are *Collomia grandiflora* and *Collinsia heterophylla* (**Chinese houses**).

GOMPHRENA

One of the most modest of flowers, *Gomphrena globosa* looks like
a long-stemmed clover, perfect for arranging with just about any sort
of informal flower, and lasting a long time in water. Stokes's tall cut-
flower strain of **globe amaranth**, 'Woodcreek', is cool and refreshing
in white or pale pink with green and white snow-on-the-mountain.
There's also a common darker violet, but it is not so interesting as
the orange and "apricot" *G. haageana* on excellent long wiry stems or
the more recent 'Strawberry Fields', which sports rich fruity-red
color and strong stems cut about 18 inches long. You can get a nice
bunch of clovers from a single, fully flowering plant by cutting the
entire plant at one time; some flowers will be large and quite developed, others smaller, and the whole delightfully casual. Globe amaranth in spring market packs at garden centers are usually shorter
bedding varieties not suitable for cutting.

Since it's a tender annual grown easily from seed, I always sow
globe amaranth a little late, in mid-May even, in a roomy spot, perhaps in place of something that failed to germinate earlier. Sow
thickly in thoroughly warm soil and give patient attention to watering, or start indoors six to eight weeks before the last frost, on a heat
mat if necessary. Provide plenty of space and full, full sun. They
should reach a good size for cutting, with lengthened stems, in about
75 days and flower plentifully over a long period in August. Four
plants are ample for arranging, but you could grow more, aiming for
a wide bowl of grassy clover.

GRASSES

The flowers and leaves of many annual and perennial grasses make
excellent company for garden flowers, though some plants are too
large for the cutting garden. You see the flowers of the grasses most

commonly dried, but many can be used fresh. Prevent them from seeding too freely.

I was surprised to discover that many annual grasses aren't necessarily easy to grow from seed, though I should try new seed suppliers before saying that too often. I wanted to experiment with Job's tears *(Coix lacryma-jobi)*, for one. In any case, several good annual grasses on my list to try for cutting are *Lagurus ovatus* (hare's tail grass), *Briza maxima* (large quaking grass), *Agrostis nebulosa* (cloud grass), *Avena fatua* (oat grass) and *A. sterilis* (animated oats), *Setaria italica* (foxtail millet) or *S. lutescens* (foxtail grass), *Phalaris canariensis* (canary grass), *Rynchelytrum repens* (champagne grass), *Polypogon monspeliensis* (annual beard grass or rabbit-foot grass), and *Hordeum jubatum* (squirreltail grass). Cut your grasses soon after the flowers have appeared.

An easy annual grain that has the feel of a grass and makes a rustic companion for sunflowers and goldenrod is **broomcorn,** *Sorghum bicolor* var. *technicum*. The big plants (start with maybe three) grow to seven feet, and you can cut several thick stems up to about 30 inches long from each plant over several weeks. The wide flower is a green brush of wiry filaments about 12 to 15 inches long, carrying small corn-like buds toward the tips. Each stem will have several marvelous long leaves, about 25 inches long, that extend out almost horizontally and give the vase a lot of presence. The leaves deteriorate before the flowers, and you may have to cut them away.

I confess I've almost always favored garden flowers over perennial grasses of any kind, but two easy choices I've grown for years are perennial **quaking grass,** *Briza media,* and **northern sea oats,** *Chasmanthium latifolium*. The former produces graceful clusters of tiny dancing oats, or "tears," in late May for superb use as filler with both elegant and casual flowers. The dainty green tears unfold on the thinnest wiry filaments, like a mobile eight inches across, from the top of a stouter stem up to 29 inches in length. I like to cut the stems before the clusters extend fully, as afterward they're liable to become entangled with each other and with other flowers; add the quaking grass last to the arrangement to prevent this. One plant forms a dense clump in full sun and produces many stems, though it's smaller than the annual quaking grass. *Chasmanthium latifolium*'s charming, dangling oat-like "flowers" in early July are marvelous with the smaller sunflowers. The green oats, tinged later in fall with soft brown and purple, make splendid companions for the difficult colors of *Salvia* *leucantha* and amaranthus. You can cut stems to about 24 inches in length from a plant grown in full sun, and 36 inches in partial shade, over a period of several months during summer. The flowers are so long lasting that I sometimes take them out of one arrangement and use them again for another. In autumn, cut the plant down (for drying, if you like) before the oats begin to drop, or you'll be over-whelmed by seedlings. Locate it near an annual bed or anywhere self-sown plants would be less of a problem; for example, away from bearded iris, where one is loathe to use the hoe. One plant grows to a good clump and can tolerate partial shade.

GYPSOPHILA

I like the annual *Gypsophila* much better than the predictable peren-nial **baby's breath,** *G. paniculata,* used so often for filler. The single 'Giant White' is enchanting by itself as a breezy cloud in a brightly colored vase, each flower as much as three-quarters of an inch across. Seed for *G. elegans,* in pink as well as white, germinates easily out-doors and self-sows. Direct sowing is a must, preferably in a rela-tively poor soil, as the plants are very sensitive to root disturbance. In cooler areas, it's one of those annuals suggested for repeat sowings every several weeks in spring, because the individual plants don't have a long period of bloom. Here it must be sown in September, in a very, very, well-drained 10- or 12-foot row (to get a good number of plants), as spring sowing is iffy. Fall-sown seed flowers in early May. Unfortunately, they're vulnerable to wind and rainstorms. The flowers need a lot of water in the vase.

G. paniculata is the more familiar florist's baby's breath, which blooms strongly in June, a classic long-lasting cut flower. Flowers are usually doubled, like the excellent 'Bristol Fairy' and 'Perfecta', and there are also pink cultivars. This is a voluminous, taprooted plant for which careful staking is always suggested in the border, though not so necessary in the cutting garden—even causing a destructive tangling of stems—but the plants do sprawl over a good bit of ground and should be given about three feet of space, making them unsuitable for small plots. You can cut the strong, widely branching stems to 24 inches, best when half or more of the flowers have opened. It may not perform well south of Zone 7, unless replanted annually, though a gardening friend reports her fine plant has lived three years in a raised bed. Fans will probably also enjoy experiment-ing with the annual soapwort, *Saponaria vaccaria.*

HELENIUM AUTUMNALE

Sneezeweed blooms at the end of July (no sneezing from this gardener), with big clusters of long-lasting red, yellow, or bronze single daisies with green or dark brown centers to arrange with heliopsis, gloriosa daisies, yarrow, tansy, and gaillardia for exuberant summer displays. The foliage is a lovely fresh green color, and the buds are tiny and delicate. The reds, like *Helenium autumnale* 'Moerheim Beauty' or 'Brilliant', are important in arranging as valuable contrast to all the golden flowers of summer, the color usually changing to bronze as the flowers age. The yellows with the light-green centers, like 'Kugelsonne', are a temptation. It's easy to cut 20-inch stems, and some thick stems will have dozens of flowers; trim the finished flowers out of the clusters before arranging.

Helenium should be cut soon after it comes into bloom in mid to late summer. (A second smaller flowering occurs in September and October.) It needs attentive watering to look its best and remain in good health; I've found it sometimes difficult to keep attractive in Zone 7 hot weather. A little light shade probably wouldn't hurt. Helenium is one of the plants that struck me, on a visit to cool wet Scotland, by the greater size of the flowers in a favorable climate. One plant forms a large clump.

HELIANTHUS

Years ago when I first considered **sunflowers**, *Helianthus annuus* and *H. debilis*, for the cutting garden, I was doubtful they'd be easy to manage or to arrange with other flowers. But they've proved themselves essential flowers for the house and have become so popular that seed catalogs devote two-page spreads to them. The summer I first grew 'Autumn Beauty', several gardeners at my community garden were growing their usual patches of 'Russian Giant' or 'Mammoth'. Between bouts of weeding, I found my eyes repeatedly feasting on the sunflowers basking in the strong sun. And remembering the red sun of the Japanese flag and the sun as the mythical ancestor of their emperor, I suddenly understood why the Japanese had just spent a great fortune on Van Gogh's "Sunflowers."

You can use sunflowers to replace early-flowering annuals and biennials that have finished, or grow them over spring bulbs. The plants grow so quickly, in 60 days or even less, that sowing at three or four-week intervals through June and sowing different types each time for the most fun will produce many long-lasting arrangements. You might begin the year in April and May sowing traditional yellows or golds and perhaps a double, and continue in June with reds and banded varieties. Planning a harvest of sunflowers for August and September is especially rewarding, as there may be little else in the garden then.

The new, smaller sunflowers easily bring this wonderful species into the house. 'Piccolo' is something of a "cut-and-come-again" sunflower with many dark-centered golden flowers, smaller than most gloriosa daisies, with long slender stems cut to about 26 inches. It's good for contrast in the same vase with larger red or banded sunflowers, and with other country flowers such as colorful amaranthus, red tithonia, and calliopsis, and tamer Queen Anne's lace and patrinia. 'Piccolo' sown in May has bloomed well into fall for me. Other small golds and oranges not even three inches wide are 'Sonja' and 'Tangina', both of which have an appealing ruff of small leaves around each flower, superb for mixed arranging. Newer, bigger, 'Soraya' has five-inch flowers, every one of them on amazingly long stems without any pinching of the first bud.

Prolific, heavily branched 'Italian White' bears pale lemon-yellow flowers with brown centers on slender stems, excellent with garden pastels and grassy plants like wheat celosia, snow-on-the-mountain, and solidaster. Grow two for mixed bouquets, more for masses of flowers. Allow plenty of space around them, as they're heavily frequented by bees and it can be frightening to wade in among them to cut; if you're particularly afraid of bees, grow sunflowers with fewer flowers, such as the larger lemony 'Valentine'.

The surprisingly short 'Zebulon', at 28 inches, is a good choice for the gardener who has the kind of neighbors who complain about sunflowers. The flowers are simple to harvest, unlike some that almost require a stepladder to pick. I've seen this type under other names, some with mixed colors. Other quite short plants are the fabulous deep-colored semidouble 'Sundance Kid', and 'Teddy Bear', brandishing puffy fully double flowers from bushy plants that need space. The latter I enjoy cutting when they're first opening and their large green centers are still flat and prominent, but you must catch them before they open fully. They mix superbly in the vase with other flowers of strong character, like globe thistle and teasel *(Dipsacus fullonum)*. Double-flowered sunflowers with shorter inner petals are sometimes described as "chrysanthemum flowered."

In the tall yellow and golden category, the relatively short petals and huge gloriously green center of 'Sunbeam' make for a cheerful appearance that the supplier describes as "the Van Gogh sunflower," and all on very long stems. This might be a good starter for those uncertain about sunflowers, as would be the lovely gray-green felted foliage of the "silverleaf" sunflowers. Arrange any of these with blue flowers, even delphinium. Six-foot 'Lemon Queen' shoulders big dark-centered lemon flowers of traditional appearance. As the first flowers are cut, smaller ones appear, so that a vase may display an appealing mix of four-to eight-inch blooms—a fine effect of the gargantuan and the merely large. A plant may produce as many as nine flowers at a time for cutting, so that one plant may suffice for those short of space, but three would be plenty. Flowers of this size, which need to rest their stems or heads against the side of a vase, need a heavy tip-proof container; a big glass block vase is ideal.

Notice that some flowers have large centers, green or brown, with short petals (the majestic nine-inch flower of 'Taiyo'), and others smaller centers and wide petal spread (prolific 'Hallo'). The dark-centered flowers are quite their most gorgeous a few days after cutting, when the heavy pollen decorates the dark disk, but that can pose a danger for vulnerable tablecloths or a good shirt. You can buy seed more and more for pollenless sunflowers *(H. hybridus)* now, 'Sunbeam' being one. Some gardeners may prefer to grow pollenless selections exclusively.

I love the reddish and banded (or "zoned") sunflowers for fall for their harvest feel. You can use these medium-sized sunflowers with smaller country flowers for exuberant arrangements; dark rust-red banded 'Velvet Queen' or 'Prado Red' and smaller 'Floristan' make handsome selections. The old favorite 'Autumn Beauty' (syn. 'Color Fashion') offers a wide range of colors running from cream to mahogany, all with banding. On a plant with dark flowers, the buds are amazing brown-black balls in green bracts that will open in the vase. Four plants provide plenty for a large bunch, and six or seven will assure you of a wider range of flower color and banding, which is the particular joy of growing this variety, because the possibilities seem endless. This type of sunflower is often seen under other names (in fact, sunflowers change their names faster than I can write them down), and I wouldn't hesitate to try them. Blue *Salvia azurea* and white boltonia have been great companions for these sunflowers in September.

Sunflowers are excellent for the beginning gardener and for children, because their culture is simple and the big seed germinates easily outside, even in hot June weather, with regular sprinkling. Don't neglect to deadhead and give plenty of water, as no sunflower likes dry soil. They may tolerate light shade. Sunflowers are much more prolific and may bloom for an extended period of six weeks and more if grown on a well-dug and well-fed soil amended with plenty of organic material. Large-flowered plants may produce daintier blooms if spaced more closely. As with many varieties that produce several flowers, pinching the first bud before it opens is a great way to lengthen the stems of the later flowers, making them all useful for cutting. Growing sunflowers may be the loveliest way to bring goldfinches into your garden in September, if you permit some to go to seed.

It's gratifying to grow these armloads of sunflowers and reflect on the prices charged for them in some flower markets. I know the first years I grew 'Lemon Queen', a single stem sold for four dollars in New York, thanks to their absolutely universal appeal. An Indian woman once spoke to me over the fence of the community garden where I spend so much of my time and requested some flowers for Puja on August seventh. Roses were best, she said, because they're scented, but the god would be pleased by a sunflower too.

The perennial **swamp sunflower**, *H. angustifolius*, produces excellent small yellow composites to rely on for fall bloom. The foliage is narrow and relatively attractive; the flowers make good companions for late-blooming gaillardias, and the dark eye livens up assortments of mums in harvest colors. Although not a coneflower, this long-lasting golden daisy will remind you of the earlier black-eyed Susan. The flowers begin in mid-October and are several to a stem cut about 18 inches in length, or much longer, and masses can be cut at one time.

This towering plant grows to an immense size quickly and should be divided and fertilized yearly. *H. angustifolius* flowers well in morning shade, but my neighbor, Augie S., uses a stout stake to keep it upright and pinches to keep it shorter. In my sunny garden, it needs no staking. A frost in early November sometimes cuts it down during bloom; my garden must be sited at the upper limits of its usefulness in the cutting garden, as it flowers so close to the killing frosts. Gardeners further north should try the very similar and hardier *H. salicifolius*, **willowleaf sunflower**, as should anyone whose soil is very dry.

If you're interested in double flowers, you can also grow *H.* × *multiflorus* such as 'Loddon Gold' or 'Flore-pleno', perennials similar to heliopsis but blooming later in the summer.

HELIOPSIS HELIANTHOIDES

False sunflower, our native *Heliopsis helianthoides,* offers fine yellow-to-orange daisies on long stems good for mixed arrangements over a long period in June. As there are cultivars of heliopsis carrying single, semidouble, to fully double flowers, you can take advantage of the many choices to select a flower form missing from your cutting garden. 'Gold Greenheart' is a big double with that flush of fresh green at the center that always makes a flower good for mixing; try 'Summer Sun' for singles. The flowers last a very long time in water, and even a young plant will flower well.

Be sure to deadhead your heliopsis to keep new flowers coming. Mildew often appears in early August and renders the foliage too unattractive for the vase, but you'll probably have already done your cutting. While heliopsis is occasionally recommended as tolerant of drought, better results come with more moisture and, where it's hot, a little shade; my plants have never looked lush in hot sun. As the plants are large, to four feet, one should be enough.

HELIOTROPIUM ARBORESCENS

Heliotropium arborescens proves to be a large perennial plant in Zones 9 and 10, but further north it's grown as a pot plant or as an annual from seed, and remains quite a bit smaller. **Heliotrope** is famous for the sweet scent of its purple or white flowers and occasionally is suggested as a cut flower as a means of bringing fragrance into the house. But the commonly available seed for the violet 'Marine' had no scent at all when I grew it, nor could I detect any from plants in a scented garden at a nearby public garden. I wonder whether you have to look for a plant grown from a cutting, if you want the real scented heliotrope. And you may have to accept short stems.

HELLEBORUS

The ethereal beauty of the **hellebores** makes them irresistible for arranging—and for collecting. Long lived and tolerant of dry shade, they're balm for the gardener with too many shady spots. You can use both the flowers and foliage, but for long-stemmed bunches, wait to cut until you see the seedpods forming in the center of the flowers, or they'll be less predictable and not keep as well. Trim away any winter-burned foliage. The pods may become large as the season progresses, but still are choice for cutting. All hellebores are poisonous.

The winter or early spring **Christmas rose,** *Helleborus niger,* rarely flowers as early as its name implies, but it's a joy to discover blooming in the depths of February. It's a plant hardy to Zone 3, yet somewhat difficult to establish. The flowers are most usually white, flushed pink, with a green center and relatively short cut stems, to about seven inches at best. They open three inches wide a week or two after they first bloom, but last only a day if you cut at that time. I have high hopes for the *H. atrorubens* (a relative of *H. orientalis*) that I've just planted, as it blooms with dark purplish flowers very early like *H. niger,* but on welcome longer stems. It's hardy to Zone 5.

The chief interest of *H. foetidus* flowers and foliage is their inspiring spring-green color in the middle of winter. These are among the smallest flowers of the garden hellebores, and on occasion develop a lovely maroon rim. The blooms may first appear in December, but they develop so slowly they're still desirable for cutting in March and April, when the flowers are larger and more widely opened. **Stinking hellebore** is a useful flower with small spring blooms—excellent with white daffodils—and you can cut the small green florets into smaller clusters for use with crocus and snowdrops for the first mixed arrangement of the year. It's not as long stemmed as *H. orientalis,* having cut stems about 10 or 12 inches. The odor of the flowers indoors is scarcely fetid and may only prompt children to ask what's cooking, but in any case, the odd smell disappears in a couple of days. One plant can grow quite large in other people's shady gardens, flowering prolifically. In my garden, the plants are short lived, but the volunteers carry on, though peculiarly of late failing to flower.

The pleasant apple-green *H. argutifolius* resembles *H. foetidus* in color and appearance, though with larger flowers and blooming later with *H. orientalis.* The clusters of pretty flowers are marvelous for filler in small bouquets with tiny daffodils, primroses, bleeding heart, columbine, lily-of-the-valley, myosotis, and *Euphorbia palustris.* It may accept more sun than other hellebores, but it's not as hardy and hasn't formed a big clump here in the coldest part of Zone 7.

The larger *H. orientalis,* the **Lenten Rose,** blooms in February and March and is good for cutting through April and May. It's a wonderful nodding flower, differing in shading from plant to plant, even flower to flower. Colors range from green and off-white to pink and plum, frequently tinged with green or speckled with crimson. Catalogs describe the highly variable color as "cream with crimson," "dusky rose," or "greenish purple," and because they're seedlings, don't allow you to choose, a good thing as it would be impossible. The pale-plum coloring of my plant is exquisite in a small bouquet with the darker plum of *Fritillaria meleagris,* the checkered lily. The drooping flowers stand more open and erect as the seedpods form, and provide welcome contrast to daffodils and tulips, Solomon's seal, old-fashioned bleeding heart, honesty, and other longer stemmed flowers of spring, though they don't need companion material. You can also "float" short stems in a low bowl so the faces turn up.

The branching cut stems are as long as 18 inches, rich with large, fingered leaves. Eight to ten stems make a big arrangement so green and lush it's hard to believe it's only April. They require very little arranging ability on the part of the grower; just drop them in a wide-necked vase. If the stems wilt, try recutting; sometimes you hear that the stem should be pricked just under the flower to prevent wilting or that the stem should be slit lengthwise. (I never do.) When I handle the stems, or move the vase, I notice faintly the same scent of the stinking hellebore, but it in no way deters me. One plant is ideal, as the mature plants grow large and flower heavily; they look so much better and take up much less room—at least temporarily—if you trim off the old leaves in late winter when the new growth is evident.

HEMEROCALLIS

Handsome reds and delicious shades of cantaloupe and exquisite green throats make modern cultivars of *Hemerocallis* irresistible, though the **daylily** is one of several plants whose flowers last only a day and aren't usually recommended for the cutting garden. Each stem should have several buds, however, so that new flowers may open over a couple of days when cut for the vase. Most plants offered in catalogs are modern hybrids, with wide petals, strong stems, and impressive green buds. Some, however, resemble the occasional garish daffodil seen at spring shows, where hybridization can be seen to have gone too far. Like iris, daylilies arrange best without other companion flowers, or at least not featured so that their coming and going in the bouquet will be noticed. Remove the spent flowers daily.

If you'd prefer simple country charm for your arranging, particularly if you want to try a daylily with mixed garden flowers, search out older hybrids with narrower petals and simple colors like lemon yellow. The common long-lived tawny daylily that is seen by the roadsides and in old gardens and that neighbors often will share is *H. fulva.* Mail-order listings commonly note whether plants bloom early or late (as late as mid-August here), or even rebloom in fall, so that you can plan a long season. Some daylily cultivars are dwarf, but not too short for cutting; others, labeled as miniature, have smaller flowers.

You can cut from daylilies in the border, but if you do plant them in the cutting garden, you'll get the greatest number of scapes (stems) by digging a deep planting area and amending the soil. You can hope to get 10 to 12 scapes per plant. In spring and early summer, see that your plants get lots of water for best performance; they may even accept a poorly drained location. One or two plants of any cultivar should be enough. I never think to cut them, myself.

HESPERIS MATRONALIS

The biennial *Hesperis matronalis,* **sweet rocket** or **dame's rocket,** is surprisingly long stemmed to be blooming as early as the third week of April and so welcome for its dense heads of sweet-smelling flowers in white, lilac, or purple. Hesperis makes an outstanding choice for spring bouquets, with globe flowers, corn cockle, camassias, cornflowers, and painted daisies all in bloom around that time. Four plants in full sun provide a good deal of flowers (with stem lengths of 24 inches), and six plants an extravaganza. While hesperis is at its most glorious when first blooming, six weeks later you can still cut shorter stems. When I've sown mixed colors I've gotten only purples, so if you particularly want white, separate seed should be ordered. It's a long-lasting flower and is quite weatherproof.

Sowing hesperis under lights in midsummer isn't always easy, but the seedlings transplant well to the garden in fall for spring bloom. I've had no luck sowing direct in autumn, though a neighbor once sowed a pack of seed outdoors and got a plant. Yet hesperis self-sows usefully in my garden—lamentably well, some other gardeners report. The young plants are weedy and undistinguished and it's sometimes necessary to get an opinion as to whether this is indeed a sweet rocket. If you can get seed-laden finished plants from friends in early summer, cut them into branches and layer on a prepared bed form-

ing a crude row, and you'll likely discover seedlings underneath when
you remove the dried skeletons in mid to late summer. The seed requires light to germinate. This is an obliging plant, as I realized
when I staked one growing in a little shade, and found it was rooted
in only a few inches of soil over a remnant of an old wall.

Hesperis accepts light shade, possibly even prefers it, and young
plants do tolerably well under deciduous trees if they aren't dug up
by squirrels. In too much shade, the flower heads are loose and the
plants need staking, as the first storm will take them over. Hesperis
doesn't live long here, but in the North it may last several years.

HEUCHERA

Coral bells are grown more and more in the border for their ornamental bronzed leaves, but for cutting, it's the *Heuchera sanguinea*
and *H.* × *brizoides* cultivars you should choose among, as coral
bells selected for their foliage won't necessarily have the best flowers.
They're often positioned in light shade in the South, but I grow my
ivory 'White Cloud' in full sun, and it blooms well over a long period in spring and early summer; perhaps it's sentimental, but I enjoy
keeping a white coral bells in the garden. In addition to the well-
known pinks and reds, there are true whites and greenish whites.
I was excited about *H. cylindrica* 'Greenfinch', with greenish-yellow
flowers on one of the longest stems of the heucheras. It was simple
to start from seed, but I couldn't keep it alive through the summer.
A fine long-lived pink with sizeable flower clusters is 'Raspberry Regal', offered as a gourmet plant at Winterthur and rightly so. Heuchera stems are astonishingly long—up to 25 inches—for so delicate
a flower, and as they're thin, stiff, and leafless, it's worth having companions in mind when choosing a coral bells for your cutting garden:
yarrow, agrostemma, hesperis, cornflowers, and *Salvia nemerosa* are
plants often in bloom at the same time. As the buds usually don't
open in water, cut when at least half the flowers have opened. You
can allow the stems to lie on an angle while conditioning in order to
take curves.

In full sun the foliage not infrequently looks burned after the heat
of summer, but that won't matter in the cutting garden, and the next
spring the plant should bloom as well as ever. Be sure to check your
coral bells in its second or third year to see if the crown has grown
out of the ground; if so, it's time to divide. Replant the new section
deeper, with the leafy crown at soil level. One plant can produce

a prodigious amount of flowers over a fairly long period, but if you want a large number of flowers at one time, get a second plant. If you find you have a real love for coral bells, try the similar *Tellima*, which blooms just a little earlier in spring.

The related × *Heucherella*'s bright pink flowers are a slighter version of coral bells and can be used in bunches for small arrangements in spring, but in the South you might as well locate it in the lightly shaded border, as it's not likely to flower heavily or live long.

HOSTA

Most varieties of **plantain lily** are not floriferous enough to grow solely for their flowers. Exceptions include *Hosta plantaginea*, the **August lily,** and its relatives, including 'Royal Standard', which have similar medium-green or yellow-green leaves, and bloom in August. They like shade but need more sun than other hostas to flower well. *H. plantaginea* bears the largest flowers, on thick stems cut to about 22 inches, and has a heavenly perfume strong enough to limit the number you'd bring into the house; you may be satisfied with just one stem in a bud vase, placed where you can smell it in the evening, as the pure white flowers open fully only at night. The splendid 'Royal Standard' has longer stems at 30 inches and a milder exquisite scent from its handsome white flowers. Because its leaves appear very late in spring, you can plant small early bulbs like glory-of-the-snow around it.

Hostas begin to bloom in mid-June here, the bulk flowering in July. The flowers are like daylilies, or iris, in that one or two buds open each day, then hang wilted from the stem a day later. They can then be twisted or trimmed off, but that quickly becomes tiresome, and after a few days in the vase, the buds also begin to drop unopened. Except for the *H. plantaginea* cultivars, it's better to use hosta stems very much in bud, and some are quite grand and exotic in appearance. (Like torch lilies, you can introduce gentle curves to the straight stems by laying them on an angle in the bucket.) The magnificent 'Sum and Substance' shoulders enormous lily-like gray-green and lilac buds, as does *H. sieboldiana* 'Elegans', but these huge landscape specimens are much too big for the cutting garden. In fact, any hosta is a waste of space in the cutting garden, as they're customarily grown for their foliage and are better located near the house or in the border.

You can add the leaves of most hostas to arrangements, with colors ranging from green to blue to chartreuse, many with variegation, and shapes ranging from small and lance like to large and umbrella like. The texture may be shiny or matte, often handsomely corrugated and puckered like seersucker, their arching habit flowing over vase rims. The leaves of the small hostas, like the lovely green and yellow early-showing 'Golden Tiara', frame the tiniest flowers and fill out little spring bouquets. Two superb large hostas with particularly handsome variegation to bring sublime spring color to sizeable arrangements are *H. ventricosa* 'Aureo-marginata' and *H. montana* 'Aureo-marginata'. The green and yellow latter appears very early in April, when it emerges spectacularly in the border with other shade-loving, early-blooming plants. The leaves of the former aren't as big, two shades of green with white, suitable for medium to large arrangements. Keep the leaves fresh when first cut by submerging them in water for a few hours.

Hosta leaves are most beautiful in spring; afterward they may be marred by insects, debris falling from trees, and burned spots from dry weather and sun. Protect them also from being stepped on just as their leaves are emerging. They're long-lived plants, easy to grow if given plenty of water (especially in a dry spring or summer), good soil, and the right degree of shade. In wet soils they'll tolerate more sun.

HUMULUS LUPULUS

The green flowers of **hops,** *Humulus lupulus,* and slender young lengths of vine are pretty drooping from a large bouquet in early to midsummer. Some flower arrangers like to twine the vine around the handles of baskets, lovely on a basket having a high arching handle. The papery flowers in July slowly become larger over a period of weeks, but they need to be cut relatively early, as the foliage becomes shabby. In the fall, however, it will be perfect for a composition of grasses, autumn berries, and the like.

Hops is a hardy, dioecious (plants being either male or female) perennial vine that can grow to 60 feet after several years. It never grew so big for me, however. 'Aureus' is a golden variety said to grow to 20 feet, and 'Sunbeam' is reputed to take light shade. My female plant, cutting actually, was given to me by my neighbor and home brewer, Joe L., who was curious about the botanical aspect of the beer-brewing process. The cutting was a short length of twiggy brown vine with eyes showing, packaged simply in a plastic bag with cultural instructions, which he found in spring at his brewing supply store. (You can also find plants from a good herb nursery, most probably mail order like Nichols Garden Nursery.) It requires good soil, adequate moisture, and patience, as the first year or two the plant stays quite small. My hops happily covers a chain-link fence, quite obscuring it, and can blanket other unsightly objects if given support. It dies back to the ground in winter. There are named varieties having various characteristics, so you could hope to find a large-flowered variety that doesn't grow so big; Sandy Mush Herb Nursery recommends 'Willamette' for big flowers. This plant is very interesting to men and provides good conversation material for parties.

HYACINTHOIDES

Spanish bluebells, *Hyacinthoides hispanica,* are foolproof spring bulbs in shades of blue, pink, and white, which flower in mid-April a few days after the old-fashioned bleeding hearts. They may be more familiar under their many old names: *Scilla hispanica* or *S. campanulata,* and *Endymion hispanicus.* Specialty bulb catalogs, the kind that have no color pictures, will have the marvelous darker shades of blue as well as white selections; the pastels seem a little saccharine to me. Spanish bluebells are particularly handsome in water with the yellow-green flowers of *Euphorbia polychroma.* You can cut stems as much as 15 inches long, a good length for one of the small spring bulbs. They multiply rapidly over a period of years and perform admirably in the shade of deciduous trees, or in full sun in the North. I discovered how well they increase when I found bulbs pushing up visibly through the soil from a veritable trove underground, and from this one spot came enough to plant a considerable area. Begin with at least a dozen bulbs and hopefully more, and locate them in the shady display garden, as in a few years each bulb will throw up many flowers, more than are needed for cutting.

The slightly smaller *H. non-scripta,* or **English bluebells,** flower about three weeks later with chives and lily-of-the-valley, strictly in blue, liking a little more moisture, and a little more sun. The stems are more slender than the Spanish, to about 12 inches cut. For me, they took their time establishing and bloom best in very wet springs.

HYACINTHUS ORIENTALIS

The commonly grown showy **hyacinth** often forced in spring (and disliked by gardeners offended by their squat sugariness), *Hyacinthus orientalis* displays single flowers thickly surrounding the stem, or rarely double flowers from heirloom varieties, a more expensive treat. The following years they offer increasingly loose flowers much prettier and easier to arrange, in many interesting colors and blooming with the early daffodils. If you routinely pass hyacinths up, give them a second thought. To grow them for cutting, you might try planting in a little shade in order to produce slightly longer stems. The best you can usually hope for is 9 to 14 inches the first year, and it's a little tricky finding the right vase for a top-heavy short-stemmed flower, one situation for which floral foam, or a heavy pin holder, makes a good solution. An order of 6 to 10 bulbs affords a good first experiment, and they'll return for many years, as many as 20 years in some gardens, so they can be a good investment. They are hardy to Zone 4.

A little more expensive, the "multiflora" type of hyacinth is valuable for its many slender stems, each with fewer florets, good for loose mixed arrangements of tiny spring flowers. These bulbs are either naturally multiflowering or have had their basal plate removed so that they will produce more stems. Three bulbs together have produced 15 or more cuttable stems of up to seven inches in length at one time. The white has made a good companion for the short-stemmed green iris *Hermodactylus tuberosa,* which blooms very early, as well as with small early tulips, checkered lilies, individual florets of *Helleborus foetidus,* and the like. There's also a soft blue. They've persisted here for many years, and they return more reliably than do the similar **Roman hyacinths,** *H. orientalis* var. *albulus (H. romanus),* which are only hardy to Zone 6.

IBERIS

Perennial **candytuft,** *I. sempervirens,* blooms in spring with fluffy clusters of small white flowers on short stems. Fix them in a small vase with Virginia bluebells and other early to mid spring flowers. It's a pretty plant hanging over the tops of walls, often remains green over winter, and accepts light shade, but you wouldn't get it first for the cutting garden. Look for tall cultivars, to 15 inches, to put in the border, and plan to cut back after flowering to keep the stems attractive.

You can also cut from the fragrant annual **rocket candytuft,** *I. amara,* in the expected white, plus pink, purple, and red, on stems 15 to 18 inches long, and from the similar **globe candytuft,** *I. umbellata,* several inches shorter. Once germinated, annual candytufts grow quickly to blooming size in 45 days and will self-sow. They're usually sown in early spring for summer flowering and are suitable for repeat sowings in summer in the North. They dislike summer heat, and in the South should be given light shade. I find them difficult to grow.

IPOMOPSIS RUBRA

At three feet tall, *Ipomopsis rubra* bears long straight stems roughly clothed with small yellow, salmon, or scarlet trumpets in abundance. Its warm coloring is just the thing with nasturtiums, golden yarrow, early goldenrods, green nicotiana, and dill. One seed catalog has been promoting **standing cypress** as a cut flower, but it doesn't offer a clue on how to grow this little-known plant. A short-lived perennial native to the West, it's usually grown as an annual or biennial sown directly in the garden, and it didn't care much for my use of peat pots in spring. Naturally choosing dry rocky slopes in its habitat, standing cypress requires a dry, well-drained soil (a good candidate for a raised bed), tolerates light shade, and will self-sow happily, even in northern Virginia, where it grows in a dry area at Green Spring Gardens Park.

IRIS

Every cutting garden must have an **iris,** though the individual flowers aren't long lasting in water. They're a major source of cut flowers from spring to summer, deserving space in the cutting garden despite the great size of some cultivars. Various types flower one after the other over a long period, offering the gardener a nice succession of bloom. Irises fall into two main groups, the rhizomatous, which are usually located with herbaceous perennials in the garden, and the bulbous, generally bought from bulb offerings. They're one of the most widely distributed flowers of the Northern Hemisphere: wherever you live, there's probably a type of iris suited to your soil and climate.

Iris to most beginning gardeners means tall **bearded iris,** sometimes wrongly called German iris. Noble plants with the fine bearing of monkshood and delphinium, their exotic beauty is apparent even to teenage boys, like the one in my car whose head snapped back to see some purple and violet bicolors as we rounded a corner. "Wow!" he said. "Were those orchids?"

The modern tall bearded irises can be extremely large flowers on thick stems cut as long as 36 inches, grander and showier than older varieties. Arrange them alone in a big vase for a dramatic display of a flower almost never seen at the florist. They may be ornately ruffled, or not, as you choose, and come in a wide range of color—the medium blues are one of their glories, as are the tremendous pure whites. For a long time, I grew a huge, fragrant pale pink for cutting named 'Pink Taffeta,' but an arrangement of it was truly enormous, and it was difficult to find a place to put the vase, though Cassidy and Linnegar in their *Growing Irises* suggest standing a large container of iris in front of the fireplace. Because you probably won't combine a large tall bearded with other flowers, pick just as showy or gaudy a cultivar as you like (bearded irises with variegated flowers are a recent novelty).

The smaller bearded irises should be the ones chosen for a modest country cottage air, or if you want them for mixing with other garden flowers like Solomon's seal, baptisia, camassia, wild parsnip, Egyptian onion, and *Nectaroscordum siculum.* You'll want to avoid using iris as the center of interest in a mixed arrangement, however, as the next day the flower may have finished, and it might be a day or two before another bud opens. You can find classes of smaller bearded iris (not dwarfs) from specialty iris growers, almost never from general nurseries, which usually offer only the big types and often a bewildering array of them. (Join the American Iris Society to see the growers' advertisements in the *Bulletin.*) Since all bearded irises periodically require division, it shouldn't be difficult to acquire interesting ones from friends and garden club plant sales. I've seen boxes of iris fans sold like bulbs at garden centers in fall, and while they'll probably grow, it seems a most depressing manner in which to acquire an iris.

You'll find the older and "historic" bearded irises in specialty iris catalogs and from local iris societies. Knowing something special about an iris makes choosing easier, I think. If you live in a "Victorian" or older house, you may like the two-tone violets (such as 'Violecea Grandiflora', hybridized in 1856), which commonly are seen in old neighborhood gardens. Purple *Iris germanica* and white *I. albicans* ('Albicans') were irises painted by Van Gogh, the last an ancient iris from the Middle East traditionally planted on graves. These are intermediate in size.

For quite small bearded irises, the Miniature Tall Bearded irises, also known as "table irises," are a treasure. These are bred to have thin graceful stems (16 to 25 inches in length) in proportion with the flower, an even easier size for arranging with other spring flowers. In the garden, they're not knocked down by storms the way large hybrids are. I asked one grower to send me a nice selection for cutting, since I wasn't familiar with cultivar names. I enjoyed 'Sand Princess', 'Violet Rose', 'Purple Heather', 'Snow Fiddler', and 'Creme Lady' for their lovely markings and soft demeanor, all delightful on the dinner table and good for mixing, though their cut stems fell at the shorter end of that range. Pretty 'Honorabile', its standards yellow and falls "brown," hybridized in 1840, was a favorite table iris of Victorian gardeners.

Bearded irises spread into good clumps, so one of any type will do for the cutting garden. If the stems fall over from rain, they should be propped up or cut right away, as the buds soon turn up to the light and will look sideways in the vase. Be careful in handling plants, because the buds snap off easily. Allow plenty of room and good drainage, and divide the year they produce more flowers than you can use. The foliage swords make excellent filler. After arranging, snip or twist off the individual flowers as they decline, and a vase of irises will seem to last for days.

Species iris catch your fancy with little trouble, though not all are simple to grow. *I. pseudacorus* blooms in bright yellow after the tall bearded have finished. The paler yellow or ivory forms are pretty as well, but the bright yellow double is a messy blob: it had to go, though it could have been saved for its big seedheads. One plant of **yellow flag** grows to a large clump in the manner of the beardeds and likes a wet spot, though it doesn't require it. I once was so fortunate to be present when a spring-loaded bud of *I. pseudacorus* opened. I had always imagined they unfurled slowly at dawn, but I was studying a stem one midmorning, debating whether to cut, when the yellow bud suddenly sprang open, all scarcely within the span of a millisecond and leaving my eyes blinking. This is the ancient iris frequently said to be the source for the fleur-de-lis, but my iris mentor, Clarence Mahan, tells me that is most likely only romantic legend, that the original source for the motif was probably the stylized image of three heads of wheat, the symbol of the Roman governors of Gaul.

The very sophisticated *I. fulva*, unique in its narrow shape and fine coppery reddish brown color, is almost an exotic in appearance; use it by itself in a modern glass vase. Some people are surprised to learn it's an iris. This great favorite of mine is easy for wet soils, as well as average conditions. Other moisture-loving irises include the beautiful **Louisiana irises**, the taller hybrids of which are ideal for cut flowers in the South, with a range of color comparable to bearded iris; I fell for white 'Clara Goula' with chartreuse veins. The branching stems carry several flowers on vigorous plants, but Clarence warns that other Louisianas will be more likely to grow old with me. Where climates are mild, many gardeners might enjoy *I. spuria* cultivars for cutting. I most usually never notice that *I. foetidissima* (**stinking iris**) has bloomed, as the small flowers are lost in foliage, but in fall the red-berried seedpods are perfect for seasonal interest. A particular attraction of this iris is that it tolerates a great deal of shade.

Beardless **Siberian iris**, hybrids of *I. sibirica*, are particularly wonderful for cutting, in rich shades of white, purple, blue, and wine red on lovely long stems with two or three flowers per spike. They range from petite with fine, narrow foliage, to larger and vigorous with more substantial foliage. You'll find showy varieties with mottling or veining, like 'Super Ego' and 'Ann Dasch'. I acquired big, floriferous 'White Sails' because Andre Viette recommended it as a cut flower, but I'd have no hesitation choosing others, including the beautiful pale yellow and white 'Butter and Sugar', expensive for so long, and daintier selections like purple and very tall 'Caesar's Brother'. Mixed arrangements of Siberians are particularly attractive when flowers of different sizes are used. Cut the stems to different lengths so the flowers are easier to see in the vase.

Siberians bloom about two weeks after the bearded irises, and the bloom may be copious. My one plant of 'White Sails' in its second spring, in well-dug soil in full sun, produced an unbelievable 106 stems over 9 or 10 days. This means Siberian irises pack many more stems into the same space as tall bearded, and so make a good choice for the small cutting garden. Because they flower so heavily, you can also locate them for cutting in the border, where missing stems won't be noticed.

Siberians grow well in ordinary gardens and thrive in wetter soil. Because the plants take a fountain shape, rather than outwardly spreading fans, they don't get filled with weeds the way the bearded do. One plant in full sun will become a large clump, yet needing no division—the best iris for gardeners with little attention to give the garden.

Japanese iris, *I. ensata (I. kaempferi)*, bloom as the Siberians are ending, and like Siberians are a glorious theme in purple and violet blue. The flowers are wider and flatter, frequently described as resembling birds in flight, and the prominent veining of cultivars is one of their most attractive features. If you have a moist or wet location, you'll love a Japanese iris for cutting, and they should still do acceptably under average garden conditions. For much too long I delayed planting Japanese iris, as I assumed my garden wasn't wet enough. They make a fabulous display on elegant slender stems with long narrow buds like colored spears, and I like it that they may take several days to open in water, but they aren't long lived in the vase. Plant only one for the cutting garden.

The **Dutch iris** (a relative of **Spanish iris**, *I. xiphium*, which blooms a few weeks later) is a hardy bulb found in bulb catalogs for planting in autumn. They're undeniably good cut flowers, though one of the most common florist flowers. I prefer them outside in the border or for giving away. These are 18 inches in length when cut, usually two flowers per stem, blooming a few weeks before the tall bearded iris. You can cut when the buds are showing a good strip of color. I found the dark blue and purple, such as 'Purple Sensation', very dark indeed. If you don't have bright rooms, stick to the medium and light colors; there are many to choose from, white through yellow, and very pretty blues.

Dutch iris are cheap and remarkably easy to grow. You'll be able to grow them fully as nice as the florist's. Given their low cost, it's a nice opportunity to plan for an explosion of flowers in a wide vase; avoid mixtures for this purpose, as they may bloom at different times. They return year after year in Zones 6 to 8, increasing slowly. From my planting, 12 bulbs produced 20 stems in their third year, and 24 in the fourth. Located in a slightly raised bed with perennial plants, Dutch iris haven't minded summer waterings or even my none-the-best winter drainage. Mark their location, as the foliage disappears in summer and reappears later looking weedy, like wild onion. A similar iris that is better for a lightly shaded, reliably moist soil, and hardier to Zone 4, is **English iris**, *I. latifolia (I. xiphioides)*. The slightly larger flower blooms two or three weeks later.

A sweet-smelling small green curiosity, known until recently as *I. tuberosa* but now called *Hermodactylus tuberosa*, flowers in late March from a hardy bulb. It has a reputation as being good for cutting, a florist flower even, though its stems are about eight inches. It makes a green filler for primroses, hellebores, and euphorbia, and lasts about three days. The common names of **snake's head iris** and **widow iris** give one pause.

KALIMERIS PINNATIFIDA

An obliging subject for cutting, like a small boltonia with doubled starry white flowers and tiny leaves, *Kalimeris pinnatifida* reminds me of an aster with double flowers and good foliage. The pretty one-inch daisies are scattered airily up and down the 18-inch branching stems for a great filler over a long period. It comes into bloom in late June and continues on through summer in a lightly shaded garden, and amazingly, you can still cut it in early October. This plant was called *Asteromoea mongolica* when I first got it, a classic southern pass-along with the odd name of **orphanage plant,** but it has changed its name, at least with some people, to **Japanese aster.**

Kalimeris is a bit lax and should be tied up or grown through a hoop. It suffers in hot sun, needing a little afternoon shade and moisture for good looks, but it's a great plant for the South. The biggest flowers come in a cool summer with good rains.

KNAUTIA

Knautia arvensis looks just like a lavender annual scabiosa, with long wiry stems cutting to 15 inches or more. **Knautia** blooms copiously in spring about a month before the perennial scabiosa (two months before the annual), and thus is a good perennial for those luckless gardeners who've given up on *Scabiosa caucasica.* It's a superb addition to large mixed arrangements of spring flowers such as camassia, hesperis, table iris, columbine, and painted daisies. One plant grows to a nice size. The smaller, wine-red *K. macedonica* is a perennial hardy to perhaps Zone 5, the color perfect for arranging with pink and white flowers and with red and white old-fashioned dianthus. Valuable for its unusual color and dark buds in the same scabious raspberry shape, it blooms heartily from late May through midsummer here (into fall in the North), but becomes untidy with smaller flowers toward the end. A good seed selection may include pastel colors.

KNIPHOFIA UVARIA

It's understandable that the yellow and orange coloring of **red-hot poker** or **torch lily,** *Kniphofia uvaria,* gives some gardeners qualms. Still, the long-stemmed spikes of the common torch lilies are especially suited to big rooms and bold arrangements, and the desirable new smaller varieties and paler colors work easily into everyday flowers and are a pleasure to fall for. Some of the lovely little pokers, like the creamy 'Little Maid' or pale yellow 'Vanilla', aren't as hardy as the big ones and may disappear over the winter. Plant them where they won't be wet in the cold months.

The various pokers bloom at a range of times through summer. 'Pfitzeri' was with me forever, flowering in late spring on magnificent sturdy stems, grander and more floriferous each year, until I felt it grew too large for the cutting garden. I was puzzled by authorities who say it blooms in late summer, but Elizabeth Lawrence *(A Southern Garden)* also found it blooms in May. A three-year-old plant can produce an astonishing 32 stems from two flushes of bloom. In the vase, it can stand by itself or emerge from a froth of lady's mantle. Smaller 'Bressingham Comet' blooms July into September, with the same glowing yellow shading to bright orange on slender spikes; and its later flowering with the zinnias, gloriosa daisies, amaranthus, and other warm colors of summer doesn't leave you wondering whatever to arrange it with.

Cut the pokers before the lower flowers open for a greenish-orange spike, and take advantage of the way the stems bend toward light by laying them on an angle in the bucket for several hours before arranging. When you position them in the vase, they'll turn upward again and take interesting curves. One plant grows into a big fellow but doesn't need division.

LABLAB PURPUREUS

An outstanding tender perennial vine at its prime in late summer, *Lablab purpureus (Dolichos lablab)* possesses splendid red stems, bronzy-green veined leaves, and fragrant purplish-pink pea-flowers. The marvelous big seedpods, in reddish purple, hang together with the flowers. It's an exotic plant, with a garden feel like that of castor bean and a sophisticated look in water. You can cut lengths of vine, with pretty tendrils and young leaves in groups of three, to trail from the vase, added to the long (to 22 inches) sturdy stems bearing pods and flowers. The water stays crystal clear for days, so use a glass vase to show off the beety stems. **Hyacinth bean** needs no companion flowers (though zinnias and small sunflowers, or amaranthus and celosia are superb), and couldn't be easier to cut and arrange. There's a white-flowered version with green leaves.

Sow hyacinth bean direct, as it resents transplanting, though where the growing season is very short, you may have to start it early in peat pots. Here, seed sown tardily in situ at the end of May blooms in late July, and when deadheaded, continues lustily through October. It should have a fence or support to climb (finished sunflowers make a good trellis), to as much as 15 feet, and relishes hot weather. Grow one plant or as many as five or six to have a good choice among stems to pick. Save a few pods for seed for next year; it also self-sows.

LATHYRUS

Lathyrus odoratus, the annual **sweet pea,** has been one of the most popular flowers of gardeners for centuries, particularly British gardeners. In Britain you'll occasionally see tiny gardens devoted entirely to sweet peas, with parallel rows of neatly built trellises making the most of little space. The delicate colors range through pink, red, blue, mauve, and white, some flushed or speckled, the flowers carried on stiff stems at most 12 inches in length (in my garden), which stand up from a vine growing to about six feet. Cut the flowering stems away, leaving the vine intact, unless you want lengths of vine for arranging. Another elegant flower likely to have short stems in June (and about as short lived) is the Shirley poppy. Shirleys combine beautifully with sweet peas, and a nice selection of small vases is an advantage in displaying them.

Sweet peas bloom from late May into early July where temperatures, particularly at night, are mild. Celia Thaxter, gardening in Maine, started hers indoors (without lights, though I can't recommend that. Possibly her conditions were very cool) by the "hundreds," and described them as blooming long into fall. Here in Virginia, gardeners must sow early-blooming strains of sweet peas, or varieties described as "heat resistant," in order to avoid the ravages of hot weather that can appear in May. American seed catalogs are fully aware of this problem and some offer good selections, while others don't trouble to offer them at all. The English catalogs showcase the fabulous "late" Spencer varieties with very large flowers in gorgeous colors, about six to each stem. These do nicely for American gardens that have a long, cool growing season, and in Great Britain, they produce stems a breathtaking 18 inches long, as we saw when we stopped to visit the Queen's little chapel near Balmoral. Standing up by the altar were buckets of sweet peas brought in for arranging by a local garden club, and the sexton allowed me to lift a few out, to marvel not so much at the flower as at the stem. Gardeners in warmer areas should try the earliest-flowering 'Mammoth' strain (up to 12 smaller flowers per stem), the midseason 'Royal Family' (also up to 12 flowers), and the "early" Spencers, or any others bred for early flowering or heat resistance. My stems manage only seven flowers at most.

We sow our sweet peas in February (because Henry Mitchell said to), the beds prepared the previous fall to loosen the soil and add nutrients, as they like a good diet. I set the biggest of tomato cages over the spot and anchor it. Others use a trellis or fence. I chip my seed with a sharp knife on a side away from the "eye" and soak it overnight before planting, usually sowing a lot to ensure success. Do not ruin things weeks later by digging around, wondering if anything is going on. Thin your seedlings to at least 10 inches apart, and pinch the vines once early to promote root growth and vigor. Where it is hot, very light shade, especially in the afternoon, may also extend their bloom. These are not the easiest plants to grow; gardeners wanting to give up on annual sweet peas can try the perennial sweet pea, or make do with the blue pea flowers of perennial baptisia and yellow *Thermopsis caroliniana*. For some reason, The Country Garden seed catalog (another jewel now gone out of business) advised that sweet pea seed not be refrigerated.

You can pick the common perennial sweet pea, *L. latifolius,* with its similar pink flower and attractive tendrils, found in late spring roadsides and wild gardens. It doesn't mind hot summers the way the annual does. A handsome named selection, 'White Pearl', grows obligingly from seed begun indoors in spring, flowering the first summer into September, and from late spring through midsummer in following years. Much farther North it blooms the last half of summer. Mixed shades of pink, and pink shading to white, are also available from seed suppliers. Even nonflowering stems are excellent for arranging, with their endearing corkscrew tendrils, green seedpods, and pretty arching buds; longer lengths of vine also make excellent filler. The stems last a long time in water if you pick off faded florets.

The perennial sweet pea is a vigorous plant, enough so that you wonder if it might take over. It should be given a fence or substantial support, growing to 10 feet, and you may cut it back ruthlessly during the growing season to keep it within bounds and reduce self-sowing.

LAVANDULA ANGUSTIFOLIA

Add the straight stems and slender spikes of the **lavenders** to mixed bouquets for their blue, violet, even pink flowers and wonderful fragrance. Cut when the flowers show color. Several of the most popular landscape forms of *Lavandula angustifolia,* such as 'Hidcote', are too dwarf for the best picking, but some good mail-order nurseries pride themselves on their selections of interesting cultivars, many as tall as 36 inches. Herb nurseries are logical places to look, too. Any lavender tall enough will be good for cutting, and as they're oftentimes as wide as they are high, you might locate your lavender in the border rather than the cutting garden. They require good drainage and benefit from lime where soils are acid. They also dislike humidity and may not be as fragrant in cool climates.

LAVATERA TRIMESTRIS

A **mallow,** whether it's a malva, malope, or lavatera, is a must for the cutting garden. The beautiful *Lavatera trimestris,* **tree mallow,** is a perennial grown as a half-hardy annual here, sown outdoors in early spring. Abundant silky lipstick-pink flowers like small hibiscus appear in mid-July on bushy plants of 'Mt. Rose', pristine white on 'Mt. Blanc', and pale pink with a lovely dark center on 'Pink Beauty'. Try them alone or with veronica, penstemons, belladonna delphinium, and meadow rue. The large flowers appear so similar to malope that you may not want to grow both in the same season, though *Malope trifida* blooms almost three weeks earlier. Lavatera is the preferred choice for many gardeners, because the stems are straighter and sturdier, and the pelargonium-like leaves are more attractive. The buds open in water.

Lavatera seems somewhat temperamental, so I'm surprised to read it's a popular florist subject in Europe. It has happened more than once that all my plants died before flowering. In cool summer areas, it will be more reliable and produce large, bushy plants for late summer and fall flowers, and even live several years. Always give it a dry, well-drained soil of good quality, and sow direct, as it doesn't tolerate root disturbance. Like malope, the plants seem to wilt badly and then die in the days after cutting, so I wait until they're in considerable flower, then cut as much as possible from any particular plant, always in the early morning or evening, as lavatera greatly benefits from picking when the day is cool. I cut the last flowers in about mid-August, then pull the plants up. Begin with about four or five.

LAYIA PLATYGLOSSA

A thoroughly charming, native hardy annual in the form of a white-tipped yellow daisy, *Layia platyglossa (L. elegans)* brings a sunny aspect to a small container of spring yellows such as leopard's bane or cushion spurge, with white iberis or spring phlox. **Tidytips** needs dry soil and cool weather, so my scraggly spring-sown plants haven't reached the 12 to 15 inches promised by the seed catalogs before the arrival of the heat. The stems are more like five inches when I cut them. This plant is a good prospect for gardens in the West, and in the East should be grown in a light, well-drained soil, possibly in a raised bed with the tiniest bit of shade.

LEUCOJUM

The bewitching white **snowflakes** appreciate a moist soil, so you can plant them in a border that receives watering in summer. The three major choices among this bulb—all of which carry several flowers to the stem, accept shade, and increase to good-sized clumps—supply pretty white bells tipped with green for spring bouquets large and small. *Leucojum vernum*, the familiar **spring snowflake**, will give you eight-inch stems, perhaps even a little longer, and comes into flower very early, in February or March, just after the white snowdrops, *Galanthus*, have ended. The similar *L. aestivum*, the **summer snowflake**, flowers over a lengthy period in April, on longer stems to 12 inches.

The largest selection, and the more expensive, *L. a.* 'Gravetye Giant' is first cuttable in early spring on strong stems of about 8 or 10 inches, eventually stretching to 21 inches later in spring with the tulips and the last breath of the daffodils. The floriferous stems are handy with old-fashioned bleeding heart, pink and white tulips like 'Sorbet', columbine, honesty, tellima, and *Euphorbia robbiae*. The easy clumps become immense with copious foliage, so you don't need many bulbs, perhaps only two or three even, for mixed arranging.

LIATRIS

The white or purple **gayfeathers** are popular with many people for mixed arrangements in July. I was unlucky with *Liatris pycnostachya* and *L. scariosa,* which always died, but *L. spicata* cultivars have lived three years and more. This last may be the best for eastern gardens. A seed strain especially for cutting, *L. spicata* 'Floristan' or 'Floristan White', is occasionally available as a nursery plant. Bulb catalogs also offer gayfeather. I like to see a few stems used modestly in an arrangement, rather than many radiating out like a sputnik, and it shouldn't be the tallest flower in the bouquet; using it with other more elegant spiky flowers, like *Veronicastrum virginicum,* helps soften it. Since gayfeather displays best in mixed arrangements, as the stiff pokers need company, it's a better perennial for the larger cutting garden that produces a fair amount of other cutting material. You may find plants in very light shade have a slenderer stem, less like a club and more attractive to the eye. The stems are about 22 inches in length when cut—the flowering spike a full 12 inches—and last a long while in the vase. Because the florets open from the top down, the stems must be cut when they first begin to open, requiring the gardener to be alert. One plant should provide enough flowers.

LIGULARIA TUSSILAGINEA

Ligularia tussilaginea is interesting for its flowering time in mid-October, a month after most plants have finished their best bloom, and months after most ligularias. The curious big yellow daisies on fleshy stems are able to withstand light frosts. You can use them alone or add them to harvest-colored mums, and along with the golden flowers of *Helianthus angustifolius,* they make one of the last mixed bouquets from the fall cutting garden. I've also seen them look delightful with small pink single mums. **Green leopard plant,** or just **leopard plant,** if you grow the spotted, is a large ornamental foliage plant for the border in moist soil and constant light shade. It wilts in even a few moments of full sun. It's an excellent low-maintenance plant (it dislikes division), which grows slowly to a large clump, green all winter in Zone 7. By the time it blooms in October, the rest of the border, unfortunately, is nothing anyone wants to look at and the flowers are never missed when I cut them. It also has a new name (a second new name, because I first knew it as *L. kaempferi*) which nobody seems to use just yet: *Farfugium japonicum.*

LILIUM

The genus *Lilium* includes sumptuous flowers to suit almost every taste, and the enormous number of species and hybrids enables the gardener with suitable conditions to have the pleasure of experimenting with new **lilies** for years. You'll find the several flowers of just one or two stems make a luxurious show, the buds opening for days after cutting and long lasting in water. Large flamboyant lilies with spots, stripes, flushed color, or elongated trumpets are difficult to use with ordinary garden flowers for mixed bouquets, but alone in water they flaunt themselves gloriously. The smaller unadorned lilies of simple color, such as white, yellow, or pink are the most likely to mix readily.

You may want to select a variety of flower shapes for the lilies in your cutting garden: the trumpet, the upward- or outward-facing like most of the Asiatics, and pendant like the Turk's cap are some of the most basic. Don't be put off by the considerable height of many lilies, as you need to leave behind two-thirds of the stem to replenish the bulb for the next year. Most accept light shade, which often lengthens their stems.

While it's a bit of a generalization, the easily grown and commonly available **Asiatic lilies** flower for the most part in early summer, the Aurelian and trumpets in midsummer, and the orientals last. A pretty, pale lemon-ice Asiatic came with our house 16 years ago, and it still blooms reliably in our well-drained shady terrace and has produced numerous welcome stem bulbs that worked their way up through the soil and were planted elsewhere. These lilies are widely available in many colors, some bulb catalogs offering mixed Asiatic collections in pastel shades, or pink and peach shades. This is a nice way to get more variety and a relatively informal lily. There are also bicolors among the Asiatics that remind you of showy tulips, the ones called "lily-flowered." The Asiatic is one of the few categories of lilies that will increase, or even hang around dependably. My lily mentors John R. and Vicki B. both rave about the new lilies called "L. A. Hybrids," crosses between Asiatics and *L. longiflorum.* They're strong plants (though not very tall), with mostly outfacing flowers, reliable over a wide area from the far North to warm South. Scheepers has them.

The **trumpet lilies** (which include the somewhat more bowl-shaped Aurelians) furnish fabulous elongated flowers on long stems. Staking is usually recommended, but you can hope you'll be cutting the flowers before the heavy heads tip over. There's less variety in color, but some have stripes or a reverse of contrasting color down the outside of the trumpet. They're easy to grow in Zone 7—less so in the far North—and should multiply, but try only a couple of these very large flowers at first. Both Vicki and John suggest 'Regale' or 'Regal' and big white 'Regal Album' as satisfactory, and Vicki has had a clump of 'White Henryi' for 30 years now.

The formal and sumptuous **oriental lilies,** species and hybrids, for the most part bloom latest in summer, valuable when fewer plants are coming into flower, but most will be short lived here and need almost to be thought of as annuals. I much admire both the white spotted ones with a stripe of yellow running down the petal from the throat and the whites flushed with pink. The species and cultivars of *L. speciosum,* particularly 'Uchida', make fine choices for cutting. Two that are more reliable than others are 'Casablanca' and 'Stargazer', the latter being an overworked florist's horse, but durable and inexpensive. Check heights when ordering. Since some new oriental hybrids for pots bloom on stems of only two or three feet, you'd be arranging these on quite short stems if you took only the recommended third of the stalk or less when cutting.

You can find smaller lilies such as *L. henryi* among the species and special hybrids in the better catalogs. These are more delicate and less formal than the big showy hybrids. The strongly orange and bristling with spots *L. lancifolium* (*L. tigrinum* or **tiger lily**) grows beautifully here in medium shade to at least six feet, propagating freely from the many black bulbils on its stems. It may be difficult to find, as it has a reputation for harboring virus. A marvelous smaller Turk's cap I was sent by mistake—*L. superbum*—orange shading to gold, and speckled, is similar but prettier than the tigers.

While sweet, the perfume of some lilies is overpowering and wouldn't be appropriate for the dining table or small space. It's the orientals that are most heavily perfumed, and the odor is stronger at night. Comments on scent are often given in lily catalogs. Watch out for lily pollen, as it stains badly: clothes, tablecloths, even paper. For that reason, florists remove the anthers from lilies they sell. Always vacuum or shake or, using a fine brush, lightly dust off pollen first, rather than wipe or wash it off (allow the pollen to dry first if it's damp). You can use scissors to remove the anthers too, outdoors preferably, but note first how much more exotic they look with all their finery.

Expect to plant lilies in the fall when they're almost dormant for a short period, and soon after you receive them, as they dry out easily. Lilies need good drainage, but sometimes it's difficult to know if a new garden qualifies as well drained; what's acceptable drainage for most plants may not be liveable for lilies, and tulips too, it seems. I lost all 12 new lily bulbs one winter in a new bed at my community garden, and it was years before I could order another lily. Begin with a few bulbs and evaluate the results, as some lilies are more intolerant of damp soils than others. While they're generally carefree, lilies are not always long lived. But if a few bulbs disappear after flowering, they'll undoubtedly have already paid for themselves in flowers.

LIMONIUM

I always felt it was a long wait for *Limonium latifolium*'s tiny lavender buds to open, but you can cut it earlier for a pretty filler in July. **Sea lavender**'s great airy heads are rather like a lavender-blue baby's breath. Give this tap-rooting perennial a well-drained location and in hot summer areas possibly a little shade. It will not like to be dug up or divided. You may want to prop up the flowering stems on twigs or upended pots to keep them off the ground, as one plant will sprawl over a good bit of space. (Save it for the large cutting garden.) It will flower heavily, but if you don't use it all, you'll find it easy to give the dried flowers away. The colorful annual **statice** *L. sinuatum* is simple to grow for flowers in early June, but for fresh flowers it's not exciting, unless you choose to use it in a rustic bouquet with solidaster, coneflowers, grasses, twigs, and the like. It has very much the papery feel and sound of an everlasting—you may decide to dry it instead. When starting statice under lights, use peat pots, because the long tap root tends to attach to the bottom of plastic pots, and it doesn't develop the kind of rootball that holds the soil together when you remove it.

LINARIA

Half-hardy annual *Linaria maroccana,* or **toadflax,** blooms for months in shades of pink, purple, red, yellow, and white where summers are cool. These are sweet flowers to arrange with chives, spring phlox, small bleeding hearts, dianthus, bluebells, all the little flowers of spring and early summer. 'Northern Lights' bears tiny, snap-dragon-like flowers on slender stems 10 to 12 inches when cut, or longer where they grow really well. The easy, quick-growing plants bloom in midspring here when started early under lights, as they like cool weather and disappear when it becomes hot. You can also sow toadflax very early in spring directly in the garden (which they really prefer), where it germinates with abandon—keep hoping the weather stays cool—or in fall where winters are mild. Pinch them once when they are young to increase bushiness. They will self-sow. *L. purpurea* is a taller perennial toadflax with pretty gray-green foliage and stems a little sturdier though still slight. It is most fetching in the garden. The narrow spike carries tiny purple flowers, pink on the selection 'Canon Went', for cut flowers lasting several days. Started in late January under lights, they're in bloom their first year by early June. Cut stems are 16 inches from young plants, longer from older plants that grow eventually to three feet.

LIRIOPE MUSCARI

Liriope muscari's strappy foliage works as greenery much of the summer for medium-sized bouquets. Cut handfuls of the narrow leaves about 15 inches long to arch gracefully from the container. Choose a tall gold and green variegated cultivar, and you'll see how handsomely the leaves complement unusual cut material like the cones of echinacea, peppers, or the seedheads of red orach. It's a ground cover for shady places and doesn't need to be located in the cutting garden, though you can grow **lilyturf** in more sun with adequate moisture. The purple or white spikes in late summer and early fall aren't an important cut flower, but you can add them in with sedum, China asters, cosmos, garlic chives, and other holdovers from summer. The flower stems in shade grow to about 14 inches, longer than those from plants grown in sun. To produce attractive new foliage each year, be sure to cut back severely all the old foliage in late winter or early spring, by far easiest to do before the new leaves are up. Water conscientiously to prevent the leaf tips from scorching. The invasive *L. spicata* is not for the cutting garden.

LOBELIA

The tall perennial lobelias are vastly different from the tiny-flowered, low-growing annual *Lobelia erinus* or *L. pendula* used for edging and containers. North American natives, they delight in lightly shaded moist or wet soils and are often short lived, but they are able to self-sow. You won't usually see them suggested for cutting, particularly not by British books, but Irene and Arno Nehrling's *Gardening for Flower Arrangement,* with its good coverage of American plants, encouraged me to try them.

The red coloring of **cardinal flower,** *L. cardinalis,* won't mix easily with most flowers, but if you're clever with grasses and foliage, you'll be able to arrange it successfully. Cut stems in my garden have been 22 inches long, the buds continuing to open in water. Recent cultivars such as 'Compliment Scarlet' have even larger flowers; the plant is quite visible at a distance. You can grow the Compliment series, which also includes blue, as biennials or annuals from seed. *L. cardinalis* needs light shade, particularly in the South, and begins to bloom in early August. It should bring hummingbirds to your garden.

I once saw a plant of *L. siphilitica* (**great blue lobelia**) in the wild, and it was impressive, though a little coarse. Great blue lobelia, which may also be white, will grow in sun or light shade, and self-sows modestly. *L. × gerardii* 'Vedrariensis', which has large, singularly rich purple flowers on long stems that bloom for a good period beginning in early July, is long lasting in water. It's a hybrid related to the previous two lobelias. All may need staking in too much shade. Begin with one of any kind.

LUNARIA ANNUA

Lunaria annua, called variously **silver-dollar plant, money plant,** or **honesty,** resembles hesperis, with its loose clusters of lightly fragrant white or purple flowers in mid-April and green or variegated foliage. Lunaria must be used soon after flowering if you want a fresh flower and especially should be cut before a rainstorm (it's not very weatherproof), as it quickly passes its prime and in just two weeks begins to make its famous seedpods. When fresh, it's clumsy enough that it is best in large casual arrangements of mixed flowers. In the last days of spring and early summer, the long stems of round, flat green seedpods are indispensable as green filler with foxgloves, iris, poppies, sweet William, nigella, larkspur, and Russell lupines, if you're so lucky to have them. The sizeable seedpods last forever in water and can even be saved for the next arrangement.

The plants self-sow well, frequently too well, and will choke out more refined plants if they're not thinned promptly. They are simple to start indoors, but don't start them too early under lights, as they may become leggy. Lunaria must be sown in the previous spring, because the plants require a full 12 months before beginning bloom. (We can wonder why it's called *L. annua.*) The small plants establish readily in the partial shade they need in hot summer areas, though they may be grown in full sun in cooler climates. The foliage looks like some ghastly vegetable during the first year and makes the gardener wonder if she's been sent the right seed. Two or three plants should be enough for arranging.

LUPINUS

The majestic **lupines** arrange handsomely with larkspur, poppies, and smaller foxgloves like 'Foxy' in late spring. While there are several lovely annual and perennial species worthy of interest, the perennial 'Russell Hybrids' are the most popular lupines for garden subjects, as they're the only lupine likely to survive most gardeners' efforts. Seed for **Russell lupines** is widely available in a rainbow of mixed or separated candy colors and bicolors. Nursery plants often are offered in mixed colors, which don't necessarily look good together for arranging, but individually they may harmonize superbly with other flowers from the garden. Better garden centers and mail-order outfits may have separated colors.

Lupines are not rewarding to grow where it's hot and humid or where the soil is heavy. As my garden endures all those unfortunate conditions, I've tried to start the Russells and several of the lovely species from seed both in the garden and under lights, but they fail to grow even passably. Purchased lupines in pots have to suffice, planted early spring or preferably fall, and as they don't live through hot summers, they are an infrequent treat. The Russells flower here beginning in mid-May over a period of three weeks, a few flowers at a time. They twist and turn considerably to the light the first day, so it's best to have them arranged loosely in the vase for ease in adjusting. They're not long lasting.

LYCHNIS

The dense flowerheads of the red **Maltese cross**, *Lychnis chalcedonica,* make energetic company for gloriosa daisies, yarrow, and coreopsis, with lots of greenery to complement the red. But like *Lobelia cardinalis,* the color is limiting. Prettier pink, white, and salmon shades from this perennial are splendid for mixed bouquets, looking appealingly like verbena, but they can be difficult to find; I've seen them on occasion at a first-rate garden center. The salmon fades deliciously to a shell pink, both colors present together, which makes it wonderful for arranging with soft purple flowers like *Salvia verticillata* 'Purple Rain', blue-green *Eryngium amethystinum,* white *Asclepias incarnata,* and shell-pink verbascums. Thompson & Morgan and Stokes have offered white or mixed colors in easy seed, flowering for me in late May of their second year, though they're described as flowering the first year from an early sowing. The cut stems are about 15 inches in length, with repeat bloom through midsummer if you're careful to deadhead. Several plants are not too many. You can try this and the following lychnis in light shade.

    L. coronaria's pink, white, or rose-red flowers on felted gray-green foliage in very late spring are irresistible. But I finally removed **rose campion** from the cutting garden because I thought it rather difficult to arrange, as the laterals are held at such wide angles from the stems. A good filler like lady's mantle or ballota gets around this problem, with nigella and *Armeria* 'Bees Ruby' to fill out the bouquet. One plant can grow quite large and self-sow heavily. The individual plants, though usually described as perennials, are not long lived.

LYCORIS

Lycoris squamigera's huge pink clusters (11 inches across) bloom on strong leafless stems as long as 30 inches. They make outstanding cut flowers, but more than five or six stems of the alluringly fragrant flowers might be too much scent for the average room. Cut when a few of the six or seven individual flowers have opened in a cluster, and snip them out as they fade. A luxuriant clump of leaves forms in spring from the hardy bulb and disappears in summer before the flower stalks—two per bulb in years of good rain—appear in early August. That's why it's called **magic lily,** because the flower stalk emerges from the ground with no leaves. It will be happy in medium-to-light shade. One neighbor tells me she believes it must be a biennial, by which she means it flowers in her garden about every other year, but most likely the absence of bloom results from inadequate moisture. Rainy springs produce the best shows, even in summers that are quite dry. South of Zone 7 you might also experiment for cutting with the less-hardy *L. radiata,* or red **spider lily,** a handsome smaller form in a deeper color, that has the advantage for the arranger of blooming in autumn.

LYSIMACHIA

A wonderful break in flower shape in June, the gently bowing white *Lysimachia clethroides* is one of the perennials most commonly recommended for cutting gardens. **Gooseneck loosestrife's** casually elegant wands mix beautifully with the shorter stems of light blue belladonna dephiniums or summer phlox; monarda is another good companion. In hot summer areas, this lysimachia performs best in moist soil and light shade, because in full sun, without extra water, the leaves burn and stems shrivel and flop. In prolonged cool June weather, which doesn't occur very often here, I notice the plant has much more upright stems. There was too much shade in my shady garden, so I had to hand this plant on to another gardener. It's invasive if left to its own devices, even choking out weeds, so divide and replant every year or two away from choice neighbors, or grow it in a large pot with the bottom cut out, set into the ground.

Also needing moist soil and tolerating light shade (even needing it to give some length to the stems), but without the charming curtsey to the flower, *L. punctata* bears soft yellow spikes weeks earlier. **Circle flower,** or **yellow loosestrife,** is not so invasive here as *L. clethroides,* though it's a pest in some gardens. It's not a terribly popular plant, but those who have it like its leafy rusticity for cutting. It is perfect with white feverfew. On a hot day, circle flower may drop its petals after cutting, but the buds still open and the stems last for days. You'll probably need to stake this one lightly too—a peony hoop might do it.

LYTHRUM

The long graceful stems of lythrum make lively accents for short-lived arrangements, but the plants are now considered noxious weeds over much of the United States, because wetlands in extensive areas of the North have become naturalized with **purple loosestrife** to the detriment of native flora. A movement has been under way for some time to end the use of lythrum in gardens and its sale by nurseries. While it's true the species are the offenders, and the named cultivars are sterile, the cultivars apparently can still pollinate the species if it

is nearby. I no longer have lythrum in my garden (and in conse-
quence no Japanese beetles), and as the petals drop too quickly in the
vase anyway, it's little loss to the cutting garden.

MALOPE TRIFIDA

You find the bushy annual *Malope trifida* mentioned in few books and
seed catalogs, yet on occasion it grows quite well here in light shade.
Mixed color packets produce mallow-like short trumpets in white and
a veined dark rose, pretty together on cut stems about 18 inches long.
Much of the luxuriant foliage must be removed after picking. Sow
in a short row of five or six plants as soon as the soil is workable in
spring, perhaps two weeks before your average last frost date, for
bloom in late June. Cutting the flowers seems to have a deleterious
effect on the plants, which become short-lived afterward; so to make
the most of my malope, I wait until they're fully in flower, then pick
in earnest over the next few weeks. They like cool weather, so by
midsummer here the plants are rangy and ready to be pulled up.

MALVA

The pink mallow flowers of *Malva alcea* 'Fastigiata' fade slightly after cutting, but as the buds continue to open in water, the stems may
even look better a day later. The white *M. moschata* 'Alba' is quite
similar. Cut when they first bloom, as their brown seedpods will develop among the new flowers. My plants situated in light shade live
the longest, and their color bleaches less, but **hollyhock mallow**
blooms amply in sun to medium shade, and even in rather dry soil.
It self-sows occasionally, a good thing, as it appears to be short lived.
One mature plant should supply enough material.

I hesitate to mention hollyhock-like *M. sylvestris* 'Zebrina', sometimes called *Althea* 'Zebrina', **tree mallow,** as it has proved a pest in
my garden through seeding too freely. It bears pretty leaves and
flowers of shell pink veined with a dark raspberry color thickly clothing the stems, charming to arrange with dianthus, nigella, balloon
flower, veronica, feverfew, and other sweet flowers, and even the
not-so-darling globe thistle. Everyone who sees it for the first time
will ask about it. A very hardy perennial often grown as an annual,
the first flowers appear in less than 60 days from a spring sowing,
and the plants reach three to four feet and bloom over a long season
where the weather is cool. In hot summer areas, Zebrinas sown in
midsummer are larger and more robust, with more stems of longer

length, blooming the following year in mid-May. You might locate them in light shade, as the flowers look pinched in full sun when the weather is dry. Allow the stems to lengthen nicely before cutting, and trim off any small brown seedpods along with the lower leaves. The buds—in fact, all malva buds—continue to open in water. Although a nuisance, 'Zebrina' is nothing like as free with her offspring as the following plant.

M. sylvestris mauritiana (or *M. s.* 'Mauritiana') matures to gigantic size, a huge cottage garden plant only suitable for the largest and wildest of cutting gardens. The large purple flowers are veined a darker purple, gorgeous against the green foliage, and bloom before the hollyhocks. Only seven or eight stems are needed for a massed arrangement. Grow just two or three of the hollyhock-like plants (the malvas have the virtue of not requiring burning of the stem ends), confine them to a corner, and prevent the setting of much seed, as it's impossible to hoe away the hundreds of tap-rooting progeny. In spite of this, some folks have happily carried away whole branches laden with seed from my plot to infest their own gardens. Certainly, don't do as I did and compost the monster without ensuring the pile is hot enough to kill seed, and then carefully distribute the menace all over the garden, particularly to those plants you most wish to coddle. I've sown this malva in the fall; perhaps smaller plants might be had by sowing in spring. It's a short-lived perennial and is very hardy.

MATTHIOLA INCANA

The fragrant seven-week 'Trysomic' **stock** *(Matthiola incana),* which I found from Shepherd's Garden Seeds, is the only reliable strain for my garden, but it is not what I had in mind when I began with stocks. I wanted the long-stemmed spires in heavenly shades of pink, rose, blue, purple, yellow, and white, so for years I tried tall annual column and mammoth stocks, and the biennial Brompton stocks. All were a disappointment, flowering too often beginning when the plants were only five or six inches tall, only once reaching 18 inches. Even the 10-week types performed poorly for me. But the sweetly fragrant seven-week 'Trysomic' stock flowers heavily in an array of colors, with many 15-inch stems per plant, and is not bothered by early heat. Shepherd's especially recommends it for areas with cold winters turning soon to hot weather. Begun in early March under lights, the plants flower in late spring and continue blooming through

June in full sun, and all summer into fall in part shade. I can make a big bunch of them in a low widemouthed vase, or use them in smaller mixed bouquets. This past year they've been pretty with sweet peas, stokesia, *Erigeron* 'Pink Jewel', and *Clematis integrifolia*, among others.

All stocks are amazingly easy to germinate and grow swimmingly in cell packs. Both seven-week and 10-week stocks may be sown outdoors in spring for summer flowers where temperatures are mild, with a second sowing for late summer flowers. Further north, I understand, most stocks will still reach only two feet in height, not florist lengths. The seed instructions advise examining your seedlings for the leaf notch, light green color, and greater vigor that indicate the plant will bear double flowers, suggesting that the others be discarded. But these clues may only be evident at cooler temperatures of around 50 degrees. I do usually select for doubles, but I get some singles anyway, and I really rather like the doubles and singles together in the vase. They look like two different types of flower, with the single resembling a phlox. Avoid both high and low temperatures for your stocks—almost all are much affected by temperature and general garden conditions. I wonder if there are many gardens they grow well in.

MERTENSIA VIRGINICA

In late March and early April, the pink buds of **Virginia bluebells** open to blue, and shown off by its pretty green leaves, it's one of the loveliest early flowers on longer stems (cut to 17 inches eventually) in spring. The blue color furnishes a valuable contrast to the season's preponderance of white and yellow. *Mertensia virginica* is another of the best of American wildflowers, perfectly accompanied by green *Euphorbia robbiae* and some of the daintier daffodils like 'Beryl', 'Jenny', or 'Minnow' (keep fresh-cut daffodils in a jar of water for a few hours at first, to drain off some of the latex that might harm the bluebells), or by *Primula veris* and *Uvularia grandiflora*, the giant merrybell. Remove a good bit of the foliage after cutting, and place them in deep water and a cool dark spot overnight to prevent wilting. The blue petals begin to drop, but the flowers last several days, especially when cut very early. The flowers attempt to turn to the light, and the stems even continue to lengthen, so rotate the vase occasionally.

The plants go dormant and disappear in summer but aren't missed where they grow with ferns and hostas in the medium shade of deciduous trees. Begin with three plants for the shady cutting garden or spring border, and you may discover for yourself that Virginia bluebells self-sow modestly where they are happy.

You might also like the similar pink buds and blue flowers of *Pulmonaria saccharata* 'Roy Davidson' (or others of the taller cultivars of **lungwort**), which has pretty spotted leaves that do not disappear in summer and make a great addition to the shady moist border. It has a much longer bloom season than Virginia bluebells. The cut stems are about six inches in late March, and later almost 10 inches.

MOLUCELLA LAEVIS

You may like to use *Molucella laevis*, or **bells of Ireland,** as a cool green mass in a handsome vase, or as a long-lasting filler with just about any flower from the garden. The long stems twist and turn to the light, appearing almost alive, and for that reason seem so fresh. The green flowers (bracts, really, the flower is small and white) are evident early while the plants are short, but you can delay picking until you get a good length of stem. You'll probably decide to cut off the green leaves that protrude up the flower spike, rather in the way of hollyhocks; I like the way some people leave a charming little tuft of leaves at the tip.

Molucella prefers cool weather and tolerates light shade. Under good garden conditions, the plants grow tall and bushy and flower long through summer into fall (and seed themselves), but since they won't produce a good length of stem in our warm weather, I've left off trying. But just half an hour out of the city, where temperatures are probably cooler at night, my friend Elaine F. grows plants in full sun for cutting with pretty stems of about 12 inches. While they're shorter than the florist's, they're popular with her customers nonetheless. The seed must be sown direct in early spring, in a moist soil, as the taprooting plants are nearly hopeless to begin under lights and dislike transplanting. Light and cool temperatures are required for germination, which may be slow. Do not fertilize.

MONARDA

Monarda didyma's unusual flower shape makes **bee balm** a valuable element of mixed arrangements; not a mere filler, yet not stealing the show, either. You'll frequently see this perennial wildflower in herb gardens, where hummingbirds may visit its whorls of tiny tubular

flowers. White and pinks like 'Croftway Pink' or 'Granite Pink'
(I never see that name any more, and I loved it) combine obligingly
with other pastels in June and July and are easier to work with than
the over-strong red color of the original species. There are a great
many cultivars to choose from, and interesting dark purples and
wine reds that are less easy to use in mixed bouquets, but that make
a singular display accompanied by snow-on-the-mountain, hosta
leaves, or the green buds of sedum. The similar lavender species
M. fistulosa is more tolerant of dry soil, but it's weedier and not the
first choice for cutting.

You can grow monarda in full sun with adequate water and
a moisture-retentive soil, but light shade is ideal. The foliage is likely
to show mildew in late August, but cutting will have ended long before then. (Mildew-resistant cultivars are offered in some nursery
catalogs.) One plant grows to a large clump, and occasional division
is necessary to prevent weediness and poor flowering.

'Lambada' monarda (*M. citriodora* or *M. hybrida* in catalogs) appeared just recently from Dutch hybridizers and was the plant I most
enjoyed the summer I first grew it. Whorls of lavender-pink bee
balm flowers rise above green bracts, the bracts flushing handsomely
with the same rosy color as they mature, the whorls spaced along the
stem in three or four wedding cake tiers beautifully green toward the
stem tip. The plants were described as growing to three and a half
feet, but mine reached only two, and the stems were not as strong as
I would have liked. Nevertheless, my 16-inch cut stems were exquisite. They use a great deal of water in the vase. You can start these
annuals under lights six to eight weeks before your frost date, for
bloom over a long period through summer.

MUSCARI

The delightful six- or seven-inch blue spikes of **grape hyacinths** such
as *Muscari armeniacum* are important for small spring bouquets with
glory-of-the-snow, primula, pansies, and the tiniest of daffodils.
'Blue Spike' is especially large. Another grape hyacinth flowering in
early April here is the surprisingly tall *M. latifolium,* in two shades of
blue. It reaches 12 inches, with cut stems over eight inches at first
bloom. Interesting seed pods follow. *M. botryoides* var. *album* and
M. azureum 'Album' produce useful slim spikes crowded with little
white pearls. Most grape hyacinths are relatively cheap; plant at least

24 at a time, in sun or light shade. If you like such tiny flowers for early picking, *Chionodoxa luciliae,* or **glory-of-the-snow,** is a cheering patch of bright blue where it thrives under our deciduous trees, with picked stems up to seven inches long. The bloom season fills three weeks in March when flowers are so appreciated. Another little flower for the tiniest posies, *Scilla siberica* ranks with the above for its intense blue. **Siberian squill** is an inexpensive bulb that is valuable for taking quite a bit of shade. Each bulb produces several stems, the clumps increasing, with cut stems about six inches long.

MYOSOTIS SYLVATICA

You won't want to miss *Myosotis sylvatica's* sweet little **forget-me-nots** in white, blue, rose, or pink, with a charming eye, for small spring arrangements. They're popular cut flowers in Europe. The biennial plants self-sow reliably even in the cracks in pavement. They are perfect for the shady garden but also enjoy full spring sunshine. The small leaves give the plant its botanical name, *Myosotis,* meaning mouse ear, says Roy Genders in *The Cottage Garden and the Old-Fashioned Flowers,* a book I can't recommend too highly for enjoyable reading, especially if you like the English poets with botanical history. Look for the tall varieties in seed packets, advertised at 12 inches. A neighbor gave me starter plants that were babies from plants she'd sown previously. Sow in spring or midsummer for bloom the next year; fall is a good time to move volunteers if they haven't chosen the right spot. Self-sown plants, which frequently end up on unimproved soil or leftover spots, are often tiny compared to plants you've installed yourself in good soil. My fall-planted and self-sown plants flower the first week of April, at the same time as the primroses, with cut stems at first about seven inches long and lengthening rapidly to 12 inches as the weeks progress. In fact, the stems lengthen even in the vase. After a few years, they may disappear and you'll need to sow a new packet. Another forget-me-not to consider is *Cynoglossum amabile,* and both are much better choices for forget-me-nots than *Brunnera macrophylla,* a charming flower in the garden but decaying horribly in water.

Forget-me-nots are beloved for picking wherever they grow. An exhibit designer once described to me how he used a single big picture of blue forget-me-nots as the last image for an American slide-show exhibit traveling in the Soviet Union during the cold war. The flower has the same common name in Russian as in English, and the picture sent a pleased stir through the audience as they took in its meaning.

NARCISSUS

Almost everyone already has some *Narcissus*. A game of ours in spring when my children were young was to scan the neighborhoods as we drove, looking for a house without a **daffodil**. After three or four months of the dark and cold of winter, these wonderful flowers begin to show and are important cut flowers for five or six weeks when so little else is in bloom.

There are hundreds of daffodils to choose among. You could use a mixture as the base of your collection, and add others of your choice to complete it, if the joy of selecting each individually isn't appealing. Mixes of daffodils work well for cutting in a way that mixes of tulips very well may not; however, there's always the danger of getting too many of only a few varieties in a mixture, so order mixtures only from the most reputable suppliers. Because I adore daffodils, I rarely buy more than a few of any one kind, to leave room to acquire more, though this is against the prevailing wisdom of large groupings of single cultivars. This sometimes requires splitting an order of 10 bulbs with friends.

It's a good idea to plan a long cutting season by paying attention to bloom time notes in the catalogs. A range of bloom dates gives you a chance to still have flowers if poor weather spoils things at some point. 'Rijnveld's Early Sensation' is a King Alfred type that blooms so early (sometimes in January) that other daffodils are scarcely showing their leaves. This is an old variety, so you don't have to despair that modern hybridization has perverted the natural life of the daffodil. 'February Gold' is a well-known choice for early flowers, and little golden 'Sun Disc' for very late.

Collect a variety of daffodil shapes as well as colors for cutting. (I like to have a fair amount of white.) You might first choose a trumpet such as 'Arctic Gold', and add large cups such as 'Ice Follies' (but only one or two of this vigorous bulb), 'Ceylon', and 'Carlton', all robust perennializers. Among small cups, a favorite category of mine, 'Birma' has a refined look, and fine old varieties like 'Barrii Conspicuus' and 'White Lady', with the kind of flowers pixies might dance with, are modestly elegant and minus the almost martial air of the tulip that some of the big daffs have. Bunch-flowering daffodils like

'Geranium' or superb 'Avalanche' will contrast nicely with the others. Too many people do not stop to see the graceful beauty of the dogwood-like white poet's daffodils, such as 'Actaea' and the wild-looking 'Pheasant's Eye', *N. poeticus* var. *recurvus*. The simple elegance of 'Pheasant's Eye', its red-rimmed green center, and late bloom time make it excellent company for large arrangements of tulips with greenery such as Solomon's seal and *Euphorbia robbiae*.

The fragrant multiflowering doubles (more than one doubled flower per stem) are some of the most charming of daffodils, looking like clusters of small white or pale yellow roses. Somewhat short 'Erlicheer' appears early when the hellebores are ripe for picking, though three or four stems might be plenty, as the fragrance of too much 'Erlicheer' can be overpowering in the house. These look best with greenery and flowers like *E. robbiae*, and *Helleborus orientalis* and *H. foetidus*, both together, and less good massed alone in the vase.

It's exciting to have a few daffodils different from the very familiar. The diminutive, very early 'Rip Van Winkle', a shaggy yellow-and-green starburst, charms me every year in a tiny vase with large hybrid crocus. Little 'Beryl' looks quite unlike any other, both in its pale straw color and sleek petals swept back from a miniature cup. The amazingly weatherproof 'Pipit' has the showy look of the reverse bicolors that makes a brilliant display in a vase. Pink daffodils like 'Accent' and 'Pink Charm' have become enormously popular.

Some of the most beautiful of the narcissi are the smaller-flowered cultivars. Unusually large daffodils are better used by themselves in the vase ("large" in catalog descriptions is your lookout), but most of the repulsive giant daffodils are only suited to viewing, as they say, at 65 MPH. Midsize daffodils on shorter stems like 'Jenny' or 'Topolino' are good for massing on the breakfast table and still being able to see over them; 'Trevithian' and extremely fragrant 'Suzy' are delicate golden **jonquils** (a class of daffodils). Along with the littlest daffodils, they produce bewitching mixed arrangements of a lovely smaller scale than the standard varieties.

Other important narcissus for arranging are the miniatures, such as 'Minnow', 'Hawera', 'Segovia', 'Sun Disc', and the delightfully old-fashioned 'W. P. Milner', a quaint dwarf with petals pulled forward toward the trumpet. 'Jumblie' has its petals jauntily swept back for a completely different effect. Among the useful species daffodils are the very early small trumpet *N. obvallaris* (the Tenby daffodil), powerfully fragrant and late *N. jonquilla* (also called 'Simplex', with

foliage unfortunately resembling onion grass to spouses), and the last
to bloom, *N.* × *biflorus*. Some have stems as long as 15 inches in light
shade, longer than suggested in catalogs, so don't assume they're too
short to be of use. These species and daintier daffodils, especially
the later-flowering sorts, are splendid for arranging with shorter-
stemmed spring flowers: primula, lily-of-the-valley, small dicentras,
euphorbia, pansies, muscari, spring phlox, forget-me-nots, *Anemone
coronaria,* and *Helleborus foetidus.* The larger daffodils overwhelm
these flowers.

Since they don't need much attention, daffodils are good candidates for an out-of-the-way part of your property. I keep mine out
of the main cutting garden to keep them from being watered in
summer. You can also plant dry-soil annuals such as calliopsis, sunflowers, or tithonia over them, but keep the shovel away. Fertilize
them yearly in the fall. Rodents do not bother daffodils.

Plenty of water in spring helps the bulbs produce the longest
stems and the biggest flowers, as does improving the soil well before
you plant, not just making holes with one of those soil corers. Top-
size daffodils are among the most difficult bulbs to plant, because
they're so large they often won't fit into the hole made by a bulb
planter. "Landscape-size" bulbs, if you can find them, are much
easier to plant and will still flower the first year. Don't be surprised if
your Dutch-grown bulbs have smaller flowers in their second year:
that's the normal course of events when the Dutch are not around,
and the flowers may look the better for it. So many modern daffodils
are lacking in modesty.

If you wish, mulch your daffodil beds in fall to prevent dirt
splashing the flowers in spring, though they often can be rinsed successfully. Bad weather now and then causes stems to bend over or
break. These can be brought inside, but if they're only leaning, they
may right themselves when the weather improves. You can pick the
flowers in bud once the color is showing. It's easier to pick stems
rather than cut; just reach low into the foliage and snap the stem to
the side. After having had a few virused bulbs, I imagine I might
also avoid spreading daffodil virus on my pruners that way.

Some say to sear cut stems in boiling water to stop the latex from
emerging and to make the flowers last longer; I never do. You can
also stand the flowers in a jar of water for several hours to get rid of
the latex. If you don't mix daffodils with other flowers, neither is
necessary. Cut the stems to different lengths for a looser look. Daf-

fodils and their stems look good in glass vases; put those that tend to face down in a narrow straight-sided vase to hold up their faces better.

I never had so much fun acquiring bulbs as at the fall meetings of the Washington Daffodil Society. There is usually a huge array of interesting varieties, small numbers of bulbs each, some in one-dollar bags and others simply free for the choosing. I got many of my favorite daffodils this way. Hunt up your local group. Daffodil societies all across the United States have wonderful shows each spring, so you can make note of your favorites and possibly even order them through the society. It's amazing to see the crowds at these shows. The daffodil must be the common man's favorite flower.

NECTAROSCORDUM SICULUM

Nectaroscordum siculum is the new botanical name recently given to the fascinating *Allium siculum.* The bulbs may be somewhat expensive, but each cluster of hanging bells (in sillier moments, my children liked to yell "Wake up!" at them) is large enough for two or three of other bulbs. As few as five of these extremely long sturdy stems (one per bulb) will disport splendidly in a tall vase in late spring and need no company, though they're handsome with tall iris (the older iris with smaller flowers) in large formal mixed arrangements with baptisia, Egyptian onion, and wild parsnip. They're sublime too with pale pink peonies and Shirley poppies, even other alliums. Cutting a long stem (as long as 36 inches) will afford a view of the reddish color inside the green bells. The stems sometimes lean over and may need staking if you want assuredly straight stems, but the ones that grow in twists and turns are perfect for interest in arrangements. The flowers are remarkably long lasting in water and develop so slowly in the garden that you have two weeks in which to cut. The foliage generally disappears by mid-June. My bulbs didn't mind the imperfect drainage that did in the nearby tulips and lilies and came back for some years, but they disappeared after one unusually cold winter.

NEPETA

Nepeta fassenii 'Six Hills Giant' is the biggest of the perennial **catmints,** with gray, aromatic foliage and subtle spikes of small lavender blue flowers in late spring and early summer. It works best as a filler, one that turns strongly to the light. This nepeta grows into a large, handsome plant under good conditions (keep it in the border), but it doesn't perform well in heat and humidity. Cut it back midsummer and it may rebloom nicely.

NERINE

Spring-planted tender bulbs in most of the United States, **nerines** bloom in autumn in shades of rose red, bright pink, and white, with a flower shape similar to a small magic lily, *Lycoris squamigera.* The flowers are very long lasting. *Nerine bowdenii* is most commonly sold, along with *N. sarniensis,* the **Guernsey lily.** The last is not cheap. In Zones 8 or 9 through 10, they can remain in the ground all year, and they may appreciate shade where it's very hot. Further north, the bulbs must be planted soon after the last frost date, as they require a long growing season. A protected location is usually suggested as a way of ensuring warm soil, and starting them early in pots is also possible. If not planted early enough, they may scarcely flower before, and risk the frosts of, mid-November. For all these reasons, northern gardeners may find them difficult.

NICOTIANA

Luckily, we have annual **flowering tobacco** to take our summer heat. *Nicotiana alata* 'Lime Green' produces green flowers for mixed bouquets even better in the vase than the garden. It's not an acidic yellow green, as are lady's mantle, patrinia, and some euphorbias, but a splendid cool lime color, especially pretty with white and pastel colors, and lovely with astilbe, eustoma, scabiosa, cosmos, even summer phlox. 'Lime Green' sometimes appeared in early June in my shady ornamental garden along with the useful pink and white nicotianas, as it had been reseeding for years, even in the brick paving. When there are fewer volunteers than before (and you may feel the self-sown plants don't appear early enough), you can hope to pick some up at the garden center to renew the process. While 'Lime Green' and its companion colors are 30-inch tall plants, be on the lookout, as garden center sorts are sometimes dwarfs, and frequently you must sow seed because there are no tall plants to be had. All will grow luxuriantly in large pots or tubs.

You can add the charming green bells of *N. langsdorfii* to bouquets, though I wish the stems were sturdier. It's also grown in light shade from seed, blooming long into fall, and reseeding in an endearing way. From curiosity I gave the little flared green trumpets of *N. rustica* a go. **Aztec tobacco,** as it's called, is easy to grow from seed in full sun and makes an intriguing, though rather coarse, filler flower for an arrangement with a tropical feel; put it with warm colors like yarrow, zinnias, and red peppers. Try only one or two of the big plants to experiment with at first. The flowers and young leaves group in awkward clumps at the stem ends; perhaps a little shade would loosen up the flowers. Pull off any petals that have passed their prime. It's cuttable only early on and lasts just two days; the related pink 'Sherazi' was no use at all, at least not in full sun. I was once surprised to see the huge white *N. sylvestris* in a cutting garden, but there is no harm trying it. The stems and foliage of the nicotianas are sticky and sometimes require rinsing away adhering dirt and tiny bugs.

NIGELLA DAMASCENA

Love-in-a-mist's feathery foliage and curious double and single flowers in shades of blue, pink, and white are easily grown and not to be missed. The popular blue *Nigella damascena* 'Miss Jekyll' and the white 'Miss Jekyll Alba' produce stiff cut stems as long as 18 inches, and stems of 'Oxford Blue' are even longer. The subtle flowers, especially the blue, seem lost unless they're bunched in groups within a mixed arrangement; the white shows up much the best. Some flattering companions are campanula, dianthus, delphinium, and green flowers such as bupleurum or alchemilla, and it's sublime to sow a great deal of nigella and use it alone as a feathery cloud in the same way that *Gypsophila elegans* looks so terrific. But the needle-leaved foliage can make a mixed arrangement look like a woman who hasn't tidied her hair unless some broader green leaves are included, such as sedum, tellima, lady's mantle, or the seedpods of lunaria.

Cut nigella when it first blooms, as it's tedious to deadhead and the new stems become increasingly shorter with smaller flowers. Many people think the interesting round green seedpods are more valuable than the flowers for June arranging, so you may choose not to deadhead. The pods rapidly change color as they grow larger, developing handsome maroon stripes until they're entirely that color, exciting in a crock with the bright golden yellow of yarrow.

In my garden it's best to sow this extremely hardy annual in place in September for bloom the next year in mid to late May. The seedlings come up reliably, even in warm weather, and are vastly superior to spring-sown plants. It's no use at all to sow nigella under lights, as it can't be transplanted. In cooler areas, spring sowing is more successful, and successive sowings will produce flowers over a longer period. It will self-sow and tolerates light shade but doesn't require it.

ORNITHOGALUM

Apparently known to some florists as **chincherinchee** (but I've only drawn quizzical looks when I've pronounced that name), *Ornithogalum thyrsoides* is a spring-planted bulb in most of the United States, as it's hardy only in Zones 8 to 10. It has pretty white flowers on stems about 12 to 18 inches in early summer. It is not reputed to be difficult, though it hasn't grown for me, and as it's a native of South Africa, eastern gardeners can't expect it to be easy. The flowers last forever in water. *O. arabicum* is another florist flower, called **Arabian star of Bethlehem**, spring-planted north of Zone 7 and flowering in summer, but disliking heat. It's also a long-lasting white flower with a distinctive black ovary. Most other species can't be recommended, as they appear to be invasive. I have one kind I'm trying to get rid of that came over from my neighbor's garden, where it has also shown its cloven hoof. Whatever you do, do not plant *O. umbellatum*, the **star** of Bethlehem.

PAEONIA

Substantial flowers for late spring, the princely **peonies** are herbaceous plants worth their space in even the smallest cutting garden. The huge blooms, six inches or more across, make a handsome dinner table display by themselves and require little arranging on their strong stems. The range of gorgeous colors from pure whites, shell pinks, through rose and red, even intriguing shades of coral, should suit anybody, and you may choose between single, anemone or "Japanese," semidouble, and fully doubled flowers. The singles and anemones display a prominent central "mound," or "boss," of stamens or petaloids, some quite enormous, and one of the most attractive features of peonies. Most cut flower gardeners will want to have both singles and doubles and will find they combine beautifully with poppies, irises, large alliums like *A. aflatunense* and the allium-like *Nectaroscordum siculum,* and other showy flowers. Some cultivars are so exquisitely scented, like roses, that I stop to breathe deeply every time I pass by (many of the best-scented varieties are older). An ex-

cellent substitute for roses for gardeners who want sumptuous flowers but prefer a low maintenance plant, no cutting garden should be
without one of these extremely hardy (to Zone 2), long-lived plants.

Popular for decades, 'Festiva Maxima' is a long-lasting early white
double, flecked with red. Pink 'Mrs. Franklin D. Roosevelt', 'Mon-
sieur Jules Elie', and 'Raspberry Sundae' and red 'Karl Rosenfield' and
'Felix Supreme' are excellent doubles that should last well in water.
Handsome examples of the "Japanese," or anemone, forms are 'Bowl
of Beauty' or 'Sonata' and, among singles, 'Krinkled White'. (I have
a similar older variety like 'Krinkled White', 'Jan van Leeuwen'.)

Since the stamens show their age days before the petals, most
double flowers appear to last longer than most singles. I usually cut
12-inch stems in order to leave foliage behind on every stem I cut
from, and because such a large flower is usually placed low in
a mixed bouquet. If you take very long stems, take only a few from
each plant. Buds cut when showing color should open in the vase.

Single-flowered peonies are less likely to need staking than
doubles, but even many doubles won't require it if you select a variety
with strong stems. Usually you'll have already cut your flowers before
they become heavy and go over. To be certain of a peony that blooms
well in hot summer areas (as the flowers age rapidly with high temperatures and may not even open), read catalogs carefully to select
a single or anemone variety that blooms early.

Once I was one of those for whom peonies didn't bloom. Replanting a little higher did seem to help; the "eyes" should be quite
near the surface. A little patience may also be required, as small
mail-ordered plants may not bloom as well as you'd like until the
third year. Buying a potted peony at a local nursery may get you
a larger plant with the eyes already set at the correct level. Since the
foliage of peonies is handsome, and even shrubby, they are superb
located in the border for occasional cutting. Plant in the fall preferably and don't crowd. One plant of any cultivar should grow to
a good clump, but few cut-flower gardeners will be able to stop at
one peony.

If your garden has too much shade for herbaceous peonies, you
may be tempted by the **tree peony,** which dislikes full sun and also
grows further south than herbaceous peonies. The big flowers are
not at all as long lasting in water, but you may like to "float" them
face up in a shallow dish for a day or two.

PAPAVER

Few flowers say so clearly that they've come straight from a garden than **poppies**. I've rarely seen them at a florist's shop. When you have poppies in your garden, people mention Monet and think you must be a master. When friends at our community garden told me a woman had been coming mornings to paint my garden, I was deeply honored, but I knew it was the poppies that brought her.

The **Shirley poppy** or **corn poppy**, *Papaver rhoeas,* is a heat-sensitive hardy annual, its prolific bloom not beginning here until June for spring-sown seed. I prefer to sow in fall to have much larger plants and more flowers by mid-May, before the heat, but in mild-summer areas they may be sown in spring (and even again later) for bloom long into summer. The single and occasionally double flowers come in a range of white, pinks, reds, and salmon, ideal for people partial to pink. They arrange themselves easily and are exceptional even with the shortest of stems. Like hollyhocks, Shirley poppies are a good choice for the front of the cutting garden to disguise any barrenness behind.

These are glorious flowers as much as four inches across, so re-markable that visitors coming into the house often don't believe they are real. Celia Thaxter, who wrote *An Island Garden,* an ethereal account of her cutting garden on Appledore Island, Maine, over a century ago, kept a room in summer filled with vases of flowers on every table and bookcase. She displayed masses of her Shirley pop-pies in over thirty glasses on a long bookcase, beginning at one end with white and proceeding through blush, shell pink, "damask rose, and tender pink," through rich pink, cherry, and crimson to close with darkest red and maroon. She says, and we can believe her, "I have seen people stand before it mute with delight." This master hand sowed a full two ounces of poppy seed each summer, about 20 dollars of seed in today's prices for bulk seed, or looking at it another way, about 5,000 packets.

Shirley poppies are not supposed to include red (though the pack-ets always do), but I like red along with the pink shades; it pleases all the more because it's unexpected, with the hand of man not quite so evident. If you need red especially, try its easy relative *P. commuta-tum,* with the central black blotch. It blooms about two weeks before the Shirleys and self-sows heavily; sow it in fall too. Occasionally one sees offered a packet of all-red *P. rhoeas,* which is the **Flanders**

poppy, sometimes called the 'Legion of Honor' poppy. 'Mother of Pearl', or 'Fairy Wings', is another lovely selection in remarkably subtle shades that is handsome with the Shirleys, but the flowers seem more fragile. Packets of seed for double flowers are available, but it's my experience the doubles don't last as long when cut.

Shirleys, and all *P. rhoeas* selections, must be sown direct in a well-dug soil. Do not cover the seed. Sow a good number, as you don't want just a couple of these plants. Broadcast seed in early October (or when it's cool, about 55 degrees) over an area three or four feet square, and you can harvest as many as 30 stems at one time from a patch that size. In late fall, thin the seedlings to several inches apart, and again in late winter or early spring to 10 or 12 inches apart. It's a serious mistake to crowd them, as the best plants are spaced well. In accommodating weather, a well-grown plant can put out as many as 15 stems, some as thick as my pencil, each with many buds on shorter stems, the entire plant up to 32 inches tall.

The drooping buds are a surprise the first time you see them. For the longest-lasting flowers, cut the buds that are becoming upright. They should open indoors the next day, when they will "surely pop," jokes my neighbor, Barbara L. The stem lengths vary from 9 to 12 inches; you can cut longer stems if you don't mind sacrificing buds, but they delight me with even the shortest stems. Unopened buds add to the beauty of arrangements; you can cut a few seedheads too, for interest. The stem ends must be charred promptly to prevent wilting; you can do five or six at a time, while standing at a gas stove. Afterward set the vase on a surface that is easily wiped up, because within a day or two they begin dropping pollen and petals. The flowers aren't long lasting—three days is tops—but they're tremendously rewarding; it's a deep pleasure to wake the next day and find the buds opened to the most magnificent flowers, the papery bud skins lying on the table. If you've given a jam jar of poppies in bud to a friend, you know the joy they'll feel at breakfast. Ruth D. says it's like Christmas in the morning when she was a child.

Shirley poppies self-sow, and young plants appear in fall and should winter over, an advantage where the dreaded hot weather comes early. When the plants decline in vigor, often by mid-June here, weed the patch well and allow them to go to seed. Don't pick every last flower, or you'll have no seed, and don't shake the seed-set stems over a very small area, or you'll have a nightmare of thinning to do. Shirleys are a particularly good choice to have coming up in odd spots and between other plants in climates where poppies are fleeting. Notice the astonishing "salt-shaker" seedpod that releases seed through little holes near the top.

The beautiful **Iceland poppies,** *P. nudicaule,* may be bigger than the Shirleys and perhaps longer lasting by a day or two, but they are less easy to grow and not so prolific. The huge luminescent flowers are five inches across, with magnificent crinkled petals in yellow, orange, salmon, pink, and ivory, on strong stems as long as 21 inches. They have the best stems for cutting of all the poppies, with the warm colors that make you love nasturtiums. I've seen the oranges provide spots of shocking color to otherwise staid arrangements of pink and white garden flowers, and all the colors are glorious with the Shirley poppies, blooming together for several weeks.

In the North, Iceland poppies may live two or three years, but it's a gamble to grow them where it's hot early in the year. They begin flowering in April, two or three weeks before the Shirleys and oriental poppies *(P. orientale)* in May. Since the plants in my garden rarely put up more than two or three new flowers at a time, many plants would be needed for large bouquets of Iceland poppies; it's easier to use fewer plants for mixed arrangements. The stem ends must be seared. If you've forgotten to sear the stems and they've wilted, try recutting and then searing. The flowers do expire after three or four days, so when long-lasting arrangements are wanted, poppies should not be used.

Like Shirley poppies, in warm summer areas the seed for Iceland poppies needs to be sown in a September or October cool spell so they'll bloom early the following spring, because with the advent of hot weather, flower quality drops off drastically. (A little shade can help.) You can also begin the easy seed earlier in peat pots under lights and plant out carefully in October; *P. nudicaule* is the only one of these annual and biennial poppies that doesn't absolutely insist on direct sowing. Watch them closely when hardening off, as the peat pots dry out quickly outdoors. My plants usually survive until spring, even though the garden is occasionally saturated in winter. Those rare plants that survive the summer may flower again in fall.

Papaver somniferum is the annual well known as the **opium poppy.** There are singles in pink, purple, and white, but "peony-flowered" doubles (sometimes called *P. paeoniflorum*) are what is usually offered. The flower resembles an extremely double peony, or a wadded ball of Kleenex, which is how discriminating vegetable gardener

Lucy C. sees it. You may also see *P. laciniatum* (also a kind of *P. som-niferum*), with deeply frilled doubles in shades of pink, salmon, and white, which make an exciting contribution to mixed flowers in June with ammi, snapdragons, *Verbascum chaixii,* and short stems of del-phinium. You can cut the flowers just opened, sear them, and enjoy them for two or three days. However, my big *P. paeoniflorum* doubles too often are a disappointment and do not open at all, even in the garden. In the future, I am only going to sow the singles.

P. somniferum is not as floriferous as *P. rhoeas,* and the cut flowers don't last any longer; nor is it any more heat tolerant. There's good reason to think they're better used for their big green seedheads in mixed bouquets of June flowers, as is *P. s.* 'Hens and Chickens'. (You'll find the seedheads of *P. rhoeas* and *P. nudicaule* are mostly in-consequential for arranging.) Sown direct in September, they flower in latest May, about three weeks after fall-sown Shirleys. The plants can reach four feet tall and appreciate moisture and light shade when it's hot.

The exciting flowers of the perennial *P. orientale* are much larger than the annual and biennial poppies, but there may not be as many of them. Colors are red, orange, salmon, pink, and white, often with a black blotch in the center, and several catalogs offer seed, which is relatively easy to start under lights. If you choose an easy color, you may be able to use **oriental poppies** in mixed arrangements that don't need to be long lasting. The huge selection of named cultivars in mail-order catalogs makes it difficult to choose just one; after years of indecision, I was finally able to buy a red at the garden cen-ter because it was the only one they had. Plant in fall in the South and early spring in the North. The foliage disappears over summer but reappears in fall, so don't think it has died, though the oriental poppy may not live long where it's hot or humid, and may need light shade in the South. Sear the ends of this one, too.

PASTINACA SATIVA

A marvelous "weed" for arranging, the true **wild parsnip,** *Pastinaca sativa,* was given to me by my fellow gardener Bessie S., who has had it volunteering in her garden for years. It took several calls (and the purchase of a bag of parsnips) to get this large, obliging biennial identified, as few garden books cover such a plant. This is not *An-gelica archangelica,* which is sometimes called wild parsnip, but the

original parsnip—brought to this continent and escaped into the
wild—from which modern named varieties of the vegetable have
been selected. Its long, white root smells like carrot or parsnips, but
don't make dinner of it, as some authorities say it is poisonous. At
the end of May, wild parsnip has wonderful big heads of tiny greenish-yellow flowers (it will remind you of patrinia or fennel), followed
by seedheads in the same shade of green, which make a superb filler,
all on long stems from a plant four feet tall. Use it with everything
from iris, Canterbury bells, and liatris to sidalcea, penstemon, and
early dahlias. Railers against weeds—Edwin Rollin Spencer in his
All About Weeds refers to it as an "ugly, worthless, dangerous weed"—
claim it seeds mercilessly, but it hasn't done so for us. Apart from
waiting for a bird to drop the wildling by, you can try sowing cultivated parsnips in spring through midsummer for flowers the following year.

PATRINIA SCABIOSAEFOLIA

In just a few years, *Patrinia scabiosaefolia* has become immensely
popular for the flower border; for a while I gave new garden books
the Patrinia test to see whether they were up-to-date. It bears wonderful sprays of long-lasting yellow-green flowers quite like mustard
on long strong stems in July or August (the plant can reach six feet),
and afterward forms tiny green seedheads that are valuable as a green
filler. **Patrinia** is useful as a companion for many summer flowers,
like cleome and phlox, and bloom continues into fall, when it can be
put with dahlias or China asters. Despite its charm, patrinia sometimes has an unfortunate smell two or three days after cutting;
I rarely notice this odor in the garden. If it smells off, reserve it for
arrangements apart from where people are sitting. One plant flowers
generously and may self-seed profusely in a moist area.

PENSTEMON

As **penstemons** make remarkably pretty cut flowers, success with
them has taken some of the bite out of my trials with delphinium.
Most penstemons are short-lived perennials that bloom the first year
from seed, though not all are reliably hardy. Graham Rice in his
Hardy Perennials makes the valuable observation that the varieties
with bigger flowers and broader leaves are less likely to be hardy than
those with smaller flowers. Penstemons must have very good drainage and shouldn't be fertilized or overwatered; many do well in dry

soil in full sun. Mulch tender selections carefully. Put your seed in the refrigerator when you get it, as penstemon appreciates cold to help it break dormancy.

The long-stemmed, very hardy (Zone 2) *Penstemon barbatus* grows like a charm from seed, performing amply in the Southeast, and while not long lasting in water, the coral-red flowers are lovely in early summer with larkspur, or simply alone in a narrow vase. It may rebloom in August if the gardener is so blessed. For the longest life, cut the stems (as much as 30 inches long) shortly after the lower flowers open; stems cut after the whole length shows color may last only a day. The airy foliage and buds are exquisite; place the vase where you'll see it up close. In the garden, the long wiry stems arch about, but they haven't usually needed staking, as the twists and curves are most attractive. Younger plants stand up better than older, and the plants grow very large, to five feet tall in good soil in a raised bed.

'Cambridge' and 'Rondo' are two smaller *P. barbatus* seed strains that bloom their first year like annuals. These are sturdy little clumps with neat foliage like stocks, the flowers like small snapdragons. The lovely mixed colors cover a rich range of pink, plum, "blue," and lavender, though the color begins to fade a day or two after cutting. The flower spikes are lush and showy, heavy with blooms and tiny buds on stems cut about 15 to 20 inches long. They last about as long as the Shirley poppies with which they are so beautiful—three days. They're perfect for medium-sized arrangements with verbascums, hesperis, table iris, nigella, and columbine, all in bloom at the same time. These penstemons are easy to start under lights and bloom about three weeks earlier when they return the next year. Plant at least four to experience the color range. The popular 'Rose Elf' is also a member of the *P. barbatus* clan.

Modest *P. digitalis* makes a good mixer, the small clusters of pinkish-white foxglove-like flowers appealing with campanula and lady's mantle in spring. It forms a good-size clump, so you need only one plant. The stems are up to about 26 inches in length, quite straight, and carry rather coarse leaves that require some removal. Give it good winter drainage—which I did not—and it may live for years, even in the East. It's one of the few penstemons readily found from mail-order nurseries. Notice that some (like *P. d.* 'Husker Red') have dark stems and foliage that may make them challenging to use for mixed arranging.

A number of hybrids popular in Britain are scarcely hardy enough to last in much of the United States, but that doesn't stop us from indulging, at least at first. For large flowers, try what seed catalogs list as *P. gentianoides* and *P. × gloxinoides* hybrids—richly colored trumpets with white throats, some almost an inch and a half wide at their splendidly flared mouths. They bloom on strong stems the first year in June and July from an early start under lights—though they aren't terribly hardy, some barely to Zone 7. Just a couple of these rewarding stems make quite an impact in water, and it's less of a shock to lose plants grown from seed.

PETUNIA

While I dislike the large flowers on squat plants of the modern hybrid **petunias** *(Petunia × hybrida)*, the tall heirloom petunias with lightly fragrant smaller flowers, such as J. L. Hudson's vigorous 'Kentucky Old-fashioned', grow to three feet and bloom on sturdy 15-inch stems that stay good-looking in the vase for days. These older types offer a simple range of color, pinks and purples, and the essential pure white. The picturesque branching habit makes them sublimely easy to fix in a loose, romantic fashion, in the same way that stokesia is so easily arranged. Pretty with feverfew and Shasta daisies, or with veronica and wild parsnip, the stems trail delightfully over the edge of the container (a particularly good choice for pedestal vases), just as they do from a window box. If you start these half-hardy annuals early under lights, you can be cutting by late May, and they may bloom until frost, even in a little shade. Another prolific petunia with even smaller flowers in pink or white, *P. integrifolia* is perennial south of Zone 8 and worth the hunt. Find it from catalogs that like to offer tender perennials.

PHLOX

The great number of species and cultivars of *Phlox* allows you to enjoy these valuable flowers over a long season, beginning in midspring and continuing through summer. Highly scented *P. divaricata* blooms in early April here, producing a cloud of lavender blue or white that compliments most other spring flowers. Bunch several stems together to make a stronger presence in a larger mixed arrangement. **Woodland phlox** is the smell of spring, though some members of the household have found the perfume too strong in-

doors and have banished it to the bathroom. You can cut stems of
10 or 12 inches from plants growing in a lightly shaded ornamental
garden rather than the cutting garden. If happy, one plant will establish a large colony and will seed freely to other locations, though
I planted the white once and never saw it again. The related *P.* ×
chattahoochee, a fine lavender blue with a red eye, is desirable for cutting but won't stay around in my garden.

Lightly fragrant *P. pilosa,* or **downy phlox,** is a lavender-pink
flower with a lighter eye. It's quite like *P. divaricata* and blooms just
after it, but *P. pilosa* has larger flowers on longer stems to almost two
feet. It has the virtue of forming a large clump in moist light shade
or a dry sunny location. Rarely seen in nursery lists, it's pretty for
picking for several weeks, though it's a bit scruffy in the garden and
occasionally is overly vigorous. Use *P. pilosa* with purple hesperis and
white *Campanula glomerata.*

The pretty **annual phlox,** *P. drummondii,* lusciously colored, is
said to like warm areas, but I wonder about that. Sow direct in
spring for flowers all summer, or early under lights in parts of the
country with hot weather, to bloom in late spring. Avoid the many
dwarf strains, but even the 18-inch versions grow only to 12 inches
for me. Pick the stems early, and use them for a delicious display on
the dinner table if they're short. I've seen others with light shade
have much more success with these, though Celia Thaxter (who gar-
dened in Maine) says it's an excellent plant for beginners.

The charm of *P. paniculata* cultivars, **summer phlox,** lies in the
big heads of strong color in pinks, salmons, purples, and white, some
with contrasting centers, though the flowers are slightly smaller here
than they are where it's cooler. A bowlful of the pink 'Bright Eyes'
lacks nothing in the way of personality. Handsome lilac and purple
cultivars are 'Franz Schubert' and 'The King'. Superb bright pink
'Eva Cullum' has a darker eye and a powerful fragrance. Mix them
all if you like rich color. After three days or so, unfortunately, the
colors begin to fade and the petals begin to drop. Good companions
for phlox are *Lysimachia clethroides, Veronicastrum virginicum,* delphinium, gayfeather, and goldenrod while still green in bud. Pick
out faded florets when arranging. Variegated phlox is intriguing, but
I've never seen a vigorous plant.

While I love all the bright colors, the early-flowering white *P. ma-
culata* 'Miss Lingard' is one phlox I've been able to grow really successfully here. It's a superb cut flower from a plant that reliably

flowers twice. It might be preferable to grow Miss L. in light shade so as to get a longer stem and possibly a looser flower head, but full sun does as well. Two plants are needed to fill a large vase, but one mature plant supplies a good deal of material. The related 'Omega' is white with the fine detail of a light pink eye, and 'Rosalind' is a desirable pink. Unlike the paniculatas, they should all flower twice if deadheaded, they bloom early, and are particularly recommended for humid areas. Because bloom times vary, 'Miss Lingard' can be flowering in late May here while other summer phlox, like 'Eva Cullum', may not be in full flower until early July. Other excellent whites to follow after Miss L. are first 'David', an exceptional long-blooming, weather-proof garden plant at its prime in mid-July, and then 'Mt. Fuji'.

Some nurseries offer comments on mildew resistance, which may throw a bucket of cold water on your enthusiasm. I like to pounce on a bright phlox of a suitable height offered by a nursery that says it resists mildew, even when they admit they found it by the road. It's not unusual to have difficulty establishing a new phlox, particularly in the South, where even if you buy from a reputable nursery, you may not get a plant that will grow. It's likely the plant is diseased, and I would look for a different source to obtain phlox the next time you order, or get divisions from friends with healthy stands.

The usual advice for summer phlox is to thin the stems in the spring to five or six, as the plant supposedly cannot support more, and to prevent mildew. If you have lots of phlox, you can experiment with pinching back some stems to delay their bloom until later. Begin with one plant of any cultivar, and expect to divide every few years.

PHYSALIS

The reddish-orange, balloon-like husks of *Physalis alkekengi,* or **Chinese lantern,** last for weeks in autumn. It's one of the colorful decorative fruits, like the ornamental pepper *Capsicum annuum,* that are handsome when brought indoors. Physalis may also be cut while the fruits are still green for use fresh with other flowers, but most people are familiar with it as an everlasting. I was surprised to be offered "physalis" on my fruit plate at a Scottish bed and breakfast, a small orange fruit with the texture of a meaty tomato and not very sweet. Looking it up in Vaughan and Geissler's *New Oxford Book of Food Plants,* I found my treat to probably have been a Cape gooseberry,

P. peruviana, a relative of the tomatillo and not the fruit of a Chinese lantern.

Chinese lantern is a perennial usually grown as an annual, in moist soil in full sun or light shade, and it may be invasive in some gardens. Unaccountably, I can't grow this plant; neither sowing several times outdoors nor setting out a purchased plant would do it, though physalis is not supposed to be difficult and is even suggested for children's gardens. The plant I purchased at a garden center was bursting out of its plastic prison—had even broken the pot, it appeared—creeping through the holes at the bottom, and leafing outside the pot as well. I was afraid it was a taste of things to come. My friend Alice N. tells me of a gardener who had to move to get away from it.

PHYSOSTEGIA VIRGINIANA

The sturdy white or pink flower spikes of *Physostegia virginiana* make good companions for a number of flowers in July, monarda and the tall butterfly weed, *Asclepias incarnata*, among them. Arrangers can make use of both colors of **obedient plant,** as the white blooms in July some weeks before the pink in mid-August, each for a long period. (Some people say the variegated form with pink flowers is good for cutting, but I've only seen weak-looking stands, including my own.) The stems are stiff and strong, cut to about 22 inches in length when grown in full sun, but avoid the short cultivar 'Vivid'. Obedient plant usually needs tying around the middle, which should be done before the stems become bent and spoiled. It often needs light shade and moist soil where the climate is particularly hot; otherwise, the foliage browns and becomes unsightly. Since it can be invasive, divide regularly to prevent problems, or else grow it in the ground in a large, deep plastic nursery pot with the bottom cut out. This is one of those basic cutting plants that will easily give you dozens of stems for massed arrangements in wide containers, if your garden is big enough to contain it.

PLATYCODON GRANDIFLORUS

Platycodon grandiflorus, **balloon flower,** blooms for many weeks in summer and into fall with pretty blue bell flowers, like campanula, opening from fully colored balloonlike buds. The flowers are a good size at more than three inches across. You'll also find cultivars in pink or white as well as some doubles; be sure to choose long-

stemmed cultivars rather than dwarfs. The pinks are what I like, as
there is no pink among cultivars of *Campanula persicifolia,* the only
long-stemmed perennial campanula to do at all well in my garden.
Cut the stems after flowering has begun, and the curious swollen
buds should open in the vase to reveal their beautiful veining. If you
particularly like the enticing balloon stage, look for 'Komachi', as the
blue balloons do not open. Some people say to burn the stem ends,
which I do.

Platycodon appears surprisingly late in spring and the foliage disappears completely in autumn, so everything you read about marking and protecting the plant from careless digging or weeding is true.
I haven't cut many stems of balloon flower, because I've torn out my
plants so many times by mistake. The plants are simple to propagate
from seed and self-sow for some people even in a brick sidewalk.
Light shade is advisable in the South.

POLEMONIUM

Polemonium caeruleum and *P. foliosissimum* are splendid, very hardy
(to Zone 2) perennials for the shady cutting garden where summers
are cool. The lavender, pale blue, or white flowers grow on long
stems in late spring to summer. The plants do not persist well in the
East, and when I had one grow nicely, I couldn't bring myself to cut
it; gardeners in the West should have more regular success. When
I see these flowers, I'm reminded of the young hero's mother in Thomas Hardy's *A Pair of Blue Eyes,* who embarrasses herself by nat-
tering on and on about her garden. She apparently has just the right
conditions at her cottage in Cornwall and finds **Jacob's ladders** all
too easy to grow, complaining "I do not care for things that neglect
won't kill."

POLIANTHES TUBEROSA

You won't want many of the sweet-smelling white **tuberoses,** as their
scent is so strong. *Polianthes tuberosa* are bulbs planted in spring in
most of the country, as they may be left in the ground only as far
north as Zone 8, but not many of us find these popular and long-
lasting florist flowers easy to grow. Where they grow well (they need
a long season, but I've seen them growing beautifully as far north as
Connecticut), they may reach almost three feet in height, two stems
per bulb with single or double flowers, and bloom from midsummer
to early autumn. Give them good drainage.

POLYGONATUM

The long arching stems of **Solomon's seal** supply indispensable green filler for graceful bouquets of lunaria, hesperis, tall columbines, old-fashioned bleeding heart, tulips, camassias, and other plants from the shady spring garden. The white bells in late April add a subtle note, but the foliage continues to be useful long after the flowers are gone. I have three kinds of Solomon's seal. The largest, and earliest, with cut stems to 30 inches, is *Polygonatum odoratum* 'Variegatum', with beautiful green leaves striped with cream, sporting the dangling pairs of green-tipped ivory flowers common to Solomon's seal. My smaller plant, which matures a few days later, with cut stems to 25 inches, is likely *P. multiflorum,* or *P. × hybridum.* It has simple green leaves without variegation and more flowers hanging in clusters of four. Both the variegated and the green look good together in a large arrangement, but the latter is also useful for arrangements where the former would be too large. They're suitable for the wildflower garden, forming good clumps in considerable shade, useful for cutting through at least July and probably longer if they've had enough moisture to keep their leaves looking fresh. The littlest Solomon's seal, *P. humile,* sports pretty, rounded green leaves and quite erect stems that cut to about eight inches in midspring for excellent filler in little bouquets.

POLYGONUM ORIENTALE

Kiss-me-over-the-garden-gate grows to seven feet and could indeed dangle its angular arching stems over a gate. Here I'll say I prefer the French name *monte-au-ciel* (climb-to-the-sky), as long as nobody makes me say it out loud—at least it's not so long. This annual, mentioned by Christopher Lloyd and Graham Rice in their very helpful *Garden Flowers from Seed* as a great plant no longer available, has just been restored to the trade with the bonus of seed catalog recommendations for cutting. While *Polygonum orientale* is not a first-rate cutting plant, for two or three days its slender pink wands may be just the thing for a certain bouquet, especially wandering out of large, billowy arrangements. There are few other flowers quite like it, with some of the character of the best border subject and the breezy informality of a weed. The long raspberry pink fingers on their relatively leafless stems hold their bright color for several days, until they begin dropping their tiny buds. Cut your stems in the cool early morning or evening, as long as 30 inches if you wish, remove almost all the leaves, and stand them in a cool dark spot for a few hours to prevent wilting. It's extremely tall and narrow and a little sparse of flower, so sow a good bit. The plants apparently like to self-sow, though I get no volunteers.

PRIMULA

The winning **primroses** of spring captivate everyone at the dining table or anyplace they can be seen closely. Bright colored or pastel, they're pretty arranged alone in tiny vases or with short early spring flowers: spring phlox, pansies, muscari, euphorbias, *Myosotis sylvatica,* and *Dicentra* 'Luxuriant'. Fabulous strains looking like the historic primroses in old prints, such as the gold laced, have reappeared recently. They unfortunately are expensive and difficult, but they're enormously appealing, with paler eyes and contrasting margins, green faces, or sophisticated colors like reddish brown.

Reliable *Primula veris,* the **cowslip,** is the first to open in my garden in earliest spring, long-lasting clusters of small strong-yellow cups with orange markings on relatively long 10-inch stems. It's a fine vase companion for *Euphorbia robbiae,* short stems of *Leucojum* 'Gravetye Giant', the light little flowers of multiflora hyacinths, and small early daffodils like 'Rip van Winkle', a spring study in yellow, green, and white.

Another sturdy little pale yellow primrose was given to me 15 years ago by my neighbor, Ruth D., which is probably a cultivar of *P. vulgaris* (syn. *P. acaulis),* **English primrose** or **common primrose.** The stems are quite short when they first flower, but several weeks later they lengthen to 9 or 10 inches. It has found its way to all the gardeners in the neighborhood, so we're bound together by our common affection for this robustly long-lived plant. It does extremely well in dry shade with summer waterings, and once survived two weeks of over 90 degrees Fahrenheit without rain or water when the vacation help failed to arrive. Ruth also gave me a similar cheerful red with a yellow eye; I have to wonder why these passalong primroses aren't in greater commerce. I like to hear of primroses that thrive to the extent they require division, as these do. You'll also discover charming doubles that look like tiny roses. Rose red *P. v.* 'Mark Viette' is one, superb in a small posy along with other primroses for variety. It returned in my garden for many years before vanishing.

P. sieboldii supplies lovely pink or white flowers here in Zone 7 and comes back every year without fail. The pink is especially choice, as the light pink petals are a darker pink on the back. The relatively big flowers in small bunches are good for bringing interest to larger arrangements of longer-stemmed greens like Solomon's seal and Lenten rose. It spreads and forms a nice clump if you give it space. The **Siebold primrose** is from Japan, but the true **Japanese primrose** is another species, *P. japonica.* It bears four or five tiers of flowers in glorious shades of red, pink, and white on quite long stems for a primrose. This is a temperamental individual that needs constantly moist or boggy soil, partial shade, and cool conditions to do well (and then it will self-sow nicely); it's not a plant for most areas of the South. People do cut them (I've never even owned one, because my soil is too dry), and they apparently last five or six days in the vase.

The very hardy **drumstick primrose,** *P. denticulata,* is an interesting variation in form, bearing small globes of pink, lavender, lilac, and white flowers so pretty for bouquets. It settles in much better in the North, in moist soil, where it may flower heavily with stems as long as 12 inches, even self-sowing. Cultivars of *P.* × *polyantha,* **polyanthus primrose,** the big, bright primroses I used to buy at the garden centers in spring, establish in other people's shady gardens, so they say, but rarely reappear for me the next year—my garden lies on a slope and it really is very dry. You can see why gardeners may feel that a primrose that can be handed around the neighborhood is a treasure. After neighbors, reliable local or mail-order nurseries like Heronswood are the next best place to look for durable primroses, then try experimenting with the kind at the garden centers or grocery stores that have been brought in as bedding plants.

Primroses should be watered well in a dry spring to get the longest stems and best flowers. Mulch them carefully so they don't dry out. You can keep your plants strong by preventing seed setting.

RANUNCULUS

It's a challenge to grow the rose-like *Ranunculus asiaticus,* or **Persian buttercup,** where hot weather appears in May and even April, but it is a pleasure nonetheless, the long-lasting flowers sublime for arranging in early June with the shorter stems of 'Connecticut Yankee' or belladonna delphinium and with seven-week 'Trysomic' stocks. The colors run from red, pink, and salmon to yellow, orange, and white. Some bulb suppliers offer special mixes in pastel or hot shades as well as picotees excitingly edged with maroon or plum. The 'Tecolote' strain is commonly available and perfect for cutting. I've been pleased to find that the flower shape sometimes varies from the usual fabulous perfect double seen in photographs, with some blooms a looser semidouble with dark or green centers. I cut the strong stems as long as 15 inches some years, but more likely 10.

In addition to bulb catalogs, seed and mail-order nurseries may offer the tubers in spring, and garden centers display them prestarted in pots. Although ranunculus tubers aren't expensive, they don't all come up for me and so seem a little more dear. Good drainage and cool weather increase your chances of success. I usually plant in late March after having soaked them overnight, though I'd like to plant earlier if they could be obtained any sooner. Allan Armitage says in his *Specialty Cut Flowers* (a guidebook for commercial growers) that since they need a chilling period, you can soak them and then store them in the refrigerator for a week or two, which to me seems a particularly good idea when the weather is too poor for planting. They bloom about 9 or 10 weeks later, several flowering stems per tuber, but they quit abruptly with hot weather. Give them a little shade where it's very warm. The foliage may reappear in fall, but ranunculus isn't hardy here, only in Zones 8-10.

R. acris 'Flore Pleno' (*R. a.* 'Multiplex') is a centuries-old hardy perennial, a double yellow buttercup just an inch across. It's a pretty little thing, known as the **common** or **meadow buttercup** or even **yellow bachelor's button,** blooming for weeks and weeks. A stem 12 to 18 inches long will have several adorable yellow buttons of varying sizes, all with a greenish heart and perfect for a little basket of late-spring flowers: dianthus, Johnnies, violets, English daisies, coral bells, and *Knautia macedonica*. This is a great plant, in miniature, for those who have difficulty with the tuberous ranunculus. But it may spread too quickly, especially in the North, if conditions are right— rich moist soil and full sun. At the bottom of its range in Virginia, the heat and dry soil in many gardens keep it largely in check. Mine eventually disappeared.

RATIBIDA COLUMNIFERA

Mexican hat is the other name for the colorful perennial *Ratibida columnifera,* with its elongated cone, like a cross between a blanket flower and a coneflower. The flowers come in golden yellow, reddish brown, and a combination of the two. One plant makes a special addition in summer to mixed arrangements of heliopsis, bronze-red heleniums, rudbeckias, and other country and prairie flowers, and the young buds are especially enchanting. It's easily grown from seed but is found in few seed catalogs (J. L. Hudson is one place to start), and it's oddly missing from most garden books. A mature plant can grow to almost four feet and likely should be staked or caged, as it leans readily. Mexican hat has a long bloom period, flowering from July well into autumn.

RESEDA ODORATA

I frankly don't detect much scent from **mignonette** here. Celia Thaxter observed in *An Island Garden* that mignonette is much more fragrant in a poor, sandy soil, which I don't have. Maybe it's the heat, too. *Heliotropium* 'Marine' is scarcely fragrant here either. But in other places we hear about, *Reseda odorata* is included as filler in bouquets for its delightful odor and is grown for its perfume rather than its plain and rather weedy-looking little cream-colored flowers. Sow this annual in place, as it dislikes transplanting—not accepting even a peat pot—with a little shade in hot summer areas. You may find mignonette performs much better where the weather is cool, on stems about 18 inches long; and as it comes to flowering quite soon, you can even sow a second crop. It's an excellent pot plant.

RICINUS COMMUNIS

You only need one or two of the immense **castor bean** plants, *Ricinus communis,* for cutting. This is a good thing, as the big seeds are expensive. Try the remarkable 'Carmencita', or another of the "smaller" forms, for their large bronzy leaves of several shades and rich pink, prickly looking seedpods all summer until frost. They're large tropical plants grown as annuals north of Zone 8, used as a screen in some gardens. The foliage and pods can be displayed together, in a large heavy container to prevent toppling. Castor bean is exotic in appearance and won't be likely to combine with most other garden flowers. After soaking the seed for 24 hours, sow outside in spring. It comes up quickly. 'Carmencita' grows to six feet in height and may need some support if it begins to lean. It should self-sow, but not in a troublesome fashion. Others of the castor bean family grow to eight and even 15 feet (less, if you keep cutting), and all are poisonous.

RUDBECKIA

The rudbeckias nicely illustrate the special charm of our native **cone-flowers**. Most are good for cutting, though the mid-July-flowering perennial **orange coneflower** or **black-eyed Susan**, *Rudbeckia fulgida* 'Goldsturm', wilts if too long or full a stem is cut (the name "black-eyed Susan" is more properly used for the wild parent of gloriosa daisies, annual *R. hirta*). Be sure to try other single rudbeckias, as you'll undoubtedly prefer them to 'Goldsturm' for cutting, though it's one of those wonderful plants that fills the garden with tiny birds in autumn, bouncing on the thin branches and devouring the seeds. If you must, use shorter stems for mixed bouquets, and cut when first blooming. Most gardeners find it self-sows a little too well.

The **brown-eyed Susan**, *R. triloba,* is an easy biennial from seed with numerous smaller golden flowers on slender branching stems with finer foliage. They're quite long lasting in the vase, even when cut after the centers have developed, but they require lots of extra water. It's a roomy upright plant with widely spreading laterals, which, when cut apart, give you numerous stems between 14 and 18 inches in length. I like it for arranging with a goldenrod like 'Peter Pan' and yellow or white zinnias for the simplest, and often the prettiest, drop-in-the-vase kind of bouquet. Or mass the lively flowers alone and enjoy their energy. You can start *R. triloba* early under lights for flowering the first summer in late July, and it should self-sow thereafter. One of these truly capacious plants should do. I suspect it will accept some shade, but it's glorious in full sun. Get your seed from J. L. Hudson.

A magnificent six-footer, *R. maxima* is the handsome **giant cone-flower** or **giant black-eyed Susan**. The unusually elongated brown cone with its ruff of yellow petals is marvelous on strong stems up to 32 inches when cut; the gardener may be surprised when the cone appears a week before the petals. The sparse stem foliage is a lovely soft blue green, but it's a plant for the large garden, as the basal foliage takes up a fair amount of room. It flowers in mid-June about a month before 'Goldsturm' and is special for displaying alone in a tall vase, or in a large mixed arrangement of yarrow, Queen Anne's lace, calliopsis, and the long wiry stems of *Allium sphaerocephalum*. Another tall rudbeckia having very long stems, *R. nitida* 'Herbstonne' bears light yellow flowers, a green cone, and gorgeous foliage, but it may require staking.

An amusing large yellow mop head, rather like a clown's wig, *R. laciniata* 'Gold Drop' makes an unusual addition to bouquets from early July into late September. **Cutleaf coneflower** has more refined foliage of softer texture and greener color, with somewhat weaker stems cut about 26 inches in length. It prefers a moist soil and must have full sun. One plant each of the above perennial and biennial rudbeckias is all that's needed for cutting.

Gloriosa daisies are short-lived perennial hybrids of *R. hirta,* superb big golden or zoned-with-brown daisies that mix well with yarrow, bronze-red helenium, tansy, coreopsis, white echinacea, goldenrod, veronica, and Queen Anne's lace, among many others. I find I miss them the year I don't grow them; they're the best of all the rudbeckias for cutting. The single and semidouble gloriosa daisies, arranged together, bring out the best in each other. These strong flowers (really any of the large golden daisies, including sunflowers) are shown off handsomely by greenery in the vase, such as hosta, Solomon's seal, euphorbia, even the seedpods of Asiatic lilies if you forgot to deadhead them.

'Indian Summer' is a florist's strain of large single golden gloriosas and is very popular. I adore the splendid big varieties heavily zoned with brown; just be sure you're getting a tall selection. The variety 'Double Gold' produces fantastic semidouble golden flowers that are a welcome break from the zoned types. One year they were the best flowers I grew, with some stems as long as 20 inches, but more usually 15. Three plants can produce about 15 flowers, five inches across with many fine buds, for cutting at one time. The huge, green-centered single 'Green Eyes', or 'Irish Eyes', is the gloriosa to grow for those who dislike dark cones, and it does mix more easily with other flowers like cosmos and zinnias. The sturdy stems can be long—up to 22 inches. An unusual gloriosa-like selection without petals, *R. occidentalis* 'Green Wizard' bears pointed green sepals and dark cones on strong stems cut to 20 inches. It's a superb green "flower" for use as filler, blooming in late spring of its second year, but it is listed as hardy only through Zone 7.

Gloriosa daisies bloom abundantly their first year and are always said to flower less well the second, so they're usually grown as annuals. They germinate easily indoors in early March for flowers in June, and self-sow modestly, though I had poor results sowing directly in the garden the one time I tried it. Light is required for germination. Gloriosas grown in my raised beds of deeply dug soil are

taller, flower more heavily, and bloom as much as two weeks earlier
than others planted in poorer soil. They tolerate dry conditions
rather well. The plants must be cut frequently to prevent legginess
and to stimulate side growth. You can grow them in light shade, but
they might require some support. You'll want four to six plants for
quantity of bloom as well as to achieve a good variety from the
zoned types.

Although older flowers may look pretty good, new ones will last
longer in the vase. The most basic clue to flower age is that the more
fully developed the center, the older the flower. Sometimes the angle
of the petals is revealing: still forward toward the center is young,
turning back and down toward the stem is older.

RUTA GRAVEOLENS

You can cut the beautiful blue-gray leaves of *Ruta graveolens* from
the herb garden for filler or foliage, with or without the pale yellow
flowers. Select a tall cultivar for cutting (many are dwarf), and handle it carefully at first, because **rue** causes skin irritation to some
people.

Owning rue is no simple matter. A determined young woman appeared at the fence one October, pointing I thought at the last few
flowers. She spoke no English, and every flower I approached to cut
proved to be the wrong one. With frustration, she finally tossed
a pebble onto what she wanted: rue. She had spotted my tiny plant
among the jungle. I cut her a good piece and she sniffed and exam-
ined it and exclaimed "Ah, ruta!" with great happiness and relief.
I watched in astonishment as she stood at the bus stop with the rue
pressed close. The previous spring I had found a hole in the ground
where my rue had been, just weeks after reading folklore that the
medicinal properties only work if the plant has been stolen. The next
time I planted it without its label.

SALVIA

The **sages** are not a first choice for cutting as, like *Linum perenne,*
they're prone to dropping their flowers and wilting, and some even
have foliage with an unpleasant odor when handled, but several are
worth space in the cutting garden. They cover the spectrum of annuals, biennials, and tender and hardy perennials. For small bouquets
from the herb garden, the tricolor and golden sages such as *Salvia*

officinalis 'Icterina' or 'Tricolor' bear colorful and variegated leaves for interest with other foliage and flowers. Cut most salvias only when the flowers first begin to open; and where the flowers are the focus, it's vital to remove almost all the foliage.

S. viridis (S. horminum) is a charming annual plant for the sunny cutting garden, neat and tidy to about 24 inches high, with colorful bracts of purple, pink, and white. It looks tatty midsummer, so harvest when it first blooms, then allow it to self-sow, when it will bloom the following year in late May. I couldn't get *S. viridis* to germinate easily in the garden but found you can start it indoors and plant out for flowers in early June.

Cultivars of perennial *S. nemerosa (S. × superba* or *S. × sylvestris)* bloom for a long time and survive heat and drought quite well. These excellent early blooming blues and purples reach heights of 18 and 24 inches. 'East Friesland' furnishes strident purple spikes for a colorful "rustic" display in May with the yellows of coreopsis and achillea, white coral bells, and gaillardias. This has always been my best perennial salvia. While some of the *S. nemerosa* cultivars, such as 'Blue Queen' or 'May Night', may flower again after cutting, 'East Friesland' does not, but it has been an outstanding performer and lives much longer than the new *S. verticillata* 'Purple Rain'. This last does bring sublime color to the cutting garden, at least until it disappears. Almost as tall as *S. nemerosa* cultivars, the dusky purple spike is larger and doesn't wilt after cutting, the flowers lasting four or five days in water. Both of these twist in a lively way to the light.

S. farinacea, **mealy-cup sage,** is a tender perennial for bedding that is often found ready to bloom in garden centers in spring. 'Victoria' and 'Blue Bedder' are two cultivars in the blue range, and 'Porcelaine's gray spikes open to white flowers, producing a lovely silvery-white effect. They're smaller sages, so get two or three. You can cut stems as long as 16 inches from June into autumn, and plants occasionally overwinter in Zone 7. These salvias take light shade and tolerate neglect fairly well, though they're a little floppy. The flowers may wilt badly (largely a problem in warm weather), but give them support against the side of a tall container, and lots of water, and they should revive. Every morning, set the vase in the sink and tap the stems to dislodge yesterday's faded flowers. Easier to find today is the related deep-colored *S. × 'Indigo Spires'*, a tender perennial also and a big plant producing quite long stems arching in the handsomest manner. Keep one plant deadheaded to produce the new spikes you need for cutting. Fall is the time to love these two with the other last blooms of the year, as the color deepens in cool weather and the stems lengthen and are cuttable until frost.

You should be able to find the showy **Mexican bush sage,** or *S. leucantha,* from a good herb nursery in spring, and in deep soil a tiny plant will become a magnificent bush five feet tall by flowering time in September. I have seen it described as blue or pink, but the plants I've known were decidedly pinky purple, with small white true flowers for a bicolor effect. Or look for the infrequently seen solid purple. *S. leucantha* bridges the seasonal gap between zinnias and chrysanthemums nicely and looks good with late-flowering cosmos and the brown oats of *Chasmanthium latifolium.* You can locate this handsome salvia in the fall border, as so much material may remain after cutting. The cut stems are longer, to 24 inches, and stiffer than many other salvias, and on a massive plant they may break off at the base. Avoid watering it from above and tie it round once if breaking becomes a problem. After cutting, provide support and a cool spot in water if the stems wilt, and they should recover. You can cut from Mexican bush into October, but as it's a tender perennial, Jack Frost will bring it down. This plant is so effective, it's well worth replacing every year, but in the far North, or where frosts come early, it may flower too late in the season to be a reliable source for cut flowers.

Gloriously blue *S. azurea* 'Grandiflora' *(S. pitcheri)* mixes beautifully with boltonia and small zoned sunflowers like 'Autumn Beauty' for a September arrangement. This tall perennial, hardy to Zone 4 and performing well in warm areas, has long waving stems that definitely need staking or the help of a tomato cage set over it. In the deep South, where autumn frosts come late, try pinching back **blue sage** once early in summer to see if it will stand shorter and straighter. Don't cut your stems longer than 24 inches, as they're more likely to wilt if you do. *S. azurea* does not produce a lot of material, but begin with one.

SAPONARIA

Two **soapworts** are used for cutting, one much better known than the other. The named cultivars of perennial **bouncing Bet** (the species is too vigorous for the garden), such as *Saponaria officinalis* 'Rosea Plena', have shaggy pink, white, or purplish-red appealingly untidy double flowers arranged in heads like a rather small summer phlox. The candy-sweet fragrance is quite strong. This soapwort isn't a substitute for phlox, however, as it's a strong-stemmed (to 15 inches at least when cut) rangy plant whose finished florets can't be easily pulled out or allowed to drop off, like those of phlox. For that reason, deadhead religiously and pick stems of bouncing Bet for bouquets when they first bloom, which isn't difficult, as the vigorous plants produce new stems over a long season, in June and July here. Companions for arranging could be white swamp milkweed, with short stems of purple garden verbena and white zinnias. Give full sun.

The elusive annual soapwort, *S. vaccaria (Vaccaria pyramidata)*, resembles gypsophila for cutting, with pretty pink sprays on branching stems, but it's scarcely mentioned in books or most seed catalogs. Look for 'Pink Beauty', which you can sow direct in spring, and possibly fall. It's supposed to be easy—in some other place.

SCABIOSA

The **pincushion flower** is one of the most glorious of all cutting flowers, with exquisite blues and lavenders and brilliant whites on long leafless stems lasting forever in the vase. As perennial *Scabiosa caucasica* can't survive high heat and humidity, light shade in hot summer areas is a requirement. I once saw a well-grown plant here, and we stood in a group wondering at it; I noticed it was not in the owner's garden the following year. It's odd how much more difficult it is than annual scabiosa.

Seed catalogs offer tempting selections of perennial scabiosa, so I succumbed and grew the perennial *S. ochroleuca* under lights. It bloomed generously in full sun the first season but became woody and less useful the next. The flower was a small version of the pale yellow flower of cephalaria and bloomed like an airy cloud around the small bushy plant. For other scabious-like perennials that may be more reliable, you can grow cephalaria or knautia.

The tall annual scabiosa, *S. atropurpurea,* is more double than the perennial, and while not as exquisitely beautiful, the annual is a much sturdier garden plant, surviving heat and humidity better. The mixed colors are usually pinks, blues, and white, with some dark plum and others strangely speckled and splotched, so if your **sweet scabious** proves to be a limited range of pastels, you might try another seed supplier. The beautiful raspberry-form buds should be cut along with the flowers, and some will continue to develop. Cut stems are about 20 inches long. If it seems that you have too many flowers—imagine that—cut them with longer stems and sacrifice some buds.

The plants are narrow and upright, spaced about eight inches apart, so that quite a few can be sown in a row for bloom about 10 weeks later, generally until frost. Plants sown direct produce many more flowers than those begun indoors, which should be started in peat pots as they dislike transplanting. Give them adequate moisture and deadhead regularly. Four plants will provide flowers for mixed bouquets, but it would be a shame not to have many more, perhaps 12.

SEDUM

Tall **stonecrops**, such as cultivars of *Sedum spectabile* and *S. telephium*, are ideal in the cutting garden for green filler, the stems cut before color begins to show. They make an excellent foil for difficult flower or vase colors. The green flowerheads are splendid in July and August, with pink or purple flowers such as annual scabiosa, eustoma, dahlias, the early Japanese anemone 'Robustissima', slim stems of liriope, and perennial sweet peas. Varieties such as pink 'Carmen' and 'Brilliant', or white 'Stardust', are good selections and are also attractive for cutting in bloom. The famous 'Autumn Joy' isn't necessarily the best choice for the cutting garden, as its brick-red color can be difficult to harmonize with other flowers. But you can always use it with small sunflowers, amaranthus, and dahlias in harvest colors for an autumn bowl, if your plant doesn't bloom in midsummer as mine does (meaning it's not the true 'Autumn Joy'). 'Matrona' is a tall soft-pink variety with eye-catching beet-red stems that are ideal for showing off through a glass vase, though in shade it disappoints by failing to color. But it's still handy for filler, as it grows tall quickly and is one of the earliest to form buds. Sedum lasts a very long time in water and may even begin to root.

Sedums are plants that you might as well get from a friend—they divide and transplant with ease and frequently have young plants sown around them. Choose when in bloom, if you can, and notice the different-shaped flower clusters, some quite tight, like broccoli almost, others loose and starry, and the leaves from fine to coarse. Sedum grown in light-to-medium shade, rather than full sun, has a longer thinner stem about 15 to 16 inches in length and a more open flower head, which is for the better. When your plants begin to fall open from the center, it's time to divide.

SIDALCEA MALVIFLORA

A pretty rose-pink **prairie mallow** or **checkerbloom** you can grow from seed rather easily is *Sidalcea malviflora* 'Party Girl'. The elegant cut flowers, with slim 20-inch stems and pretty foliage, make ravishing company with ranunculus, liatris, penstemons, *Verbascum chaixii,* and dill, or Queen Anne's lace. Harvest when the first flowers are opening, as the plants can look ratty later, with finished flowers dotting the stems. While the buds continue to open in the vase, the individual flowers begin to fade badly a day or two after cutting, making sidalcea better for short-term arrangements.

Checkerbloom flowers the first year from seed, and as the seedlings transplant well, you may find it worth your time to buy seed rather than nursery plants. When sown indoors here in early February, 'Party Girl' blooms in June, about four months from sowing. Set two or three plants in good soil; those that live into the second year should form a nice clump that also blooms in June, though on the whole, it's not long lived. Checkerbloom accepts light shade and may appreciate it where summers are hot.

SOLIDAGO

Everyone recognizes **goldenrod,** an easy native plant for the July, August, and September cutting garden, the robust golden or lemon-yellow flowers familiar from the roadside. They are ideal for casual arrangements, valuable in the late summer doldrums for an ample bouquet for a big vase, or a bright addition to mixed garden flowers, especially sunflowers and gloriosa daisies. If you cut stems before the buds open—they linger in a pretty state for weeks—you'll find they're splendid as filler, and the yellow-green color is exceptional. You'll see tall stands of various cultivars in English and European gardens, where they're popular, but in the United States it's difficult to find much to read about goldenrods beyond the admonition that they do not cause hay fever, an idea I never had but have been soundly disabused of.

The plant sent to me as *Solidago* 'Peter Pan' has been just what I wanted, and at five feet, is quite a bit taller than the suggested height. It produces sturdy cut stems at least 25 inches long, beginning bloom in mid-July (early for a goldenrod), the arching spike like a big astilbe, splendid for massing in a big vase, but the dense flowerhead is big enough to be suitable only for large arrangements.

Splendid *S. rugosa* 'Fireworks' is an aptly named relatively tall selection from a much different species, blooming later, with finer foliage
and airier stems far easier for arranging with other garden flowers.
Try pairing it with a white aster. Its height is much less in a dry season. Another goldenrod with quite unusual but desirable character is
S. sphacelata 'Golden Fleece', almost a ground cover and somewhat
scruffy in the garden, producing shorter (cut to 15 inches) stems with
tiny rounded leaves and small yellow flowers thickly covering the
spreading spikes. It's useful because the flowerhead is not so large as
other goldenrods, and it is interesting with late summer and early fall
zinnias, white cosmos, even dahlias, and especially grasses and seedheads. Allan Armitage and Niche Gardens recommend *S. caesia* for
cutting, and I've just set my first plant in the garden.

Gardeners with enough space and an interest in late summer and
fall arrangements may want several different cultivars; I once saw
a superb bouquet at the Brandywine River Museum in Chadds Ford,
Pennsylvania, in late August, using pokeweed, sedum, astrantia,
large drying allium heads, greenery, and three kinds of goldenrod,
much of it probably cut from their extensive garden of native plants.
Most goldenrods form large clumps, producing a great deal of material, occasionally requiring staking, and growing taller with maturity.
If you love solidago, you'll also want to try its relative × *Solidaster
luteus*.

× SOLIDASTER LUTEUS

The tiny pale yellow flowers of × *Solidaster luteus* 'Lemore' (the
large × symbol tells you it's a rare inter*generic* cross between a solidago and an aster, and you don't pronounce it) perform handily as
a filler, a joy with rudbeckias, wheat celosia, snow-on-the-mountain,
cleome, and small sunflowers in mid-July. This is earlier than most
goldenrods or asters. The cultivar 'Yellow Submarine' is a deeper yellow. My solidaster sprawled terribly the first years I had it, the flowers useless, but on the theory that it needs treatment like a phlox, or
even like *Aster pringlei* 'Monte Cassino', I now thin the multitude of
soft stems by half in the spring and keep watch that new stems don't
sneak in. Then I enclose the plant with a small cage of low wire
fencing—the kind used for edging—to keep it upright, and give it
additional staking as it grows, as its heavy head hangs over at flowering. The stems grown this way are straight and strong, to about
18 inches when cut, with fine sprays of flowers. One plant flowers
heavily.

STACHYS BYZANTINA

Arrangers occasionally use *Stachys byzantina (S. lanata),* or **lamb's ears,** for its interesting velvety-gray leaves early in the year, popular now for wedding bouquets. A handsome selection with large leaves is 'Helen von Stein', or 'Big Ears', which may be less vulnerable to rot in the South. I've never had the urge to use either leaves or flowers for bouquets, but I always feel a pleasant surprise when I see the flowers used in a casual arrangement. Remove the leaves as they decline to keep the arrangement looking fresh. One plant forms a large clump, in light shade if necessary, and may self-seed.

STOKESIA LAEVIS

I've eliminated, and inadvertently killed, many plants from the cutting garden over the years, but never the reliable *Stokesia laevis.* The two colors, most usually blue and white, look wonderful put together, and the white is also a fine companion for other white flowers and for gray-green ones, such as *Eryngium planum.* A pale yellow **Stokes' aster** is sometimes heard of. Because of the angular branching of the stems, only a few are needed to fill an average vase. The wide cornflower-like blooms close up with the arrival of evening and open again the next day; the first time I saw this, I thought my flowers had wilted—what a pleasure to see them open again the next morning. For this reason, it's not suitable for a dinner table arrangement.

Stokesia blooms mid-June and survives full sun admirably during dry, hot summers. The long-lived plants grow large slowly, and even self-sow. You'll want two plants to make a big bunch.

TAGETES ERECTA

I grow few **marigolds,** *Tagetes erecta,* for cutting, though they're often recommended for that purpose. The strong scent of their foliage, so redolent of the garden, is welcome indoors only a few times a summer, though if you remove most of the leaves, you'll have dispensed with most of the smell. Burpee describes its "white" 'French Vanilla' as odorless, and for the most part it is. But ironically, this absence of odor is in some small way unsatisfying, and I find myself quite enjoying the scent of the original in small doses.

Burpee began the search for a white marigold years ago and still is one of the few seed suppliers that has them. They are, more accurately, a soft, pale creamy yellow, pleasant with old-fashioned flowers such as zinnias, lavatera, veronica, and *Malva* 'Zebrina', and also for an all-white bouquet. Cut white marigolds early when they're small and the center still tight and green, and they're really very charming.

Lately, the big bright orange or yellow marigolds have the half-fashionable appeal of many decades past. Look for the taller marigold varieties with big flowers, such as 'Crackerjack', which are sometimes difficult to find in the catalogs' throngs of dwarfs; tall seed strains are often found under the subcategory of "African" (in British catalogs) or "American" marigolds (rather than "French," *T. patula*, though they're all from Mexico). These are the thing for big spots of color with other heat lovers like peppers and blood-flower. Seeds of Change offers an unusual strain of tall single marigolds, pale lemon-yellow 'Moonlight' and orange 'Pesche's Gold', with a single row of lightly ruffled petals. I like them; you can use more of them in a bouquet than you might of the doubles, and they look great with the 'Old Mexico' type of little zinnias, but most gardeners won't lose their hearts to them. I found their foliage pleasantly scented.

If you grow your cutting flowers in the vegetable garden, a great tactic with annuals like marigolds, the scented varieties should help repel pests there. Choose an area of the garden of low fertility, as rich soil causes the plants to sprawl and flower sparsely; since cosmos is similarly inclined, you might plant them together. They're easily grown, long-blooming plants that children might like to sow directly in their own cutting patches. They are excellent for hot summers, even accepting very light shade. You can sow marigolds late when it's too warm for other annuals: a sowing at the end of May (five weeks after my average last frost date) gives me flowers in mid-August.

TANACETUM VULGARE

Vigorous *Tanacetum vulgare,* or **tansy,** flowers from early July into September with clusters of small, flat yellow buttons that are extremely long lasting and indispensable in a wide range of mixed arrangements, though it's unlikely you'll cut a great deal, as the ferny and profuse foliage has a strong odor like chrysanthemum. Heliopsis, reddish helenium, rudbeckias, zinnias, and salvia are among the many good companions for tansy in mid to late summer. If it has been cut when it first opens, it will often be the last flower in the vase to fade. Don't get fernleaf tansy, *T. v.* 'Crispum', for cutting, as its ornamental curling foliage is unnecessary for cutting purposes, and the plant is somewhat shorter and may not flower as well.

In full sun tansy stands erect and never needs staking. Most descriptions suggest three feet as its height, in contrast to my experience of four to five feet. The plant grows rapidly and will probably need division after only one year; reset just a small piece, and don't plant it close to anything precious, as it can run faster than you can. Find this plant from an herb nursery.

TELLIMA GRANDIFLORA

Plant the long-lived *Tellima grandiflora* in the perennial patch to help fill out bouquets over a long period in May. **Fringecups** adds picturesque charm and subtlety to almost any late spring arrangement and is particularly useful for large bouquets. Like coral bells and blooming a week earlier, the flowers are carried on long, strong arching stems to 32 inches, but the small fringed bells are largely greenish white, sometimes shell pink, and the stems not so stiff as coral bells. The pretty leaves, low on the stems, look attractive at the neck of the vase. Tellima prefers light shade, and the English, with their limited experience of the extremes of garden possibility, say it tolerates dry soil. My plants have always flopped about in a little too much shade, but I never tie them up, as they take the most delightful twists and turns to the stems. Plants in less shade should flower more heavily, but probably also straighter. Tellima can be almost impossible to find in nursery catalogs, but it's easy to grow from seed under lights. Plan for two plants at first. The seedlings are minuscule while first growing but will be large enough to set out in 8 to 10 weeks in a moist soil.

THALICTRUM

The exquisite foliage and clusters of tiny flowers of **meadow rue** furnish clouds of delicate interest for elegant arrangements. *Thalictrum aquilegiifolium* bears purple, mauve, or white fluffy flowers on good stems in late spring, with beautiful columbine-like leaves. *T. delavayi (T. dipterocarpum)* and the similar long-blooming *T. rochebrunianum* are the larger of the garden meadow rues, with long-stemmed—cut to at least 24 inches—white or purple flowers with yellow centers in midsummer. This last is self-supporting and performs adequately in hot weather, blooming in late June with a second flush in August. The individual purple flowers, while small, are bigger than the little fuzz balls of the others and form a huge panicle 10 or 11 inches across. My plants of *T. delavayi* in medium shade (partial shade is better) required staking, as the long stems leaned over from the base to lie on the ground. *T. flavum (T. speciosissimum)* has yellow flowers with pretty foliage in summer that are worth cutting.

Light shade is strongly recommended for thalictrum in the South; in full sun the plants suffer terribly in hot, dry weather. One plant of any species is a good starting point for the cutting garden.

THERMOPSIS CAROLINIANA

Quite like an earlier-flowering baptisia, *Thermopsis caroliniana* carries pea-flowered racemes of a pretty shade of light lemon yellow in April. The fairly long stems, about 20 inches when cut (longer in a cool, wet spring), bloom at a convenient time for use with tulips, honesty, poppy anemones, Solomon's seal, and the very last daffodils. In the vase, they arch toward the light and form graceful curves. Hardy to Zone 3, **Carolina lupine** performs excellently with a little shade and extra moisture in the Southeast, but like *Veronicastrum virginicum,* if the soil is too dry in full sun, the plant screams bloody murder. It forms a good-sized clump and doesn't like to be divided.

TIARELLA CORDIFOLIA

I keep *Tiarella cordifolia* 'Wherryi' in the shady border to cut from, as it's a treat with other spring wildflowers for tiny bouquets, with primroses and columbines, and the small tulips produced by bulbs in the ground for several years. **Foamflower's** low clump of pretty leaves produces a multitude of slender pale pink flower spikes on stems about eight inches long when first flowering, 14 inches in the third week of bloom. Bunch the little stems together for more impact in the vase; the leaves are useful as well. Grow two to three of these very hardy plants for cutting in moist, organic soil, and they'll flower for as much as a month. If you have the space, one plant of *T. cordifolia,* the species, should spread to form a two-foot mat.

TITHONIA ROTUNDIFOLIA

The individual flowers of **Mexican sunflower,** *Tithonia rotundifolia,* are nowhere near as big as the usual notion of sunflower, though the bushy plants grow as big as an annual can get in one year. The glossy orange-red or yellow daisies open about three inches across, with heavily velveted stems cut about 18 inches in length. 'Torch' grows four to six feet and should have longer stems than the shorter 'Gold-finger', both orange red. I used to see 'Yellow Torch', but I've always grown the wonderfully exuberant red, as yellow daisies are easy to come by in other genera. Since it's rather rustic in appearance, titho-nia always looks best in some sort of crock or simple container and needs no companion flowers, though small sunflowers like 'Tangina' or 'Sonja' are terrific choices. Be gentle when picking, as the stems crush easily; it's not a flower to crowd carelessly in the bucket.

Tithonia is a tender annual, quick to grow from seed, flowering here in early July from a mid-April sowing, or sown in June for fall flowers. It's well suited to hot, dry areas, and for planting over those bulbs that shouldn't be watered in summer. Tithonia suffers ne-glect well, save for deadheading, and shouldn't be fertilized or even watered, so they say, though I find it difficult to never water a plant. Sow in place, as the seedlings react badly to transplanting, and space them generously. Two or three plants should provide a good display, and may even self-sow.

TRACHELIUM CAERULEUM

Modest *Trachelium caeruleum* bears subtle, dusky violet-blue flowers with bronzy foliage that can occasionally be seen in florist shops. **Throatwort** is the common name I've never heard it called. It's a tender perennial hardy to Zone 8, grown as an annual in cold cli-mates. I was at first skeptical of success with this flower in my gar-den, as it needs five or six months to reach flowering size, yet is re-puted to hate hot weather. You can begin seedlings under lights in mid-January, and while the plants are initially tiny, they grow rapidly and are good candidates for repotting, even a cold frame. Plant out immediately with the coming of the last frost date. They flower in July, tolerating partial shade, and don't seem as bothered by the heat as some other sufferers. Cut throatwort back occasionally to keep it in good shape during a hot summer if you're not using the flowers, because the plant will brighten up considerably with cool fall weather. Cut stems have been 13 inches long at the most in my gar-den, but the plants grow taller in mild climates.

TRACHYMENE COERULEA

Trachymene coerulea (Didiscus), or **blue lace flower,** reminds me of a small blue Queen Anne's lace, growing in an airy open fashion

with widely spaced little pincushiony flowers in mid-June for delicate addition to mixed bouquets. I like to arrange this annual loosely
with large airy heads of dill; the colors of lavender blue and greenish
yellow look sublime together. Blue lace flower relishes cool weather
and can't be sown outdoors in spring here, as it doesn't have enough
time to mature before summer arrives, but it also dislikes root disturbance, requiring peat pots to transplant successfully, preferably
into light shade. One plant supplies a dozen stems of about 16 inches
in length, but no more, as it flowers sparsely once the heat arrives.
In climates with mild summers, sow outdoors in spring in a light
soil, with full sun or partial shade, where it may grow two to three
feet tall.

TRADESCANTIA VIRGINIANA

The **spiderworts**, *Tradescantia virginiana (T. × andersoniana)*, are
particularly pretty for spots of entrancing color, running through
white, pink, purple, and blue; some tinged with blue or a violet center. The buds droop from short stalks at the top of thick fleshy stems
and are open one to three at a time, closing at night; a cut stem
(about 14 inches long) will have open flowers every day for 10 days.
Just under the cluster of buds are two awkward leaves, one to each
side and frequently quite long—presumably giving spiderwort its
name—that may be cut away before mixed arranging or left on for
their curious interest, however clumsy, in a vase of spiderworts. Better selections for cutting will have shorter leaves—it's good to observe this when choosing your plant, which you may be able to get
from a friend. After a few hours in deep water in the vase, the leaves
recharge and hold themselves a bit more attractively. Spiderworts are
peculiar, and I always think someone more clever than I must know
what to do with them.

A clump grows large in a well-drained soil, even invasively, producing a sea of messy foliage that should not be fertilized. Spiderworts tolerate light shade and extra water where it's hot, though they
become weedy and bloom only passably in medium shade. They
flower heavily for several weeks, and if cut back, may rebloom (with
smaller flowers) in cool weather later in the season, but they bloom
longer in the North than in the South.

TRITELEIA LAXA

The pretty blue and violet-blue flowers of *Triteleia laxa* 'Queen Fa-
biola' appear in long-lasting loose clusters in June on wiry leafless

stems. Exuberant mixed with gold gloriosa daisies and veronica, with the stems bunched together for clusters of blue, the flowers go part way toward lifting my spirits after the deaths of my agapanthus. The stems are sometimes only 12 inches long, but they can be as long as 16 inches. You'll occasionally find this plant in bulb catalogs under the name *Brodiaea*. Buy at least a dozen bulbs for a spot in full sun. Plant them in autumn in Zone 6 and south, where they should return, and in spring in the North.

TROLLIUS

The long-stemmed perennial **globeflowers** are a great favorite of mine in late spring and summer, looking variously like big buttercups, small yellow roses just opening, or golden ranunculus. If you acquire plants from the three largest *Trollius* species, you'll have a six-week season of bloom, and occasionally a second flush of flowers. Mature buds will open in water.

The smaller yellow *T. europaeus* cultivars such as 'Superbus' usually bloom early. Following that are the many *T.* × *cultorum* cultivars in shades of yellow to deep orange; the recent 'Alabaster' is a creamy white from this group, and 'Earliest of All' has flowered here in earliest May for arranging with some of the prettiest flowers of midspring. Blooming last, the marvelous big *T. ledebourii* 'Golden Queen' *(T. chinensis)* is a glowing orange on magnificent longer branching stems, easily 34 to 38 inches when cut, and of a slightly different appearance, the flower more open and the stamens more prominent and irresistible to my eye. It needs additional moisture to perform well.

Globeflowers flourish in cool growing seasons, but they suffer terribly in dry weather, and in the East they don't grow well in Zone 7 and further south (excepting in those infuriatingly rainy *El Nino* springs). I bought a few plants recently when two seasons of good rains had dulled my memory. It's not a satisfactory location—too much sun and not enough moisture—and the flowers are sparse. You'll find this plant an opportunity for a wet cutting garden, and it's always safe in the South to provide afternoon shade. Anyone who loves trollius might also like the tiny flowers of *Ranunulus acris* 'Flore Pleno'.

TROPAEOLUM

The intriguing **nasturtiums,** with their charming, round green or prettily variegated leaves and marvelous glowing colors are always worth growing. I feel I should wear a Hawaiian shirt when I see them. Monet in his garden had nasturtiums on both sides of a wide gravel path, the vines creeping into the path toward the center. Celia Thaxter also adored them, arranging them in sweeps of color along a mantel, progressing from pale yellow through "gold, orange, scarlet, crimson, to the blackest red." The deliciously scented flowers are held away from the vine in the same way as a sweet pea. Fix them with anything warm blooded—golden yarrow, dill, flowering tobacco, marigolds, bloodflower, *Verbena bonariensis,* maybe a short-stemmed goldenrod like 'Golden Fleece'. While the stems are usually short at only eight or nine inches, they make a tropical presence in a low bowl, perfect for the dining table. In the cool weather of fall (nasturtiums are tender annuals important to the fall cutting garden) or areas of mild summers, the stems reach 12 inches. Be sure to include lengths of vine to trail the wonderful foliage over the vase's edge—the tiniest leaves at the growing tips have all the delight of miniature sand dollars. After a day's adjustment to the vase, they'll hold up their leaves for the best display, and you can reposition any flowers now hidden by the foliage. The sinuous manner of growth makes nasturtiums seem alive in the vase, more like potted plant than bouquet, though they aren't long lasting. Nasturtiums from the *Tropaeolum minus* family—the variegated 'Alaska' is one— don't produce vines as long as the *T. majus* strains and are said to "mound," but for arranging, they are of more than adequate length. You'll be able to find separated colors, too.

Easy to germinate, nasturtiums must be sown direct a week or two before your last frost date (or as late as July to flower in September). They bloom in early June but need cool conditions to perform decently. Avoid rich soil. I sometimes hesitate to grow them, as they're magnets for aphids, though some years there are no aphids at all and the plants are glorious. Once I began nasturtiums early in peat pots to get them flowering before the aphids were about, but transplanting stress stunted them dreadfully, and the aphids appeared shortly after. Try insecticidal soap. Two plants may suffice, especially of the *T. majus* kinds, which are almost too rambunctious for a small plot.

TULBAGHIA VIOLACEA

Blooming over a long season from early June into October, but supposedly tolerating only light frosts, **society garlic,** or *Tulbaghia viola-*

cea, is well known to gardeners in Zones 9 and 10, though it has lived through several mild winters here in Zone 7. The pretty lilac-pink allium-like flowers are held on a wiry scape to 20 inches and have just a mild scent of garlic or onion, discernible only by sniffing directly at the flower. In October the stems can reach 32 inches. They are pretty for additions in bunches to mixed bouquets, lasting four or five days. While the leaves of most alliums do smell of onion when cut, the foliage of society garlic gives off a particularly pungent odor when cut or bruised and should never be brought indoors, or the house will require airing for days. It can cause quite a commotion at one's mother's house. One plant develops a generous clump of foliage that persists most of the year. Difficult to find in the North, society garlic travels well and so can be begged from relatives and friends in the deep South.

TULIPA

Tulips come quickly with the late daffodils and, like daffodils, are a flower people have prized for centuries. Charles Mackay's account of the vases of tulips on the tavern tables where Dutch speculators ate great dinners and traded in tulip bulbs is transporting. If you haven't read his history of the 17th century tulipomania, you may like to find a copy of his *Extraordinary Popular Delusions and the Madness of Crowds*.

The first fairly long stems come with the Single Early and Fosteriana groups, which bloom relatively early. 'Apricot Beauty' is justly popular for its flushed salmon pink and apricot coloring, gorgeous when it opens to reveal its pale yellow base. 'Sweetheart' is a lovely soft yellow and white flamed flower, like Easter candy with 'Apricot Beauty' and pink daffodils. An excellent early white tulip is 'White Emperor' ('Purissima').

The many Triumph, Darwin Hybrid, and Single Late (cottage) tulips are the most familiar for cutting, with quite long stems. Be sure to try the "Rembrandt-type" tulips, which you can recognize by their streaked and flamed colors. The insides of these tulips, as they open and hang over the vase, are just as beautiful as the outside. Marvelous choices are yellow flamed with red 'Olympic Flame' or 'Vlammenspel', white flamed with red 'Beauty of Volendam' and 'Sorbet', and orange with light purple 'Princess Irene'. Mixed Rembrandts are often advertised, and they may do just fine if you don't mind the bulbs coming up at different times. In fact, I wouldn't order any mixed tulip selections unless I could use the flowers individually.

Selecting tulips from the various bloom periods may be a lot more satisfying than having all your flowers come up at once; on the other hand, sometimes an explosion of tulips is wanted. Ten or twelve of any kind are usually a minimum to plant, with big arrangements of tulips requiring 30 or more. An exception is possibly the peony-flowered (also known as Double Late) such as the old favorite 'Angelique', which opens so wide and full that just three or four in a small vase may be very satisfying, but you'd still need to plant at least six to make certain of four in bloom at the same time. They're also splendid with mixed spring flowers. The parrots are outrageous enough at first experience, that a few may suffice. As a chaser of variety, I enjoy fewer of more kinds of tulips, to put in narrow vases and examine up close.

Bunch-flowering tulips like 'Modern Style' or 'Happy Family' have the charming characteristic of producing several flowers of different sizes on the same stem, for a natural garden look. You can cut the little flowers off separately for use in smaller bouquets. The lily-flowered tulips are among the last and best for cutting, bridging the gap until the iris and peonies appear. 'White Triumphator' is a useful white, 'Mariette' a fantastic rich pink, and 'Ballade', violet with a white edge, looks almost tropical as its petals open to the fullest. Tulips are one flower that look increasingly exotic as they age and that can often be kept around until the petals drop off.

The fabulous colors of tulips are their greatest feature. The more boldly colored the tulip, the more suitable it may be for the vase than the garden—better a garish tulip than a gaudy daffodil to my way of thinking. Most yellow tulips are uninteresting because the just-finished daffodils are so predominantly yellow, but yellow *Tulipa viridiflora* 'Hummingbird' with its green feathers is another matter. All the viridifloras make good picking, green-and-white 'Spring Green' especially. The so-called black tulips, such as 'Queen of the Night' or 'Black Parrot', are a handsome deep maroon or wine purple and need to be placed in a bright room so you can see them properly. They're much more attractive than you might suppose, both in the garden and in the vase. You can put them with the luxurious foliage and flowers of old-fashioned bleeding heart, early hosta leaves and Solomon's seal, or with white tulips for a "black and white" effect. White tulips are endlessly useful. Some catalogs weigh too heavily in the direction of soft colors for their tulip selections, so when you find a catalog with more than pretty pastels, order from it and stay on their list.

One of the few long-stemmed flowers in spring, the yellow mustard from wintered-over plants in the vegetable garden (or found on the wayside), makes a fine companion for tulips. Try mustard arranged with huge, white peony-flowered 'Mt. Tacoma'. Wintered-over collard greens also furnish a handy light-yellow long-stemmed spring flower. You may also find euphorbias useful, particularly *E. robbiae, E. palustris,* and *E. polychroma,* which bloom at staggered dates in spring. Tellima, honesty, Carolina lupine, *Helleborus orientalis,* and *Leucojum* 'Gravetye Giant' are also pretty with tulips. (Most of these plants make good use of partially shady areas.) I occasionally cut tulip stems with one or two leaves, particularly on short-stemmed flowers, as leaves suggest the garden so strongly and look lovely through glass vases, but leave the others behind to replenish the bulb.

When considering heights of tulips given in catalogs, remember that you'll likely be cutting the flower in bud or at opening, and the stem at that time may be several inches less than the ultimate height; beware of anything described as lower than 12 inches. Early tulips can be quite short, but still work massed in a low, wide bowl; crowd them in so they hold each other up. Some years, warm weather conditions cause tulips to bloom on quite short stems. You can always pull your tulips, rather than cut, for the longest stems and the most leaves, but those bulbs will definitely not return the next year.

Anyone who has cut tulips from the garden knows how frustratingly pliant their stems become. Tulips need support immediately after cutting to allow them to stiffen as much as possible, as they won't straighten out by themselves. Wrap them in stiff paper to above their heads for support, or find a tall and narrow florist container, and stand them in deep water overnight, but remember that tulips are *supposed* to lean over and let you admire their glorious interiors. They continue to lengthen after cutting, and even turn to the light, making it easiest to arrange them in a casual fashion so their movement won't spoil everything. Look in antique or museum reproduction shops for the interesting old vases with holes in which to insert tulip or other bulb stems.

Tulips are particularly susceptible to poor winter drainage; a slope is usually a good choice, or a raised bed. The flowers in following years will be smaller and fewer, but delightful for working into little posies. These second- and third-year flowers will appear as much as two weeks before new tulips, lengthening your tulip season. If you don't need to try for a second year of bloom, you can even plant them in shady spots. I've planted tulips on the north side of our house, and the flowers bloomed adequately.

Are tulips worth the expense to grow for cutting? They rarely increase and live long lives as do many daffodils, though some I have are now at least 12 years old, all yellow. Fosteriana and Darwin Hybrid tulips are usually the longest lived. But you'll be able to grow varieties you won't see at the florist, and you'll have the charming smaller flowers of the following years. Some catalogs offer "perennial" tulips, which they say should bloom for five years. Many herbaceous perennials in my garden don't live that long!

UVULARIA GRANDIFLORA

The little-known **giant bellwort** or **merrybells**, *Uvularia grandiflora*, though not at all a giant, bears curious dangling flowers with fine stems and soft green leaves for posies in early spring. The modest yellow "bells" bring interest as well as filler power to mixed bouquets of little daffodils like 'Beryl', primroses, Virginia bluebells, small bleeding hearts like 'Luxuriant', cushion spurge, and other little spring blooms. The stems cut to 12 or 13 inches long. Wildflower gardeners with moist shady spots will appreciate it especially; my big colony blooms heavily alongside the Virginia bluebells in deciduous shade, and forms a fine perennial stand with watering in dry spells. It may self-sow. The foliage tends to disappear in summer, but it isn't missed in the shady garden with ferns and hostas to fill in. You may need to find merrybells from a native plant catalog.

VALERIANA OFFICINALIS

Garden heliotrope, or **common valerian,** *Valeriana officinalis,* produces long cut stems (18 to 20 inches and more) of tiny pale pink or white flowers in large rounded clusters as much as five inches across, not unlike an expanded white *Centranthus ruber.* It's an ancient herb considered pleasantly fragrant, even described as "vanilla scented," though I can't bear the smell when the flowers are first opened. They last quite a while in water, and as the scent dissipates a few days after cutting, the flowers are useful for mixed arranging in early summer. One plant grows to a vigorous clump, blooming for an extended period if kept cut back. Valerian tolerates light shade and overly moist soil, but it suffers terribly in hot weather—mine usually endures a black death in July, but a fresh clump of green appears in August. It may self-sow modestly. The American Horticultural Society notes that it "has the disadvantage of attracting cats," though what the cats do with it I do not know.

VERBASCUM

The intriguing **mulleins** are a little fragile for cutting, occasionally wilting and dropping petals, but splendid for a short display. The majority are short-lived perennials or biennials that you can start indoors from seed in January for bloom the same year. I set them out in the garden in March or April here. A few are too large and imposing for cutting, but others grace the prettiest arrangements. They're much better known in England (Thompson & Morgan offers a good selection of seed) than the United States, where seed or nursery catalogs may include only a few.

Verbascum phoeniceum 'Flush of White' has been the first to bloom here in mid-May from an early sowing indoors. It is a branching plant with spikes of pure white flowers opening up the stem, pleasant with many late-spring and early-summer flowers. The plants are not tall for me in the first year, the stems measuring about 15 inches when cut.

Started early from seed, or sown the previous fall, the distinctive 'Southern Charm Hybrid' blooms about two weeks after 'Flush of White'. A range of unusual softly colored spires on a larger plant, branching well from the base, the lovely colors of dusky pink, buff, and palest cream yellow, all with a handsome violet eye, combine attractively with white verbascum, ammi, columbine, and the pastel colors of the *Lychnis chalcedonia* hybrids, the cut stems from 18 to 26 inches in length. Some seed lists may have a similar selection under another name, such as *V. phoeniceum* 'Mix' or 'Hybrids'. The plants may rebloom in the fall if cut back after flowering and then bloom heavily the next year, about two weeks earlier, with longer stems. If they're felled by a hard rain, stake them up right away. Both of the above may accept light shade.

V. chaixii 'Album' blooms a week later, in early June. It's a good mixer, with white flowers with a purple eye on a sturdy spike. *V. chaixii* has yellow flowers. These are less fragile than other verbascums, and a little taller. You may find that *V. chaixii* 'Album' self-sows, and it may also bloom again in fall.

V. blattaria is another you can grow from seed started early, for bloom in mid-July. A pretty white flower, flushed pink with a violet eye, on spires rather like *V. phoeniceum,* its delicate color is dreamy with salvias, cosmos, delphinium, blue sea hollies, rosy plumed thistle, and others of the casually elegant garden flowers of early to mid summer. Each plant produces a main spike with abundant laterals, rising from an intriguingly flat rosette, for cut stems about 20 inches long. It looks pinched in warm sun and dry weather, but in cool weather it's glorious, to almost five feet, an excellent keeper whose buds continue to open in water. *V. blattaria* self-sows copiously for flowers in mid-June; the unwanted plants are easily weeded out, but you might go easy on yourself by disposing of most of your finished plants before they go to seed. All the verbascums appreciate a good watering in dry weather, and the flowers look better for cutting the next day.

VERBENA

Most of the **verbenas** are on the tender side. One of the hardiest (to Zone 6) is the airy, long-stemmed *Verbena bonariensis* or **tall verbena.** You can keep it in the border rather than the cutting garden and pick from it occasionally for added interest to mixed bouquets. It's an odd, dusky violet flower on stiff stems that drops its small petals a little too easily, but it does good work as a filler. Bunch the cut stems together and add them to casual bouquets of zinnias, salvias, gloriosa daisies, and small sunflowers. It's an easy perennial that grows quickly to blooming size from seed sown early under lights or direct outdoors, and the plants self-sow in a helpful manner, continuing to bloom even in hot, dry weather—the best plants appear in droughty summers. It doesn't take much space and, like dill, comes up between other plants. *V. bonariensis* blooms at the very end of May, continuing over a long period into autumn and generally disappearing over winter. In the far North, you may need to reseed each year if it doesn't volunteer. Two or three plants are plenty for occasional picking. Also a tall perennial, *V. hastata*, or **blue vervain,** is said to be good for cutting, but as I've not been able to grow it from seed, I need to find a plant to buy. The flowers are violet, pink, or blue.

Annual (or tender perennial) garden verbenas also bloom all summer on sprawling plants with branching stems carrying small clusters of glowing purple, red, lavender, rose, and white flowers. 'Homestead Purple' and white 'Snowflurry' are splendid choices. Excellent ground covers for cutting from the border, they look best at the edge of a raised bed or at the top of a wall. Their wiry curving stems, 12 to 14 inches in length, fill out a casual summer bouquet with spots of glorious color. Find these at good garden centers or specialty mailorder nurseries, but don't expect them to be hardy above Zone 8. Light shade is acceptable.

VERONICA

The many perennial cultivars of **speedwell** are indispensable for spiky flowers for medium-sized arrangements. The flowers resemble foxtails, and it's difficult not to stop by the vase and feel their "fur." White veronica, like the relatively tall *Veronica spicata (V. longifolia)* 'Icicle', is especially useful for mixed bouquets. I like to have at least two plants of different colors, at the moment 'Icicle' and pink *V. longifolia* plants I grew from seed, Park's 'Pink Shades'. Both of these stand quite a bit taller than many other cultivars, with flowers appearing in late spring and early summer. A slightly shorter veronica to grow from seed, *V. gentianoides*, has larger bluish-white florets to the 15-inch stems, the petals dropping too easily, like a verbascum. But because it blooms four to five weeks before the others, you can grow it in the border for occasional picking with *Centaurea montana* and geums in late April, around the time of the tulips. The flowers continue to open and are pretty for several days, twisting enchantingly around to the light, but the plant does not produce new flowers like other veronicas. Popular 'Sunny Border Blue' is a little too compact and stubby for the best cutting, but do look for the longstemmed white veronica relative, *Veronicastrum virginicum*.

While veronicas bloom over a long period, most are at their best for cutting only in the first few weeks, as succeeding flowers become increasingly small and tatty. Young plants flower best. 'Icicle' has been more obliging than others, still attractive and cuttable at the end of August. The center spike in each flower cluster opens first, so cut it out if it has gone past its prime. Veronica needs a moist, well-drained soil to reach its potential, and it appreciates very light shade where summers are hot. It's easily grown from seed, flowering the first year, and both seed and nursery catalogs have interesting selections.

VERONICASTRUM VIRGINICUM

The lovely tapering white (occasionally pale pink) spires of *Veronicastrum virginicum,* also known as *Veronica virginica,* appear in early July. The flowers are pretty for use with phlox, penstemon, cleome, globe thistle, feverfew, snow-on-the-mountain, and many of the dressier country flowers. Cut **Culver's root** or **Bowman's root** when the central, topmost flower first begins to open for stems 18 inches and longer. After the first cutting, the big plant (one will do) blooms a second time in mid-August, each original stem bearing clusters of smaller foxtails. In full sun it appreciates a moist soil, and in hot weather wilts noticeably without it.

VIOLA

This important genus has a long history of cultivation and a complicated family tree. If you locate plants or seed for **sweet violets,** *Viola odorata,* you'll have the descendants of the traditional violet sold in the Athenian flower market three hundred years before the birth of Christ, as well as the flower the gardener probably chose for his mistress to wear in the traditional English song "The Seeds of Love." The modern **pansy** *(V. × wittrockiana)* and later the smaller **viola** *(V. × williamsii)* were created in the early 1800s by crossing *V. tricolor,* the "wild pansy," with other species of violet. All of these were grown mostly for cutting or exhibition, rather than bedding as they are now.

Pansies are lovely for picking in March and April, with stems as long as four inches, and in May lengthening to seven. The large size of some flowers, three inches and more across, make pansies important for small bouquets. They offer glorious blues for fanciers of that color—and just about every other color and bicolor imaginable, including "black." Read seed catalogs closely to find strains said to have long, strong stems. Nichols Garden Nursery, for example, offers seed packets for a florist strain called 'Oregon Giants'; and years ago Thompson and Morgan offered a Tall Cut Flower type, to 10 or 12 inches, gone from the catalog just as it came to my attention. But everyday pansies cut perfectly well. There are pansies with and without "faces," and with waved and ruffled petals. Bunches of the starry glory-of-the-snow make a delicate early companion for the small vase, as do primula, muscari, and tiny daffodils in just another week or two.

Pansies are actually very hardy perennials, which is why they can be planted in autumn to bloom off and on during the winter. (Note that some catalogs refer to certain varieties as "Winter Flowering.") They begin their best show in spring. Sowing seed outside in fall hasn't worked for me, but pansies are easily started from seed indoors, requiring darkness for germination. They should be planted out when small, in autumn where summers are hot, and in full sun, or light shade if need be. Well-developed already-flowering plants should be cut back when planted. Any pansies you start from seed in mid to late winter can begin hardening off about six weeks later if the weather permits. This requires diligence when the weather is still cold; it's essential to expose them to strong sunlight only gradually, beginning with early morning or late afternoon, because they're easily burned (and their growth permanently checked). They can be planted out when the ground is workable and will be flowering by late April here, continuing through June (where the growing season is cool, the *Viola* family blooms long into summer). Two to six pansy plants will suffice for additions to mixed bouquets, or many more if you want large bunches. It's important to deadhead.

Although the stems may be only about six inches grown in full sun, a big bunch of **Johnny-jump-up** or **heartsease**, *V. tricolor*, packed into a short vase makes a captivating show in spring. The three colors vary for the most part along a theme of purple, blue, and gold, some with delicious whiskering, and in addition you'll find pure "black" and pure yellow. Hybrids like 'King Henry' or 'Helen Mount', found at good garden centers or grown from seed, may have surprisingly long cut stems to eight inches and more, with small faces delightful with spring phlox, euphorbia, Spanish bluebells, and Lenten rose for a charming contrast of flower size.

I like Johnnies for the shady border, as they're agreeable with other early spring plants, develop longer stems, and it does no harm to cut from them there. In full sun you can lengthen the stems by

planting or sowing among early developing upright plants like cornflowers or larkspur, where the shade and support produce strong
stems that on occasion may reach 15 inches. Johnnies are one of those
plants whose seed I have an easier time germinating in late winter
under lights for spring planting, than in the warmer late summer for
fall planting. Five or six plants, started in February and set out in
spring, produce a nice bunch in May. Self-sown plants bloom by
early April, but some people, perhaps those with light soils, find
these plants spread too easily. Stokes has a good selection of seed,
including seed for many modern garden violas, which are much like
small pansies.

XERANTHEMUM ANUUM

An annual usually classified as an everlasting, *Xeranthemum anuum*
supplies charming small white, purple, or pink flowers that you can
also use fresh. They may be single or semidouble. Each **immortelle**
plant flowers heavily in summer where temperatures are moderate,
and you can harvest by grasping the stems of each plant in a handful
and cutting at the base. The seed germinates without much difficulty
in the garden, but not infrequently the young plants shrivel and die
in a hot summer. If you like them, the crisp and papery everlasting
strawflower, *Helichrysum bracteatum,* also cuts fresh, with an excellent color range of red, yellow, pink, and white on long stems. It's an
annual for full sun. Skip the dwarfs.

ZINNIA

Few other plants in late summer offer such intense reds and oranges
and coral pinks and such huge flowers as the **zinnia,** sometimes four
and a half inches across. The genial cactus varieties I adore, the flowers so large that just eight or nine fill a wide-mouth jar. Dahlia-
flowered zinnias possess a more refined petal arrangement on an
equally large bloom. The "lilliputs" are a little more elegant for a tiny
tea-table decoration than the six-inch giants; you can even set
a small bottle of them into the center of a bundt cake. A lively companion for zinnias is the green-centered gloriosa daisy 'Green Eyes',
as well as tiny sunflowers, hyacinth bean, goldenrod, gomphrena,
salvias like 'Purple Rain', garden verbena and *V. bonariensis,* and
grasses. But zinnias never require companions.

   To get a more formal look from zinnias, try solid-color massings of a favorite color. Stokes Seeds has a nice range of separated colors in both dahlia-flowered and cactus-flowered long-stemmed cutting selections. White shows up infrequently in packets of mixed colors, and is especially useful, so you may need to sow 'Snowman' or 'Polar Bear' if you want a lot of white flowers (because the whites show their flaws all too readily, cut them early while the center is still greenish).

Zinnias are such a mainstay of the late summer garden that they can become wearisome; sowing several different types weeks apart makes for more variety. This could be an early sowing of a large bright red like 'Firecracker' or 'Big Red'; followed a month later by white dahlia-flowered and the useful tall green 'Envy' to use together; and then again in three or four weeks with mixed colors of the cactus zinnias, or the long-stemmed smaller flowers of 'Oklahoma' or *Z. peruviana* 'Bonita'. There are also fairly long-stemmed small flowers in solids and bicolors in yellows, golds, and browns like zesty *Z. haageana* 'Old Mexico' on 12-inch cut stems, which make a rustic "mixed" arrangement all on their own, or with marigolds and bloodflower. When sowing a separated color, 8 to 10 plants may do, but for mixed colors, unless there is little room, fewer than twice that number might be a lost opportunity. Several seed catalogs promote 'Blue Point' as a top strain for cut flowers, and they are beautiful.

The flower stems lengthen after a few weeks, assuming you've chosen tall varieties. Some of the new hybrids are so vigorous that cut stems may be close to 24 inches long and plants to almost five feet. I like to cut a few half-opened flowers as well; while they won't continue to open, they make the arrangement look just picked. Handle the stems carefully, as they sometimes bend just under the flower. Foliage below the waterline must be removed, and even then the water will grow cloudy, so you may want to avoid a glass vase. Vase water stays cleaner longer if you carefully pull off, rather than cut, the lower leaves, because tiny bits of leaf are left when scissors are used.

Zinnias require less effort for great effect than just about any flower. They are quick-growing annuals, blooming in about seven weeks, even in a little shade, invaluable for planting in spaces vacated by early flowering plants, or sowings that failed. There is little point to starting them early under lights, as the plants resent transplanting and perform better sown direct. The seed germinates amply even in warm, dry weather, with one daily watering, which means you can still sow it successfully in June for flowers in mid-August. For this reason, zinnias are one of the best plants for growing between the spring harvesting of many fall-sown hardy annuals or biennials and the next fall sowing or planting of, say, agrostemma, hesperis, corn-flowers, or poppies.

August is the month of zinnias, but if you'll be away, sow them earlier for June and July. They can't be relied on for fall flowers: by mid-September flower production slows markedly and mildew de-faces the foliage, though some years they last into October and can be used with asters and dahlias and other remnants of the summer season.

Appendix 1
Growing Seed under Lights

Among my favorite times of year as a new gardener was the arrival
of the seed catalogs and the delicious moments I stole out of busy
days to examine them. I wish I could have again my first few assig-
nations with these jewels from the day's mail. They once arrived just
after Christmas, making the new year something to look forward
to, but they now appear even before Thanksgiving. This seemed
a shame at first, but it does allow you to purchase your seed to be
ready for January sowings.

When your seed arrives, put the packets of seed that require chilling, like delphinium, penstemon, rudbeckia, larkspur, and linaria,
directly into the refrigerator. It's horrifying to discover the seed you're
about to sow should have been in the fridge the past two weeks. You
can store your other seed there as well.

Pots, Cell Packs, and Trays

In January I bring the trays, cell packs, and small pots up from the
basement for their bath. Warm water and dish soap, plus bleach to
10 percent of the solution make up the cleanser. During a season,
I don't wash the trays every time I put in a new batch of pots or cells
to germinate.

My local garden center stocks both a cheap white plastic tray with
a raised clear plastic top and a sturdier green plastic tray of various
sizes without tops. The flimsy tray and top combination, filled with
cell packs, stays in the basement or on the refrigerator top for germi-

nating, and the cell packs move into the sturdier trays after growth has begun and to go outside for hardening off. The sturdy ones are worth buying, in part for the peace of mind of watering a well-made tray without pinholes or cracks that sits on a shelf over a light fixture. I prefer short white plastic labels, as they are reusable and easily washed at the same time as the pots and trays, and because they don't interfere with the cover or the lights above. If they've been inscribed in pencil, the notations can be erased for the next use.

The garden center also sells plastic cell packs, the most useful being the four-pack and six-pack, and they can be used again and again if you take care not to break them when removing plants. The trays are sized so that eight cell packs fit evenly. Annuals bought at garden centers come in these same packs, which you can save. The taller— by an inch and a half—single cells that herbs sometimes come in are useful for starting taprooters like baptisia or bloodflower and quick growers like feverfew.

Lights

My lights are rigged on our storage shelves in the basement from cup hooks screwed into the underside of the shelves, two hooks for each fixture. The hooks support each end of the four-foot fluorescent fixtures dangling below from lightweight chains bought at the hardware store. Each chain runs in and out of prepunched holes in the mounting surface of the lights, the free end of the chain attaching to itself with an S hook above the fixture. The chains are raised or lowered from the cup hooks to keep the bulbs two to six inches above the plants as they grow. If you suspend them so the plants are easily tended at table height, you'll thank yourself.

The fixtures came from an electrical supply house, where they refer to them as shop lights. I have three, and I know people who use eight or ten, but you really can do quite a lot with only one or two. The bulbs are ordinary fluorescent bulbs from the same source, and they don't need to be anything specially advertised to be better for plants. They'll be on 16 hours a day; an ordinary household timer turns them off at 11 P.M. and on again at 7 A.M. Although they're cooler than incandescent bulbs, they still heat things up a bit, so occasionally when germinating something that would really rather begin life at 55 degrees, I place the tray on the cool concrete floor next to the bottom shelf. The bulbs dim gradually with age, so you'll need to replace them before they burn out.

Seed Sowing

Occasionally plastic cell packs, and even individual peat pots, have inadequate drainage holes. You can cut off the tip of a plastic corner with scissors, or push a pencil through what should be the hole in the peat pot. A decent hole is important not only for drainage but also to permit bottom watering.

Seed-starter mix, bought bagged at the garden center, is sterile and free of insects and weed seeds and won't require messy baking in the oven. It's not a true soil, but it saves the trouble of preparing special soil yourself. The brand I buy no longer says "sterile" on its packaging, but I have no trouble with it.

Pour your best guess at the amount of seed-starting mix needed for the day into a clean bucket and add a small amount of hot water (more readily absorbed than cold), stirring until evenly moist. It shouldn't be wet or soggy. Fill the cells to the brim (they'll settle as they are watered), and lightly tamp with your finger.

Add the label with plant name, date, germination temperature, and a note if it needs light or darkness. Only the barest of abbreviations is necessary. Such information is readily available from seed companies or from books like Peter Loewer's helpful *Annual Garden*, but if I have no information on the depth, I'll put some at the depth of the seed's thickness, and a few more on the surface. Press the seed gently into the soil. If you're starting seed with children, save the largest seed for them. Record each sowing in your seed journal, leaving a line for the results later and suggestions to yourself for next time. These notes will save you from repeating mistakes.

Usually three seeds for annuals are adequate, and four to five for perennials. For expensive seed, which usually means less in the packet, you can put fewer in each cell and take the risk that some cells won't germinate. But the end result will be more plants. Transplant extra seedlings into those empty cells, handling them by a leaf rather than by the stem, so as not to break the stem.

Don't use the same cell pack for different types of seed. If you did, when the first cells germinated, you'd need to remove the pack from under the cover even though the other type of seed had not yet germinated. If you don't want to use all the cells in a pack, leave some empty, or use single pots. Not using all the seed in the packet on the first try also leaves you another chance later; if starting bupleurum early doesn't work, you'll still have seed to sow in the garden in March.

After sowing the seed, cover it lightly with mix; if the instructions say "just cover," it's easiest to sift on dryish mix. Bottom water lightly if your soil is dry by setting each pack briefly in a pan of water. Water less in seasons of high humidity. Don't water from above, other than a quick misting with a sprayer, or you'll disturb the seed. Attach the clear plastic cover, loosely if you think necessary, and place the tray under the lights, unless it's a seed requiring darkness to germinate. This procedure works well with other equipment, like the plastic sweater boxes some people swear by.

You can also sow all the seed first in one larger pot placed in the germinating tray, and after germination transplant the young seedlings into the individual cells or pots they are to be grown in. This makes a great deal of sense if large numbers of one kind of plant are to be grown: the many cell packs needed would overfill the available germinating trays. If you're only going to grow a few, however, it's an easier matter to skip that seedling transplant stage.

Plants that won't grow properly if their roots are disturbed need to be started in peat pots. The very tiniest pots dry out too quickly; three-inch diameter pots are about right in my experience. Use quite moist soil to avoid soaking the pots themselves through bottom watering. Later, water gently from the top, around the edge, using a small houseplant watering can with a narrow spout, to prevent a destructive rush of water. Peat pots are so prone to mold that I no longer shut them up tight; leave the lid ajar and mist the soil top occasionally, or leave the lid off the tray and place a rectangle of clear plastic on top of the pots. A warmer place, like the top of the refrigerator, seems to work better than a cool basement at keeping down fuzzy growths, but the seed may need frequent misting. You can easily tell when peat pots need watering: the pot becomes dry and stiff to the touch, and its weight feels light when you pick it up.

Germination

I keep a thermometer in a tray under the lights, and one occasionally on the floor, so I know what conditions are, not that I ever do much adjusting—our old basement at any season is usually between 65 and 75 degrees. That's a perfect germinating temperature range for a great many plants, though a bit warm for penstemon, delphinium, or stocks. Those I manage to start with the tray set on the cold floor, where the thermometer reads about 62 degrees in winter. Thermostatically controlled heating mats are available for gardeners whose conditions run in the other direction, and for seed that needs higher temperatures. I once spent 12 days trying to start a peanut plant for a school project; I set a second pot on a heat mat, and it germinated in two days. Heat mats are also useful for drying out cells soggy from overwatering. Remember that soil above a heat mat dries out sooner, and if there is a cover on the tray, the heat may build too high. Keep the soil fairly moist, and the cover ajar or off. After germination, young plants prefer somewhat cooler temperatures, perhaps 60 degrees, so those with cool rooms can take heart.

A few plants need total darkness to germinate. Place clean, new aluminum foil loosely across the cells in their tray and keep them in a dim place where you won't forget them. The trays have to be checked daily, because without the raised cover there's no room underneath the foil for a seedling to grow straight and they become extremely leggy without light. (As they germinate, peel back the foil to expose the seedling in each cell and put the tray under the lights.)

When you find more than half the cells in your germination trays have sprouted, bottom water and return them to the lights without covers. Put sun lovers toward the middle of the bulbs, where the light levels are highest. At this point, your attention is required daily. Withhold fertilizer until the young sprouts have shown one or two true pairs of leaves, in addition to the first pair of cotyledons. Mix a liquid fertilizer to only half the strength recommended for mature plants, and use it in place of plain water for bottom watering; when the plants are larger, you can water carefully from the top. Young plants in seed-starter mix must be fertilized regularly or they won't continue to grow.

Seedlings

Permit the several seedlings that may grow in each cell to develop a few pairs of leaves before you select the one to keep growing on. When growing mixed colors, don't select only the first to germinate, or only the strongest, as it may result in flowers all of one color.

I often select the healthy seedling that is closest to the center of the cell, or an equal amount of early and late risers. Some seed packets, such as delphinium, warn that the best colors come from smaller seedlings.

It's less disruptive to use a pair of nail or embroidery scissors to snip out unwanted seedlings than it is to pull them out. In the case of plants like tellima and foxgloves, which have almost microscopic seedlings, I may not thin them for a while in case some mishap causes a few to succumb. Forgetting to water is the usual problem. Some seedlings use up their water sooner than others, and peat pots may need daily watering rather than the two to four times a week for plastic. Keep in mind whether the plant is sensitive to poor drainage; the soil shouldn't appear soaked, and it may be a good thing if it looks a little dry. I haven't had much problem with seedling death caused by disease; more often it's caused by some unnatural disaster, such as the installation of a new furnace blowing black soot over the entire basement.

You may need to move into larger pots those seedlings like fever-few that surprise you by their rapid growth. Raise the lights as the plants grow taller to keep the bulbs two to six inches above the fo-liage. A small household fan, set on a timer to come on for a few hours at low speed, and not placed too close to the plants, will simu-late a gentle breeze and strengthen stems. I've always meant to do this. It may cause plants to dry out faster, but it can also help prevent disease. In a heated room, you may need to provide a source of hu-midity, as the air otherwise may be too dry in winter. Basements in old houses rarely have this problem.

Hardening Off

When the plants become large and planting times for each species are within about two weeks, the trays come up from the basement to harden off. Hardening off means to introduce your plants gradu-ally to sunlight, wind, and temperature variations: in other words, weather. Allow about ten days to two weeks for the process. A cold frame allows you to harden off plants earlier than you could other-wise and provides shelter against poor weather; it can also stress your plants severely if you forget to raise the lid on a sunny day. Don't underestimate the damage done by too much sun the first few days;

begin the hardening off in the late afternoon and early morning, bringing them in midday.

Biennials, hardy annuals, and perennials like pansies and delphinium can tolerate much more cold, even prefer it, than other plants, and so are ready to harden off first. Next come the plants that can't take much frost or heat and must be planted soon because they'll be finished off by the coming summer: *Trachymene coerulea* and *Ammi majus* are two. Last to harden off are tender annuals such as globe amaranth and ageratum.

The trays sit out on my partially shaded south-facing back porch for two hours a day at first, not in strong sun or wind, increasing their exposure gradually. You can set them in an open cardboard box as shelter from wind and hard rain. By the end of a week to 10 days, the plants are out all day and come in to sit on the kitchen floor at night. If night temperatures are not too near freezing, and the plants can accept it (not tender annuals), I leave them out at night thereafter. They dry out much more quickly now and require frequent watering, with plain water, if they are under stress. You'll need to protect them from cats and squirrels, which love to dig into cell packs. I resorted to the stuffed toy cat, Tico, to sit out beside them on the porch, and I even drew scary faces on a paper bag with a soup can inside to keep it from blowing away. After seeing me do this for years, my son built me a lovely chicken wire cover under which fit two trays of seedlings. In just a few days of hardening off, the seedlings are so lush and green that I realize again what torture it must be for plants to grow indoors.

Planting Out

The very hardy plants that tolerate frosts can be planted when they're ready, and when the average last frost day arrives in spring, you can begin putting the remaining plants in their places in the garden, remembering that frosts may still occur after that date. If your area has a local gardening guide like our *Washington Star Garden Book*, you may find it has maps of the average frost dates for fall and spring. Plant on a cloudy day, if possible, and shade plants from strong sun for a couple of days afterward. In the absence of better materials, I'll even stick twigs into the ground at an angle over the little plant and drape some chickweed over it as a tent. If a plant looks stressed, cut back some of the foliage to give the roots time to adjust. Peat pots must be set gently into the ground, first tearing off the upper part protruding above the soil line, to keep air from wicking moisture out of the pot. Water well the first weeks.

Now you can turn off the lights, stack the pots and trays, and take a deserved break. There's no doubt that starting seedlings indoors is careful work requiring patient attention to detail. To go away for a week while there are young plants germinating may call for house-sitting assistance even more capable than that employed for pets. But the fact is that sowing seed out in the garden often doesn't succeed for even the most experienced gardener. Starting seed indoors under lights may be the only way to include some of the most desirable plants in the cutting garden.

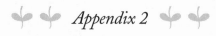

Appendix 2

Volunteers in My Garden

Whether a plant self-sows depends partly on climate and soil conditions. Some of the following volunteer here only rarely, others do so copiously. Many additional plants for cutting will self-sow in other places, perhaps in your garden.

BOTANICAL NAME	COMMON NAME
Alcea rosea	hollyhock
Allium tuberosum	garlic chives
Amaranthus cruentus	prince's feather
Anchusa azurea	Italian bugloss
Anethum graveolens	dill
Anthemis tinctoria	golden Marguerite
Antirrhinum majus	snapdragon
Aquilegia, various	columbine
Asclepias currasavica	bloodflower
Aster novae-angliae	New England aster
Aster novi-belgii	New York aster
Aster pringlei 'Monte Cassino'	September flower
Atriplex hortensis	mountain spinach, orach
Begonia grandis	hardy begonia
Bellis perennis	English daisy
Bupleurum griffithii	thoroughwax
Calendula officinalis	pot marigold

BOTANICAL NAME	COMMON NAME
Celosia, various	celosia
Centaurea cyanus	cornflower
Centranthus ruber 'Alba'	red valerian
Chasmanthium latifolium	northern sea oats
Chrysanthemum leucanthemum	ox-eye daisy
Cleome hassleriana	spider flower
Consolida, various	larkspur
Coreopsis tinctoria	calliopsis
Cosmos bipinnatus	cosmos
Cynoglossum amabile	Chinese forget-me-not
Daucus carota	Queen Anne's lace
Dianthus barbatus	sweet William
Digitalis purpurea	foxglove
Dipsacus fullonum	teasel
Echinacea purpurea	purple coneflower
Emilia javanica	tassel flower
Euphorbia marginata	snow-on-the-mountain
Euphorbia polychroma	cushion spurge
Foeniculum vulgare	fennel
Gaillardia, various	blanket flower
Helianthus annuus	sunflower
Helleborus foetidus	stinking hellebore
Helleborus orientalis	Lenten rose
Hesperis matronalis	sweet rocket
Lablab purpureus	hyacinth bean
Lilium lancifolium	tiger lily
Linaria maroccana	toadflax
Lunaria annua	honesty, money plant
Lychnis coronaria	rose campion
Malva alcea 'Fastigiata'	hollyhock mallow
Malva sylvestris	tree mallow
Mertensia virginica	Virginia bluebells
Myosotis sylvatica	forget-me-not

Nicotiana, various	flowering tobacco
Nigella damascena	love-in-a-mist
Papaver rhoeas	corn poppy, Shirley poppy
Pastinaca sativa	wild parsnip
Phlox divaricata	woodland phlox
Ricinus communis	castor bean
Rudbeckia triloba	brown-eyed Susan
Rudbeckia fulgida	orange coneflower
Salvia viridis	sage
Sedum spectabile	stonecrop
Solidago, various	goldenrod
Stokesia laevis	Stokes' aster
Tropaeolum majus	nasturtium
Uvularia grandiflora	merrybells
Verbascum blattaria	mullein
Verbena bonariensis	tall verbena
Viola tricolor	Johnny jump-up

In addition, I've known the following plants to volunteer in nearby gardens:

Alchemilla mollis	lady's mantle
Arum italicum	arum
Cheiranthus cheiri	wallflowers
Ipomopsis rubra	standing cypress
Lavatera trimestris	tree mallow
Patrinia scabiosaefolia	patrinia
Platycodon grandiflorus	balloon flower
Primula japonica	Japanese primrose
Valeriana officinalis	common valerian
Verbascum chaixii	mullein

⚜ ⚜ *Appendix 3* ⚜ ⚜

Sources and Suggested Reading

Some of my nicest gardening opportunities have been gifts of plants I might never have chosen myself. Black tulips bought by my spouse at the airport in the Netherlands are the first that come to mind. Other instigators include Mary Beth R., who grew only annuals and cut me a handful one day long ago, and another who shocked me by remarking that she loved dahlias. Excellent plants may come from neighbors. Some plants like irises are available in catalogs in such a multitude of forms that it's difficult to choose even with a picture, so it may be as satisfying to keep an eye on the gardens of neighbors and friends and beg a section at division time; you may not get to know the name, but you'll have a plant you know you like. If you garden at a community garden, you'll encounter all kinds of plants you'd never know to grow otherwise, and attending horticultural society plant sales will keep you flush with new treasure.

Every year I place orders from several of my favorite suppliers, which keeps their catalogs coming. I like to order from nurseries in my part of the country when it's possible, because I expect they're more likely to offer plants that succeed here, and their catalogs make valuable reference material. Once I found myself going back to lock my car because I'd left a certain list on the front seat. But I avoid catalogs that advertise MINIATURE HOLLYHOCKS!!! without identifying them as *Sidalcea malviflora*, or use lens filters to exaggerate color, and I dislike the use of forced bulbs photographed in pots but pictured to suggest they're growing in the garden. It's worth seeking out better bulb catalogs than some of the illustrated ones that arrive unsolicited. Some of these specialty catalogs include no pictures but do have a tremendous selection for those who know what they want, and the supplier will likely prove more reliable.

A good garden center or local nursery is an excellent place to acquire those plants you'd like to choose while in bloom: iris, dianthus, peonies, oriental poppies. Don't forget your local herb nursery. When a mail-order plant succumbs repeatedly, try it again in a pot from a local source.

Avoid most shortcuts to selecting cut-flower plants such as the collections offered in catalogs—"Dahlias for Cutting," "Blue Cutflower Mix," or "Annuals for Cutting"—almost always a hodgepodge, and tricky to care for in the case of seed since you don't know what will be germinating. If, however, you know you'll like almost anything in the category, such as "Sunflowers for Cutting" or "Cornflowers for Cutting," then it may be a way to acquire variety at low cost. The following suppliers should offer most of the plants mentioned in this book.

Sources for Seed

W. Atlee Burpee & Co.
300 Park Ave.
Warminster, PA 18991-0001
800-888-1447. Catalog free
www.burpee.com

Cook's Garden Seeds
PO Box 5010
Hodges, SC 29653-5010
800-457-9703. Catalog free
www.cooksgarden.com

J. L. Hudson, Seedsman
Star Route 2, Box 337
La Honda, CA 94020
No phone. Catalog $1.00

Nichols Garden Nursery
1190 Old Salem Rd. NE
Albany, OR 97321-4580
541-928-9280. Catalog free
www.gardennursery.com

Park Seed
1 Parkton Ave.
Greenwood, SC 29647-0001
800-845-3369. Catalog free
www.parkseed.com

Seeds of Change
PO Box 15700
Santa Fe, NM 87506-5700
888-762-7333. Catalog free
www.seedsofchange.com

Select Seeds Antique Flowers
180 Stickney Hill Rd.
Union, CT 06076-4617
860-684-9310. Catalog free
www.selectseeds.com

Shepherd's Garden Seeds
30 Irene St.
Torrington, CT 06790-6658
860-482-3638. Catalog free
www.shepherdseeds.com

Stokes Seeds
Box 548
Buffalo, NY 14240-0548
800-396-9238. Catalog free
www.stokeseeds.com

Thompson & Morgan
PO Box 1308
Jackson, NJ 08527-0308
800-274-7333. Catalog free
www.thompson-morgan.com

Territorial Seed Company
PO Box 157
Cottage Grove, OR 97424-0061
541-942-9547. Catalog free
www.territorialseed.com

Twilley Seeds
PO Box 4000
Hodges, SC 29653-4000
800-622-7333. Catalog free

Nursery Sources

Canyon Creek Nursery
3527 Dry Creek Rd.
Oroville, CA 95965
530-533-2166. Catalog free
www.canyoncreeknursery.com
Interesting perennials

Heronswood Nursery
7530 E. 288th St.
Kingston, WA 98346
360-297-4172. Catalog $8.00
www.heronswood.com
*Primulas, euphorbias, rare
perennials*

King's Mums
PO Box 368
Clements, CA 95227
209-759-3571. Catalog $2.00
www.kingsmums.com
Tender and hardy mums

Klehm Nursery
4210 N. Duncan Rd.
Champaign, IL 61822-9559
800-553-3715. Catalog $4.00

www.klehm.com
Peonies, perennials

Niche Gardens
1111 Dawson Rd.
Chapel Hill, NC 27516
919-967-0078. Catalog $3.00
www.nichegardens.com
Asters, phlox, perennials

Plant Delights Nursery
9241 Sauls Rd.
Raleigh, NC 27603-9326
919-772-4794. Catalog 10 stamps
or box of chocolates
www.plantdelights.com
Unusual perennials, some tender

Sandy Mush Herb Nursery
316 Surrett Cove Rd.
Leicester, NC 28748-5517
Thurs-Sat only: 828-683-2014.
Catalog $6.00
Tender and hardy perennials

Shady Oaks Nursery
1101 S. State St.
PO Box 708
Waseca, MN 56093-0708
800-504-8006. Catalog $4.00
www.shadyoaks.com
Shade perennials

Andre Viette Farm & Nursery
PO Box 1109
Fishersville, VA 22939
800-575-5538. Catalog $6.00

www.viette.com
Perennials, iris, peonies

White Flower Farm
PO Box 50
Litchfield, CT 06759-0050
800-503-9624. Catalog free
www.whiteflowerfarm.com
Perennials, bulbs, lilies

Bulbs, Tubers, and Corms

Aitken's Salmon Creek Garden
608 N.W. 119th St.
Vancouver, WA 98685
360-573-4472. Catalog $2.00
Iris

B and D Lilies
PO Box 2007
Port Townsend, WA 98368
360-765-4341. Catalog $3.00
www.bdlilies.com
Lilies

Brent and Becky's Bulbs
7463 Heath Trail
Gloucester, VA 23061
877-661-2852. Catalog free
www.brentandbeckysbulbs.com
Hardy and tender bulbs

Chuck Chapman Iris
RR #1 (8790 Hwy #24)
Guelph, ONT
Canada 91H 6H7
519-856-4424. Catalog $2.00
Iris

Dutch Gardens
PO Box 2037
Lakewood, NJ 08701-8037
800-818-3861. Catalog free
Hardy and tender bulbs

The Lily Garden
4902 N.E. 147th Ave.
Vancouver, WA 98682-6067
360-253-6273. Catalog $1.00
Garden lilies

McClure & Zimmerman
108 West Winnebago St.
PO Box 368
Friesland, WI 53935-0368
800-883-6998. Catalog free
www.mzbulb.com
Hardy and tender bulbs

John Scheepers, Inc.
23 Tulip Dr.
Bantam, CT 06750
860-567-0838. Catalog free
www.johnscheepers.com
Hardy bulbs, lilies

Sea-Tac Gardens
20020 Des Moines Memorial Dr.
Seattle, WA 98198
206-824-3846. Catalog free
Dahlias

Swan Island Dahlias
PO Box 700
Canby, OR 97013-0700
800-410-6540. Catalog $4.00
www.dahlias.com
Dahlias

Suggested Reading

For new gardeners, I always suggest Pamela Harper and Frederick McGourty's *Perennials: How to Select, Grow & Enjoy* (1985) and its companion books on annuals and bulbs by HP Books; I still turn to them. Along with several of the following, they offer valuable basic gardening instruction as well as plant information. Taylor's Guides to Gardening, such as *Taylor's Guide to Bulbs* and *Taylor's Guide to Annuals,* are excellent illustrated sources for a range of plant categories and garden types. Two essential garden references for me now are Allan Armitage's *Herbaceous Perennial Plants,* second edition (1997) and *Perennials for American Gardens* by Clausen and Ekstrom (1989). The former is particularly valuable for gardeners in the South and contains priceless information on plant culture (including on some bulbs), but the latter includes plants missing from Armitage's work. When I need more than these two can offer, I heft the big *Hortus Third* (1976, compiled by the Liberty Hyde Bailey Hortorium at Cornell University) off the reference shelf at the library, which doesn't yet have the more up-to-date *Index of Garden Plants* by Mark Griffiths (1994). For identifying flowers, the pictures in Roger Phillips and Martyn Rix's two-volume *Random House Book of Perennials* (1991) and the companion books on bulbs and herbs are invaluable, as is the American Horticultural Society's *Encyclopedia of Garden Plants* (1989). Nancy Bubel's *The New Seed Starters Handbook* (1988), Peter Loewer's *The Annual Garden* (1988, which includes grasses, vines, and foliage), and *Garden Flowers from Seed* (1991) by Christopher Lloyd and Graham Rice are three I refer to for seed-starting. For after-harvest care of flowers, you might find *The Complete Book of Cut Flower Care* by Mary Jane Vaughan (1988) helpful. Two books on growing cut flowers as a small business are (in Kansas) Lynn Byczynski's *The Flower Farmer* (1997) and (in California) *Growing Flowers for Market* by Mike Madison (1998). And for a very personal account of a cutting garden, Celia Thaxter's *An Island Garden* is the one to read.

Appendix 4

A Sequence of Bloom
with the Dates of First Flowers

The reader of a garden book naturally wonders when the plant will bloom for *me* when reading that it flowers "in late May" or "early fall." I usually subtract almost a month for a book written from upper New England, and I add several weeks to information arriving from the lower South. A more reliable method for estimating the likely date of bloom in another garden lies with identifying plants flowering at the same time. "Blooming with the Siberian iris" identifies a period of the garden year familiar to gardeners almost anywhere. The following chart lists many plants for cutting *in chronological order of their median bloom dates* in my Zone 7a locale. Plants near each other on the list may bloom together in other gardens, and you can try them as companion material for your cutting garden. If you know when certain of these plants bloom in your garden, you can make educated guesses regarding others by examining the chart.

You can also anticipate the consequences of various gardening practices by, for example, comparing the result of sowing *Papaver rhoeas* in fall, which will bloom with foxgloves and sweet William, and of sowing the same poppies in earliest spring, blooming over three weeks later with Shasta daises and veronica. I should caution that, as some plants proceed to full bloom quite slowly after producing their first flower, it may be two or more weeks after the dates listed here before certain plants are at their prime. Boltonia, chrysopsis, and fall asters are notable for this behavior. A specimen in shade may also bloom some days later than the same plant in full sun, and dry weather sometimes delays bloom.

I recorded the dates of the first flower's opening (from my garden and several nearby gardens) in my journals over a period of twelve years, and the median date determined each plant's order on the list. Many had numerous entries recorded over many seasons, but where only one date was available, it was placed in the median column; where two dates existed, the average of the two (in parentheses) dictated the plant's placement on the list. The decade includes several very cold winters, and several particularly mild ones.

Those plants noted as "sown fall" or "planted fall" were usually sown (seeds) or planted (plants) in the garden in September or October (at the time of *Salvia azurea* or *Aster tataricus*). Those sown under lights in winter, noted as "winter/lights," were begun indoors January through March, with the perennials and biennials (requiring longer to reach maturity) begun first, hardy annuals next, and tender annuals last. "Late winter" here is February (before the snowdrops), and "earlist spring" is March (with the crocus). The dates for hardy bulbs are largely for bulbs that have been in the ground for several years.

Readers will suspect correctly that I consulted the list included by Elizabeth Lawrence in her classic *A Southern Garden* for her method of presentation. The differences here are that only cutting plants have been included, and they've been arranged in order of bloom rather than alphabetically. I've also omitted reference to length of bloom, as most plants are at their best for cutting when they first flower. While this book does not cover roses, I included dates for several roses to locate the rose season in the chronology. Please consult chapter 6 for more information on each plant.

	DATES OF FIRST BLOOM		
PLANT	FIRST	MEDIAN	LAST
Viola × *wittrockiana* (planted fall)		all winter	
Helleborus foetidus	Dec	Jan	Jan
Narcissus 'Rijnveld's Early Sensation'	Jan 6	Feb 7	Feb 10
Bellis perennis (planted fall or self-sown)	Feb	(Feb)	Feb
Galanthus elwesii	Jan 27	Feb 12	Mar 7
Crocus species	Feb 6	Feb 13	Mar 4
Helleborus niger	Feb 20	(Feb 21)	Feb 21
Narcissus	Feb 21	Mar 3	Mar 23
Crocus hybrids	Feb 26	Mar 7	Mar 25
Primula veris	Feb 21	Mar 10	Apr 2
Helleborus orientalis	Feb 12	Mar 12	Mar 30
Anemone fulgens	—	Mar 15	—
Leucojum aestivum 'Gravetye Giant'	Mar 10	Mar 16	Apr 7

Viola tricolor (planted fall or self-sown)	Feb 27	Mar 18	Apr 1
Chionodoxa luciliae	Mar 12	Mar 22	Apr 1
Iberis sempervirens	Mar 22	(Mar 22)	Mar 22
Pulmonaria 'Roy Davidson'	—	Mar 24	—
Doronicum cordatum	Mar 18	Mar 24	Mar 27
Hyacinthus orientalis/H. multiflorus	Mar 10	Mar 25	Apr 2
Primula vulgaris, species and hybrids	Mar 17	Mar 28	Apr 9
Hermodactylus tuberosa	Mar 13	(Mar 29)	Apr 4
Helleborus argutifolius	Mar 13	Mar 29	Apr 4
Scilla siberica	Mar 22	Apr 2	Apr 6
Mertensia virginica	Mar 23	Apr 2	Apr 9
Primula denticulata	—	Apr 3	—
Euphorbia amygdaloides var. *robbiae*	Mar 20	Apr 3	Apr 18
Anemone coronaria (planted fall)	Feb 23	Apr 4	Apr 14
Tulipa	Mar 20	Apr 4	Apr 9
Bellis perennis (sown fall)	—	Apr 5	—
Cheiranthus cheiri (sown fall)	Apr 2	(Apr 5)	Apr 7
Iberis amara (sown fall)	—	Apr 5	—
Muscari armeniacum	Mar 25	Apr 7	Apr 15
Brassica oleracea (2d yr)	Mar 30	Apr 7	Apr 8
Uvularia grandiflora	Apr 1	Apr 7	Apr 13
Muscari latifolium	—	Apr 8	—
Phlox divaricata (blue)	Apr 1	Apr 9	Apr 17
Brassica juncea (2d yr)	Apr 5	(Apr 9)	Apr 12
Lunaria annua	Mar 29	Apr 10	Apr 20
Muscari botryoides var. *album*	Mar 30	Apr 10	Apr 13
Fritillaria meleagris	Mar 30	Apr 10	Apr 14
Viola tricolor (winter/lights)	—	Apr 11	—
Aurinia saxatile 'Citrinum'	—	Apr 11	—
Myosotis sylvatica (self-sown)	Apr 1	Apr 11	Apr 13
Ranunculus acris 'Flore Pleno'	Apr 3	(Apr 11)	Apr 19
Dicentra spectabilis	Apr 5	Apr 11	Apr 14
Narcissus 'Thalia'	Mar 29	Apr 12	Apr 14
Primula sieboldii	Mar 30	Apr 12	Apr 23
Erythronium 'Pagoda'	Apr 1	Apr 12	Apr 17
Hyacinthoides hispanica	Apr 1	Apr 12	Apr 22
Thermopsis caroliniana	Apr 11	Apr 13	Apr 16
Dicentra eximia 'Luxuriant'	Apr 5	Apr 14	Apr 16
Euphorbia polychroma	Apr 7	Apr 14	Apr 20
Geum × *borisii*	Apr 10	(Apr 16)	Apr 21

PLANT	DATES OF FIRST BLOOM		
	FIRST	MEDIAN	LAST
Tiarella cordifolia 'Wherryi'	Apr 2	Apr 22	Apr 23
Papaver nudicaule (planted fall, sown fall)	Apr 13	Apr 23	Apr 27
Narcissus poeticus var. *recurvus*	Apr 16	Apr 23	Apr 29
Hesperis matronalis (planted fall, self-sown)	Apr 11	Apr 25	Apr 30
Convallaria majalis	Apr 16	Apr 25	Apr 29
Hyacinthoides non-scripta	Apr 19	Apr 25	Apr 27
Polygonatum odoratum 'Variegatum'	Apr 10	Apr 26	May 1
Centaurea cyanus (self-sown or sown fall)	Apr 11	Apr 26	Apr 29
Camassia leichtlinii 'Blue Danube'	Apr 24	Apr 26	Apr 29
Aquilegia vulgaris (self-sown)	Apr 19	Apr 26	May 2
Salvia 'East Friesland'	—	Apr 27	—
Iris, tall bearded	Apr 22	Apr 27	May 1
Tellima grandiflora	Apr 26	Apr 27	Apr 27
Polygonatum multiflorum	Apr 15	Apr 28	May 1
Euphorbia palustris	Apr 16	Apr 28	May 6
Heuchera sanguinea/H. × *brizoides* hybrids	Apr 23	Apr 28	May 12
Phlox pilosa	Apr 26	Apr 28	May 7
Iris, Dutch	Apr 23	Apr 29	May 7
Heucherella 'Bridget Bloom'	Apr 25	(Apr 29)	May 3
Campanula glomerata 'Joan Elliott'	Apr 24	Apr 29	May 1
Camassia cusickii	Apr 20	Apr 30	May 6
Campanula glomerata 'Alba'	Apr 24	(Apr 30)	May 5
Allium schoenoprasum 'Forescate'	Apr 26	May 1	May 5
Knautia arvensis	Apr 28	May 1	May 4
Dianthus × *allwoodii* 'Doris'	—	May 2	—
Aquilegia 'Nora Barlow'	Apr 23	May 3	May 14
Allium aflatunense	Apr 25	May 3	May 12
Calendula officinalis (winter/lights)	Apr 26	May 3	May 6
Dianthus 'Mountain Mist'	Apr 27	May 3	May 5
Nectaroscordum siculum	Apr 27	May 4	May 10
Allium neapolitanum	May 2	May 4	May 6
Rudbeckia 'Green Wizard' (2d yr)	—	May 4	—
Chrysanthemum coccineum	Apr 27	May 5	May 8
Cynoglossum amabile (self-sown, planted fall)	May 4	(May 5)	May 5
Chrysanthemum leucanthemum 'May Queen'	May 4	(May 5)	May 6
Verbascum 'Sou. Charm' (2d yr, planted fall)	May 3	May 6	May 12
Paeonia, herbaceous	Apr 30	May 7	May 17
Malva s. mauritiana (sown fall, self-sown)	May 5	May 7	May 22

Allium christophii	May 6	May 7	May 16
Gypsophila elegans 'Giant White' (sown fall)	May 2	May 8	May 8
Baptisia australis	May 2	May 8	May 16
Rosa 'Zepherine Drouhin'	Apr 22	May 9	May 15
Papaver rhoeas (sown fall, self-sown)	May 4	May 9	May 20
Dianthus barbatus	Apr 27	May 10	May 13
Valeriana officinalis	May 2	May 10	May 12
Centranthus ruber	May 3	May 10	May 22
Baptisia alba	May 4	May 10	May 18
Anchusa azurea 'Dropmore'	—	May 11	—
Viola × *wittrockiana* (early spring/lights)	—	May 11	—
Dianthus × *allwoodii* 'Laced Romeo'	Apr 27	(May 11)	May 24
Papaver orientale	May 2	May 11	May 15
Papaver commutatum (sown fall, self-sown)	May 7	(May 11)	May 15
Dictamnus albus 'Purpureus'	—	May 11	—
Clematis integrifolia	May 10	May 11	May 11
Linaria purpurea (2d yr)	—	May 12	—
Bupleurum griffithii (sown fall, self-sown)	May 4	May 12	May 15
Achillea × 'Moonshine'	May 10	(May 12)	May 14
Rosa 'Dainty Bess'	—	May 13	—
Digitalis purpurea 'Foxy' (planted fall)	May 11	(May 13)	May 14
Trollius europaeus 'Byrne's Giant'	May 12	(May 13)	May 13
Penstemon 'Rondo' (2d yr)	—	May 14	—
Alchemilla mollis	Apr 26	May 14	May 28
Consolida ajacis (sown fall)	May 10	May 14	May 19
Chrysanthemum corymbosum	—	May 15	—
Digitalis purp. (self-sown, planted prev. sprng)	Apr 26	May 15	May 16
Consolida 'Blue Cloud' (self-sown)	Apr 27	May 15	May 18
Trollius ledebourii 'Golden Queen'	May 14	May 15	May 30
Delphinium 'Conn. Yankees' (winter/lights)	—	May 16	—
Matthiola i. 'Trysomic Stock' (winter/lights)	—	May 16	—
Iris pseudacorus	May 6	May 16	May 23
Cirsium japonicum (2d yr, winter/lights)	May 10	May 16	May 25
Gladiolus byzantinus	May 12	May 16	May 20
Iris sibirica 'White Sails'	May 13	May 16	May 23
Kniphofia uvaria 'Pfitzeri'	—	May 17	—
Malva 'Zebrina' (sown fall, self-sown)	May 15	May 17	May 22
Agrostemma githago (sown fall)	Apr 24	May 18	May 20
Tradescantia × *andersoniana*	Apr 24	May 18	May 24
Knautia macedonica	—	May 19	—

PLANT	DATES OF FIRST BLOOM		
	FIRST	MEDIAN	LAST
Polemonium caeruleum	May 4	(May 19)	June 3
Campanula medium (planted fall)	May 13	May 19	May 27
Consolida ajacis (winter/lights)	May 15	May 19	June 5
Bupleurum griffithii (winter/lights)	—	May 20	—
Rosa 'Heritage'	—	May 20	—
Erigeron 'Pink Jewel'	May 14	May 20	May 20
Dianthus superbus (winter/lights)	May 17	(May 20)	May 22
Ruta graveolens	—	May 20	—
Salvia horminum (self-sown)	—	May 21	—
Campanula persicifolia	May 8	May 21	May 26
Nigella damascena (sown fall)	May 10	May 21	May 25
Iris louisiana 'Clara Goula'	May 14	May 21	May 22
Digitalis grandiflora	May 16	(May 21)	May 26
Iris fulva	May 21	May 21	May 22
Penstemon digitalis	May 16	(May 22)	May 27
Coreopsis tinctoria (winter/lights)	—	May 24	—
Papaver somniferum (sown fall)	May 17	(May 24)	May 31
Chrysanthemum parth. 'White Wonder' (2d yr)	May 20	May 25	June 4
Penstemon barbatus 'Coccineus' (winter/lights)	May 21	(May 25)	May 28
Lychnis coronaria (2d yr, self-sown)	May 22	(May 25)	May 27
Lathyrus odoratus (sown late winter)	May 22	May 25	May 31
Lychnis chalcedonia mixed colors (2d yr)	May 22	May 25	June 4
Delphinium 'Pacific Giant' (2d yr)	—	May 26	—
Delphinium × *belladonna* (2d yr)	May 19	(May 26)	June 2
Briza media	May 20	(May 26)	June 1
Nicotiana langsdorfii (winter/lights)	May 25	(May 26)	May 27
Lathyrus latifolius (2d yr)	May 25	May 26	May 29
Allium caeruleum	—	May 27	—
Astrantia major	May 10	(May 27)	June 13
Phlox maculata 'Miss Lingard'	May 21	May 27	June 5
Lysimachia punctata	May 23	(May 27)	May 30
Coreopsis grandiflora	May 23	May 27	June 1
Verbena bonariensis	May 24	May 27	June 2
Linaria purpurea (late winter/lights)	—	May 28	—
Cosmos b. 'Sensation' (winter/lights)	—	May 28	—
Nepeta fassenii 'Six Hills Giant'	May 11	May 28	June 8
Verbascum 'Southern Charm' (winter/lights)	—	May 29	—
Armeria plantaginea 'Bees Ruby'	May 22	May 29	June 3
Veronica spicata 'Blue Peter'	May 23	May 29	June 1

Chrysanthemum carinatum (winter/lights)	—	May 30	—
Astilbe × *arendsii* hybrids	May 25	May 30	June 6
Achillea millefolium hybrids	May 26	(May 30)	June 6
Ammi majus (winter/lights)	May 27	May 30	June 1
Aruncus dioicus	May 27	May 30	June 8
Asclepias incarnata 'Ice Ballet'	—	May 31	—
Iris foetidissima	—	May 31	—
Delphinium belladonna (winter/lights)	May 27	(May 31)	June 4
Tropaeolum majus (sown early spring)	May 30	May 31	June 7
Scabiosa ochroleuca	—	June 1	—
Ratibida columnifera	—	June 1	—
Tulbaghia violacea	May 4	June 1	June 12
Lilium, Asiatic hybrids	May 27	June 1	June 7
Antirrhinum majus (winter/lights)	May 30	June 1	June 2
Brassica juncea (sown late winter)	May 31	(June 1)	June 1
Catananche caerulea	—	June 1	—
Cephalaria gigantea	—	June 2	—
Centaurea macrocephala	—	June 2	—
Gaillardia × *grandiflora* 'Burgundy' (2d yr)	—	June 2	—
Ranunculus asiaticus (planted early spring)	—	June 2	—
Anthemis tinctoria (planted fall, sown fall)	May 23	June 2	June 9
Anethum graveolens (winter/lights)	June 1	(June 2)	June 3
Gaura lindheimeri	—	June 2	—
Rudbeckia h., gloriosa daisy (winter/lights)	May 15	June 3	June 17
Verbascum blattaria (self-sown)	May 27	(June 3)	June 10
Lavandula angustifolia	May 27	(June 3)	June 10
Consolida ajacis (sown earliest spring)	May 28	(June 3)	June 8
Salvia horminum (winter/lights)	—	June 3	—
Gypsophila paniculata	—	June 4	—
Nicotiana alata (self-sown)	May 25	June 4	June 9
Triteleia laxa 'Queen Fabiola'	May 28	(June 4)	June 12
Alcea rosea (sown fall, planted fall)	June 1	June 4	June 7
Euphorbia marginata (self-sown, sown spring)	May 22	June 5	June 18
Pastinaca sativa	May 27	June 5	June 7
Penstemon barbatus 'Coccineus' (2d yr)	June 5	(June 5)	June 5
Malva alcea 'Fastigiata'	June 4	June 6	June 7
Verbascum chaixii	June 5	(June 6)	June 7
Salvia farinacea (2d yr)	—	June 7	—
Veronica longifolia 'Pink Shades' (2d yr)	May 21	June 7	June 14
Scabiosa atropurpurea (winter/lights)	May 30	(June 7)	June 15
Achillea ptarmica 'The Pearl'	June 7	(June 7)	June 7

PLANT	DATES OF FIRST BLOOM		
	FIRST	MEDIAN	LAST
Nicotiana rustica (early spring/lights)	—	June 7	—
Achillea filipendulina 'Parker's Variety'	May 23	June 8	June 13
Asclepias tuberosa	May 30	(June 8)	June 17
Heliopsis helianthoides 'Summer Sun'	June 2	(June 8)	June 14
Lythrum cultivars	June 5	June 8	June 13
Penstemon barbatus 'Rondo' (winter/lights)	—	June 9	—
Astilbe × arendsii 'Ostrich Plume'	May 30	June 10	June 20
Veronica spicata 'Icicle'	June 7	(June 10)	June 12
Penstemon gentianoides (winter/lights)	—	June 10	—
Papaver rhoeas (sown early spring)	—	June 11	—
Iris ensata cultivars	May 29	June 11	June 14
Chrysanthemum × superbum (Shasta daisy)	May 23	June 12	June 20
Hemerocallis fulva	June 1	June 12	June 16
Amaranthus 'Prince's Feather' (sown spring)	June 5	June 12	June 27
Emilia javanica (self-sown)	June 11	(June 12)	June 13
Anethum graveolens (self-sown)	June 12	June 12	June 22
Eryngium planum	—	June 13	—
Chrysanthemum parthenium (winter/lights)	—	June 13	—
Sidalcea 'Party Girl' (2d yr, winter/lights)	May 31	June 13	June 24
Stokesia laevis	June 4	June 13	June 23
Eryngium amethystinum	June 12	June 13	June 27
Gypsophila elegans 'Giant White' (sown spring)	—	June 14	—
Daucus carota (sown fall, self-sown)	June 9	June 14	June 20
Coreopsis tinctoria (self-sown)	June 1	June 15	June 17
Trachymene coerulea (winter/lights)	June 14	(June 15)	June 16
Humulus lupulus	—	June 15	—
Scabiosa caucasica 'Fama'	—	June 16	—
Phlox drummondii (sown spring)	—	June 16	—
Delphinium 'Magic Fountain' (Jan/lights)	May 16	June 17	June 20
Lysimachia clethroides	June 8	June 17	June 19
Crocosmia 'Lucifer'	June 13	June 17	June 20
Monarda didyma cultivars	June 13	June 17	June 23
Platycodon grandiflorus	—	June 18	—
Echinops ritro 'Vietch's Blue'	June 16	(June 18)	June 19
Rudbeckia maxima	June 18	(June 18)	June 18
Allium sphaerocephalum	June 12	(June 19)	June 25
Saponaria officinalis 'Rosea Plena'	—	June 19	—
Euphorbia corollata	June 16	June 19	June 28

Digitalis purpurea 'Foxy' (winter/lights)	—	June 20	—
Helenium autumnale 'Moerheim Beauty'	—	June 20	—
Gladiolus × *hortulanus* (planted spring)	June 17	(June 20)	June 22
Polygonum orientale (sown spring)	—	June 20	—
Alcea 'Ind. Spring'/'Majorette' (win./lights)	June 21	(Jun 21)	June 21
Astilbe taquetii 'Superba'	June 14	June 22	June 28
Cleome hassleriana (self-sown)	June 20	(June 22)	June 23
Papaver somniferum (sown spring)	—	June 22	—
Cosmos bipinnatus (sown spring)	June 19	(June 22)	June 24
Echinacea purpurea	June 13	June 23	June 28
Agrostemma githago (sown spring)	—	June 23	—
Agastache 'Blue Fortune'	—	June 24	—
Gladiolus callianthus (planted spring)	—	June 24	—
Kalimeris pinnatifida	—	June 24	—
Thalictrum rochebrunianum	June 21	June 25	July 1
Malope trifida (sown spring)	—	June 25	—
Godetia amoena (sown spring)	—	June 26	—
Amaranthus caudatus (sown spring)	—	June 27	—
Phlox paniculata 'David'	June 16	June 28	June 30
Phlox paniculata 'Eva Cullum'	June 25	June 28	July 2
Asclepias incarnata	June 21	June 29	July 6
Calamintha nepeta nepeta	June 25	(June 29)	July 2
Zinnia (sown spring)	—	June 29	—
Dipsacus fullonum (sown fall)	—	June 30	—
Helianthus annuus (sown spring)	June 14	(June 30)	July 15
Lilium auratum platyphyllum	—	July 1	—
Dianthus superbus (2d yr)	—	July 1	—
Trachelium caeruleum (winter/lights)	—	July 1	—
Physostegia virginiana 'Alba'	June 22	July 1	July 4
Veronicastrum virginicum	June 27	July 1	July 2
Liatris spicata 'Floristan White'	June 22	July 2	July 4
Lobelia × *gerardii* 'Vedrariensis'	June 26	(July 2)	July 7
Callistephus chinensis (spring/lights)	—	July 2	—
Lilium superbum	June 23	July 3	July 7
Lilium lancifolium (L. tigrinum)	June 30	July 4	July 13
Tanacetum vulgare	July 3	July 4	July 6
Crocosmia 'George Davidson'	July 4	July 4	July 5
Monarda citriodora 'Lambada' (spring/lights)	—	July 5	—
Chasmanthium latifolium	July 4	July 5	July 6

PLANT	DATES OF FIRST BLOOM		
	FIRST	MEDIAN	LAST
Lobelia cardinalis	—	July 6	—
Atriplex hortensis (sown spring)	—	July 7	—
Tithonia rotundifolia (sown spring)	—	July 7	—
Agapanthus 'Bressingham Blue'	July 6	(July 7)	July 7
Cleome hassleriana (sown spring)	—	July 7	—
Solidago 'Peter Pan'	July 5	(July 8)	July 10
Lathyrus lat. 'White Pearl' (winter/lights)	—	July 9	—
Gaillardia g. 'Burgundy' (winter/lights)	June 30	(July 9)	July 18
Lavatera trimestris 'Mt. Rose' (sown spring)	—	July 10	—
Rudbeckia triloba (self-sown, spring/lights)	July 7	(July 12)	July 16
Rudbeckia 'Goldsturm'	July 5	July 13	July 17
Celosia 'Flamingo Feather' (sown spring)	July 8	(July 13)	July 17
Rudbeckia laciniata 'Gold Drop'	July 6	(July 13)	July 20
Scabiosa atropurpurea (sown spring)	July 10	(July 13)	July 15
Sedum 'Matrona'	July 10	(July 13)	July 15
Artemisia lactiflora	July 10	(July 14)	July 17
Verbascum blattaria (winter/lights)	—	July 15	—
Kniphofia 'Bressingham Comet'	July 8	July 15	July 21
Alcea rosea 'Chater's Doubles' (2d yr)	—	July 17	—
Limonium latifolium	July 13	(July 19)	July 24
× *Solidaster luteus*	July 9	July 20	July 21
Sorghum bicolor technicum (sown spring)	—	July 22	—
Lablab purpureus (sown spring)	July 21	July 22	July 26
Allium senescens	—	July 23	—
Lobelia siphilitica	—	July 26	—
Lycoris squamagera	July 18	July 26	Aug 5
Eupatorium purpureum	July 19	July 26	July 31
Helenium autumnale 'Kugelsonne'	July 24	July 29	Aug 8
Gomphrena glob. 'Woodcreek' (sown late May)	—	Aug 1	—
Anemone tomentosa 'Robustissima'	July 28	Aug 1	Aug 8
Callistephus chinensis (sown spring)	—	Aug 2	—
Hosta plantaginea	July 19	Aug 2	Aug 16
Asclepias curassavica (self-sown)	July 23	(Aug 4)	Aug 15
Sedum spectabile 'Meteor'	—	Aug 6	—
Begonia grandis (self-sown)	July 29	Aug 8	Aug 31
Dahlia (planted late spring)	July 29	Aug 9	Aug 15
Hosta 'Royal Standard'	Aug 6	(Aug 10)	Aug 13
Physostegia virginiana 'Vivid'	—	Aug 14	—

Ageratum h. 'Cut Wonder' (sown late May)	—	Aug 14	—
Boltonia asteroides 'Pink Beauty'	Aug 6	Aug 14	Aug 14
Chelone lyonii	Aug 14	Aug 15	Aug 25
Allium tuberosum	Aug 15	Aug 22	Aug 26
Aster novae-angliae 'Alma Potschke'	Aug 22	(Aug 23)	Aug 23
Solidago sphacelata 'Golden Fleece'	Aug 25	(Aug 26)	Aug 27
Boltonia asteroides 'Snowbank'	Aug 18	Aug 27	Aug 31
Chrysopsis 'Golden Sunshine'	Aug 20	Aug 27	Aug 31
Salvia azurea	Aug 24	Aug 28	Aug 30
Caryopteris incana (planted spring)	—	Aug 28	—
Solidago rugosa 'Fireworks'	Aug 29	(Aug 30)	Aug 31
Anemone japonica cultivars	Sept 3	(Sept 5)	Sept 6
Salvia leucantha (planted spring)	—	Sept 10	—
Aster laevis 'Bluebird'	—	Sept 12	—
Aster pringlei 'Monte Cassino'	Sept 11	Sept 14	Sept 14
Aster tataricus	Sept 12	Sept 15	Sept 18
Chrysanthemum nipponicum	Sept 19	(Sept 21)	Sept 23
Chrysanthemum × *morifolium*	Oct 1	Oct 6	Oct 11
Helianthus angustifolius	Oct 10	Oct 12	Oct 14
Ligularia tussilaginea	Oct 10	Oct 15	Oct 18
Chrysanthemum pacificum	Nov 5	(Nov 6)	Nov 6

Notes: (2d yr) indicates date in second year for plant that may bloom its first year; (winter/lights) indicates plant sown under indoors lights in winter; (sown fall) refers to seed sown outdoors in fall; (planted spring) refers to plant installed in the garden in spring. As indicated, the dates for some entries are applicable for both sown and planted plants.

Index of Plants

Page numbers in boldface refer to the main entries in chapter 6. You may find additional page citations by looking up both botanical and common names, remembering that some plants have several common names.

Index of Subjects and Names